NATIONAL
GEOGRAPHIC
KiDS

ALMANAC 2015

A European common frog makes a splash diving into clear water.

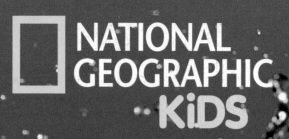

ALMANAC 2015

NATIONAL GEOGRAPHIC
WASHINGTON, D.C.

National Geographic Kids Books gratefully acknowledges the following people for their help with the *National Geographic Kids Almanac 2015*.

Curtis Malarkey, Julie Segal, and Cheryl Zook of the National Geographic Explorers program; Truly Herbert, National Geographic Communications; and Chuck Errig of Random House

Amazing Animals

Suzanne Braden, Director, Pandas International

Dr. Rodolfo Coria, Paleontologist, Plaza Huincul, Argentina

Dr. Sylvia Earle, National Geographic Explorer-in-Residence

Dr. Thomas R. Holtz, Jr., Senior Lecturer, Vertebrate Paleontology, Department of Geology, University of Maryland

Dr. Luke Hunter, Executive Director, Panthera

Dereck and Beverly Joubert, National Geographic Explorers-in-Residence

"Dino" Don Lessem, President, Exhibits Rex

Kathy B. Maher, Research Editor, NATIONAL GEOGRAPHIC magazine

Kathleen Martin, Canadian Sea Turtle Network

Barbara Nielsen, Polar Bears International

Andy Prince, Austin Zoo

Christopher Sloan

Julia Thorson, translator, Zurich, Switzerland

Dennis vanEngelsdorp, Senior Extension Associate, Pennsylvania Department of Agriculture

Going Green

Eric J. Bohn, Math Teacher, Santa Rosa High School

Stephen David Harris, Professional Engineer, Industry Consulting

Catherine C. Milbourn, Senior Press Officer, EPA

Brad Scriber, Senior Researcher, NATIONAL GEOGRAPHIC magazine

Paola Segura and Cid Simões, National Geographic Emerging Explorers

Dr. Wes Tunnell, Harte Research Institute for Gulf of Mexico Studies, Texas A&M University–Corpus Christi

Super Science

Tim Appenzeller, Chief Magazine Editor, NATURE

Dr. Rick Fienberg, American Astronomical Society, Press Officer and Director of Communications

Dr. José de Ondarza, Associate Professor, Department of Biological Sciences, State University of New York, College at Plattsburgh

Lesley B. Rogers, Managing Editor (former), NATIONAL GEOGRAPHIC magazine

Dr. Enric Sala, National Geographic Visiting Fellow

Abigail A. Tipton, Director of Research (former), NATIONAL GEOGRAPHIC magazine

Erin Vintinner, Biodiversity Specialist, Center for Biodiversity and Conservation at the American Museum of Natural History

Barbara L. Wyckoff, Research Editor (former), NATIONAL GEOGRAPHIC magazine

Culture Connection

Dr. Wade Davis, National Geographic Explorer-in-Residence

Deirdre Mullervy, Managing Editor, Gallaudet University Press

Wonders of Nature

Anatta, NOAA Public Affairs Officer

Dr. Robert Ballard, National Geographic Explorer-in-Residence

Douglas H. Chadwick, wildlife biologist and contributor to NATIONAL GEOGRAPHIC magazine

Drew Hardesty, Forecaster, Utah Avalanche Center

History Happens

Dr. Sylvie Beaudreau, Associate Professor, Department of History, State University of New York

Elspeth Deir, Assistant Professor, Faculty of Education, Queens University, Kingston, Ontario, Canada

Dr. Gregory Geddes, Lecturer, Department of Global Studies, State University of New York–Orange, Middletown-Newburgh, New York

Dr. Fredrik Hiebert, National Geographic Visiting Fellow

Micheline Joanisse, Media Relations Officer, Natural Resources Canada

Dr. Robert D. Johnston, Associate Professor and Director of the Teaching of History Program, University of Illinois at Chicago

Dickson Mansfield, Geography Instructor (retired), Faculty of Education, Queens University, Kingston, Ontario, Canada

Tina Norris, U.S. Census Bureau

Parliamentary Information and Research Service, Library of Parliament, Ottawa, Canada

Karyn Pugliese, Acting Director, Communications, Assembly of First Nations

Geography Rocks

Glynnis Breen, National Geographic Special Projects

Carl Haub, Senior Demographer, Conrad Taeuber Chair of Public Information, Population Reference Bureau

Dr. Mary Kent, Demographer, Population Reference Bureau

Dr. Walt Meier, National Snow and Ice Data Center

Dr. Richard W. Reynolds, NOAA's National Climatic Data Center

United States Census Bureau, Public Help Desk

Dr. Spencer Wells, National Geographic Explorer-in-Residence

Contents

Your World 2015

8

Amazing Animals

18

Going Green

82

Awesome Adventure

100

Super Science

118

Fun and Games

154

Culture Connection

174

CONTENTS

Wonders of Nature
200

History Happens
222

Geography Rocks
254

Dai women in Yunnan, China, have buckets of fun at the Water Splashing Festival. The Buddhist celebration takes place every spring.

Animal Discoveries

From "WALKING" SHARKS to FLYING FROGS, here are some species recently found in the wild.

Epaulette Shark

Forget swimming: One of the newly discovered species of epaulette shark can also "walk" on its fins along the ocean floor. Discovered off the coast of Indonesia, *Hemiscyllium halmahera* feeds on bottom-dwelling invertebrates in tide pools and coral reefs. Another cool fact? It can survive for about an hour in the low-oxygen conditions of tide pools by increasing blood flow to its brain and shutting down less essential body functions.

Cambodian Tailorbird

Discovered outside Cambodia's bustling capital of Phnom Penh, this orange-topped warbler was first spotted at a construction site. It gets its name for the intricate way it "tailors" its nest by weaving leaves together.

Olinguito

This may be the cutest new species discovery yet! The olinguito—found in a forest in Colombia, South America—is described as a "cross between a teddy bear and a house cat." And with its big, wide eyes, round ears, and fuzzy, orange-brown coat, it's easy to see why this carnivore can be mistaken for a furry friend. But this animal isn't so cuddly: The canopy dweller has sharp, curved claws, along with textured foot pads, to allow it to grip branches and climb trees high in the Andes Mountains.

Helen's Flying Frog

This amphibian, discovered close to Ho Chi Minh City in Vietnam, uses its huge webbed feet and hands to parachute across the lowland ever-green forest canopy. But one of these large, white-bellied frogs was simply sitting on a log when it caught the eye of researcher Jodi Rowley, who later named the species "Helen" after her mom.

The 100th Anniversary Sinking of the *Lusitania*

THE *LUSITANIA*

The captain of the R.M.S. *Lusitania* had been warned. The year was 1915, World War I raged across Europe, and the German government declared that all Allied ships would be in danger of attack in British waters. Still, the British ocean liner set out on its planned course from New York City, New York, U.S.A., to Liverpool, England, with 1,900 passengers and crew members on board.

The *Lusitania* never made it. On May 7, 1915, as the ship cruised along the southern coast of Ireland, a German submarine, also known as a U-boat, torpedoed and sank the ship. It took less than 20 minutes for the giant ship to plunge to the murky depths of the Atlantic Ocean, taking more than 1,100 people along with it.

The event sparked outrage around the world from those who believed the Germans' act was unlawful. In the United States—home to nearly 130 of the *Lusitania* victims—public opinion on Germany swiftly shifted from a neutral standpoint to a strong desire to declare war on the country. Two years later, the U.S. officially entered World War I, joining the Allied powers to defeat Germany in 1918.

Now 100 years later, the sinking of the *Lusitania* remains a key turning point in World War I's time line. This year, people around the world will mark the anniversary with memorial services to honor those who lost their lives on the *Lusitania* and commemorate this monumental event that helped shape our world's history.

SURVIVORS FROM THE *LUSITANIA*

LUSITANIA MAY 1915

ELEPHANT SIGN LANGUAGE

While elephants don't sit around chatting with each other like you and your friends do, they do express emotions through gestures similar to sign language. After studying a family of African elephants in the wild for decades, biologist Joyce Poole noticed that subtle movements and gestures were actually ways in which the pachyderms communicate.

"I noticed that when I was narrating the elephants' behavior to others, I was able to predict what they would do next perhaps 90 percent of the time," Poole says.

What are some of the ways elephants express themselves? If one feels threatened, it may spread its ears out wide to appear bigger (top right) or stand up on a log or an anthill to look taller. A mama elephant may show her little one love by wrapping her trunk around her calf's leg or belly, or by touching its mouth. And an elephant who wants to initiate a game might wiggle its head from side to side or lie down on the ground, hoping others may clamber on top.

They display a sense of humor, too: After repeatedly observing elephants appearing to trip and fall in front of her car, Poole figured out that the animals were just messing around. "It is one of the behaviors that led me to say that elephants have a sense of self and a sense of humor," says Poole. "They *know* that they are funny."

HEADS UP!

I WANT TO GO THIS WAY. LET'S GO TOGETHER.

I'M FEELING UNEASY OR AMBIVALENT.

SPACE BALLOONS

Just how high can balloons travel? How about all the way to Saturn? That's just what a team of scientists in the United States is working on. The hot-air balloon is being designed to orbit Saturn's biggest moon, Titan. It will also transport equipment on unmanned missions and possibly send photos back to Earth.

But getting a balloon to withstand Titan's extreme environment is no easy feat. Temperatures hover around 300 degrees below zero Fahrenheit (-184°C) on Titan. Researchers developing the balloon hope that a specially created material made of polyester fibers will do the trick.

While the balloon is still being tested, scientists plan to get it off the ground soon. And once it takes off? There's hope that this type of balloon mission can continue in the future to shed more light on some of the greatest mysteries of our solar system—and beyond.

NATIONAL GEOGRAPHIC KiDS SCANNER

SCAN THIS PAGE!
GET BONUS MOBILE CONTENT! Download the free NG Kids scanner app. Directions on inside front cover.

One-Way Ticket TO MARS

AN ARTIST'S DEPICTION OF MARS ONE'S PLANS FOR COLONIZING THE RED PLANET

Forget a dream vacation to Tahiti or Disney World. How about a trip to Mars? The only catch is that you may never come back. At least that's what Dutch-based company Mars One is proposing through a project they say will send four people on a one-way mission to Mars in 2023. But this trip's not just about exploring: Mars One wants to colonize the red planet, too. So, after eight years of full-time training, the select crew will travel to Mars in 2023 and live there for the rest of their lives. Sound scary? Not to everyone: More than 200,000 have already applied!

REAL-LIFE
Lightsabers?

Darth Vader, watch out! Physicists at Harvard University and the Massachusetts Institute of Technology (MIT) in Massachusetts, U.S.A., created a real-life system that behaves like a lightsaber in the Star Wars movies. By binding together photons—massless particles of light—in a special optical material, laser beams of light can be pushed and pulled, just like the beam of a lightsaber. So while you may not be able to fight the Dark Side with your saber just yet, you may be able to do so one day without having to travel to a galaxy far, far away.

SPONGEBOB
SQUAREPANTS 2

KUNG FU PANDA 3

HOTEL TRANSYLVANIA 2

HOT
MOVIES
in 2015*

- SpongeBob SquarePants 2
- The Penguins of Madagascar
- Jurassic World
- Hotel Transylvania 2
- Kung Fu Panda 3
- Alvin and the Chipmunks 4
- The Smurfs 3
- Star Wars: Episode VII

*Release dates and titles are subject to change.

KING RICHARD III FOUND IN PARKING LOT!

You just never know what—or who—may be buried beneath your feet. Case in point: Researchers recently discovered the skeleton of King Richard III, who died in battle in 1485, under a parking lot in England. The remains, unearthed during an archaeological dig by the team from the University of Leicester in the United Kingdom, matched the DNA of a living relative of Richard, giving researchers proof that the skeleton in fact belonged to the famed leader. This discovery solved the decades-long mystery surrounding the whereabouts of his body.

Can Dogs Sense Emotions?

Your pooch may know you better than you think. A recent study shows that dogs yawn more in response to their owners' yawns than they do to strangers' yawns. To test the pets, researchers had the dogs watch both their owners and strangers yawn or pretend to yawn. The result? The dogs in the study yawned more in response to their owners' yawns and yawned less when they saw fake yawns. This, researchers say, suggests that pups can actually sense their owners' emotions. No wonder your pup is considered man's best friend!

15

Cool Events in 2015

Songkran Festival

Thailand gets wet and wild in this countrywide water fight!

April 13–15

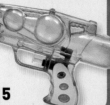

World Turtle Day

Come out of your shell and celebrate turtles big and small!

May 23

FIFA Women's Soccer World Cup Canada

Watch the best soccer players in the world kick it in Canada. Score!

June 6–July 5

International Left-Handers Day

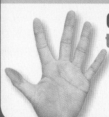

Give a high five to your favorite southpaw today!

August 13

International Chocolate Day

Treat yourself to an extra cupcake today. Sweet!

September 13

Rugby World Cup

The world's best rugby players are set to scrum in matches all around England.

September 18–October 31

International Music Day

Turn up the tunes as you celebrate all things music. Did someone say dance party?

October 1

150th Anniversary of Alice in Wonderland

Lewis Carroll's famous character is 150 years old. And she still doesn't look a day over 7.

November 26

SAND SCULPTING CHAMPIONSHIPS

Each February, some of the world's best artists head down under for the annual Australian Sand Sculpting Championships in Surfers Paradise along the continent's Gold Coast. But this competition isn't just about building simple castles: Artists use more than 198 tons (180 MT) of sand to mold and carve elaborate designs, like amazingly real-looking animals, mythical creatures, fierce pirates, and crazy faces. Hoping to see the sculptures for yourself but don't live down under? There are similar competitions around the world in places like Fort Myers Beach, Florida, U.S.A.; San Diego, California, U.S.A.; Jesolo, Italy; and Fiesa, Portugal.

sports funnies
uh-oh!

Pro soccer players are superfierce, but they can be superfunny, too! As we gear up for the FIFA Women's World Cup Canada 2015, here are some players caught in some silly positions!

Christie Rampone of the U.S.A. makes a kick during the finals match against Japan in the 2011 FIFA World Cup in Frankfurt, Germany.

Brazil's Aline Pellegrino chases the ball during a 2012 soccer match against the U.S.A. in Chiba, Japan.

Amazing Animals

Emperor penguins leap and glide at floe's edge on the Ross Sea's Cape Washington in Antarctica.

WHAT IS Taxonomy?

Since there are billions and billions of living things, called organisms, on the planet, people need a way of classifying them. Scientists created a system called **taxonomy**, which helps to classify all living things into ordered groups. By putting organisms into categories we are better able to understand how they are the same and how they are different. There are seven levels of taxonomic classification, beginning with the broadest group, called a domain, down to the most specific group, called a species.

Biologists divide life based on evolutionary history, and they place organisms in three domains depending on their genetic structure: Archaea, Bacteria, and Eukarya. (See p. 131 for "The Three Domains of Life.")

Where do animals come in?

Animals are a part of the Eukarya domain, which means they are organisms made of cells with nuclei. More than one million species of animals have been named, including humans. Like all living things, animals can be divided into smaller groups, called phyla. Most scientists believe there are more than 30 phyla into which animals can be grouped based on certain scientific criteria, such as body type or whether or not the animal has a backbone. It can be pretty complicated, so there is another, less complicated system that groups animals into two categories: vertebrates and invertebrates.

Chinese stripe-necked turtle

SAMPLE CLASSIFICATION
LLAMA

Domain:	Eukarya
Phylum:	Chordata
Class:	Mammalia
Order:	Artiodactyla
Family:	Camelidae
Genus:	*Lama*
Species:	*glama*

TIP
Here's a sentence to help you remember the classification order:
Dear Phillip Came Over For Good Soup.

BY THE NUMBERS

There are 11,092 vulnerable or endangered animal species in the world. The list includes:

- **1,140 mammals**, such as the snow leopard, the polar bear, and the fishing cat.
- **1,313 birds**, including the Steller's sea eagle and the Madagascar plover.
- **2,110 fish**, such as the Mekong giant catfish.
- **847 reptiles**, including the American crocodile.
- **835 insects**, including the Macedonian grayling.

- **1,948 amphibians**, such as the Round Island day gecko.
- **And more**, including 21 arachnids, 723 crustaceans, 236 sea anemones and corals, 164 bivalves, and 1,707 snails and slugs.

Vertebrates Animals WITH Backbones

Fish are cold-blooded and live in water. They breathe with gills, lay eggs, and usually have scales.

Amphibians are cold-blooded. Their young live in water and breathe with gills. Adults live on land and breathe with lungs.

Reptiles are cold-blooded and breathe with lungs. They live both on land and in water.

Birds are warm-blooded and have feathers and wings. They lay eggs, breathe with lungs, and usually are able to fly. Some birds live on land, some in water, and some on both.

Mammals are warm-blooded and feed on their mothers' milk. They also have skin that is usually covered with hair. Mammals live both on land and in water.

Bird: Bald eagle

Fish: Clown anemonefish

Invertebrates Animals WITHOUT Backbones

Sponges are a very basic form of animal life. They live in water and do not move on their own.

Echinoderms have external skeletons and live in seawater.

Mollusks have soft bodies and can live either in or out of shells, on land or in water.

Arthropods are the largest group of animals. They have external skeletons, called exoskeletons, and segmented bodies with appendages. Arthropods live in water and on land.

Worms are soft-bodied animals with no true legs. Worms live in soil.

Cnidaria live in water and have mouths surrounded by tentacles.

Worm: Earthworms

Cnidaria: West Coast sea nettle

Arthropod: Red-kneed tarantula

Cold-blooded versus Warm-blooded

Cold-blooded animals, also called ectotherms, get their heat from outside their bodies.

Warm-blooded animals, also called endotherms, keep their body temperature level regardless of the temperature of their environments.

21

Incredible Animal Friends

GORILLA GOES APE FOR RABBIT
ERIE, PENNSYLVANIA, U.S.A.

IS IT TIME FOR MY HOPPING LESSON?

Samantha the western lowland gorilla seemed to like her new roommate, Panda the Dutch rabbit. But her keepers at the Erie Zoo grew worried one day when the rabbit hopped over to Samantha's favorite stuffed animal. They knew the ape was crazy about her toy and feared the 200-pound (91-kg) Samantha might get upset if the rabbit got too close. But the gorilla didn't sweat it. She just moved the toy so Panda could pass by. That's when keepers realized the roomies were best buds.

Too shy to live with other apes, Samantha was paired with the rabbit to keep from getting lonely. Keepers introduced them slowly, first letting the duo see each other through a mesh screen. Eventually, Panda moved into the ape's exhibit. "Almost immediately, they were sitting side by side," zoo CEO Scott Mitchell says.

The pair was practically inseparable. They liked watching visitors walk by their exhibit together, and Samantha often let the rabbit nibble on her hay. Keepers even saw the gorilla stroke Panda under his chin. Says Mitchell, "Their friendship was one of a kind."

THANKS, I THINK I SMELL GREAT TOO!

PUP BABYSITS PIGLETS
ORANIENBURG, GERMANY

I KNEW PIGGING OUT WOULD MAKE THEM SLEEPY!

The litter of boar piglets living at the Lehnitz animal sanctuary loved trying to get piggyback rides from their best bud, Baby the French bulldog. "Sometimes, one of the boars will try to scramble onto Baby's back," says Norbert Damm, who works at the sanctuary. "She'll just playfully shake the piglet off."

The football-size boars arrived at the sanctuary where the dog lives after they were found alone and freezing in a nearby forest. "Baby cuddled with them, just as their mom would've done," Damm says. The pup stuck close to the pigs afterward.

The fuzzy crew enjoyed dashing around the garden together and snuggling up for naps until the boars were big enough to move to a nature reserve. Guess you could say these guys were hog wild about each other!

BABOON BEFRIENDS BUSH BABY
NAIROBI, KENYA

I'M NOT SAYING WHO, BUT ONE OF US NEEDS A BATH.

It's easy to see that Dina the yellow baboon and Bushy the bush baby are best friends. They're always giving each other bear hugs—even when they're on the move. Bushy wraps her arms around the baboon's tummy and holds on upside down as Dina crawls around their enclosure at the Nairobi Animal Orphanage.

The critters bonded after arriving at the reserve as infants. Now, the baboon protects her pal from other animals and makes sure Bushy eats enough. Bushy, who's naturally nocturnal, even changed her sleeping schedule so she's awake at the same time as Dina. "The friendship is rare," primate expert Barbara Smuts says. "But the animals are great for each other."

Bet you didn't know

6 phenomenal **facts** about **families**

1 European **shrew** families often **travel** with each member **holding** on to another's tail.

2 Born on land, **poison dart** frog tadpoles **wriggle** onto a parent's back for a ride to water.

3 Cassowaries— **large flightless** birds—are raised by their **dads.**

4 Up to **700** black widow **spiders** can hatch from one grape-size egg sac.

5 Mother elephants use their **trunks** to lift newborns to their feet.

6 **Meerkats** can have up to **12 babies a year.**

APE BRUSHES TEETH

WHERE'D I PUT THE MOUTH-WASH?

Central Kalimantan, Borneo

Siswi the orangutan would make a dentist proud. The 34-year-old ape has been spotted scrubbing her teeth with a toothbrush! So, does Siswi scrub her chompers to prevent cavities? Not exactly. She's likely copying people she's seen brushing their teeth at a nearby river (not to mention she may enjoy the minty taste of toothpaste). Yet another reason might explain why the animal cleans her teeth—she's getting ready to mug for the camera. "Siswi's much more likely to start brushing if someone's about to take a picture," orangutan expert Biruté Mary Galdikas says. "She's a bit of a diva."

CAT HAS TWO FACES

TALK ABOUT MEOW MIX!

South Florida, U.S.A.

This is one two-faced cat. Venus's unique mug is divided down the middle—one side is jet black, while the other is light orange.

Why does Venus have such a dramatic look? Every animal's body contains sets of genes passed down from parents. These microscopic molecules determine how the animal will look, including the color of its skin, hair, or fur. "It's possible that the genes that decide fur color came together in an unusual way in Venus," cat researcher Leslie Lyons says. "This may have led to her odd coloring." Who wouldn't want face time with this cool cat?

25

DO ANIMALS LOVE EACH OTHER?

I t's a boy! Romani the Asian elephant has just given birth. After nursing, the baby falls asleep and his mom positions herself directly over him. All is quiet in the barn, and the elephant keeper dims the lights. Then this first-time mom does something remarkable: Like a human mother tucking her child into bed, she gently covers her baby with hay.

Is it love? Scientists used to say that love belonged only to humans. Now they aren't so sure. Jaak Panksepp, a neuroscientist at Washington State University, believes that feelings such as love are hardwired into animals' brains and control their behavior.

The most important sensation is the need to feel good. Like people, many animals feel good when they have something to look forward to—and somebody they care about. Keep reading for more stories of animal love.

MOM, LEAN DOWN... I'VE GOTTA TELL YOU A SECRET.

CARE BEAR

One day, Else Poulsen, a zookeeper at the Detroit Zoo, puts extra branches in Triton the polar bear's enclosure. Why? Poulsen is playing matchmaker. She's bringing a second bear, a female named Bärle, to live with Triton. One look at Bärle turns Triton to mush. It takes a while, but he eventually wins her over with gifts of sugar maple branches.

Later, their cub is born. In the wild, Triton would be long gone. Male polar bears don't stick around once mating season is over, and they do not help raise their young. But Triton continues to bring Bärle gifts, including a plastic toy that Poulsen fills with small treats such as raisins. "They have a strong bond," Poulsen says.

A PRESENT? FOR ME? YOU'RE SO THOUGHTFUL!

HOW COME YOU ALWAYS GET TO SIT UP FRONT?

SISTER ACT

Glitter and Golden are the oldest twin chimpanzees known to survive in the wild. And they're very close. How close? Their bond is so strong that they even share food—a rare sight in the wild.

Take, for instance, when Golden and their mother are pigging out on freshly hunted monkey meat, a special treat for chimps in the forests of Tanzania. But no fair—Glitter doesn't have any! A frustrated Glitter holds out her hand and begs. While the mom ignores her pleas, Golden hands over some of her meat. She has no reason for doing that, unless, of course, she truly loves her twin.

DEVOTED DAD

I'M STARVING! DID DAD TELL YOU WHAT'S FOR DINNER?

In India's Ranthambore National Park, two orphaned Bengal tiger cubs are missing. Their mother died, and the cubs' den is empty. Has the ruling male tiger killed the defenseless babies?

Forest rangers set up camera traps and catch a photo of a male tiger named Zalim. But one of the missing cubs is also in the picture! Zalim isn't preying on them; he's traveling with them. It turns out he's taken over the role of the mother. For example, when the cubs kill a goat, Zalim lets them eat it instead of taking it for himself as most males would do. And when another tiger threatens one of his "kids," Zalim makes the bully back off. This is one big cat that's really earning his stripes.

UM, YEAH. YOU DEFINITELY HAVE FISH BREATH.

SPECIAL DELIVERY

It's lunchtime at the Philadelphia Zoo. A keeper brings a bucket of catfish to the otter exhibit, and an otter mom and her five hungry pups come running. But not Banjo, the pups' dad. At 19, Banjo is one of the world's oldest otters.

The otters start chowing down, except Banjo. He never worries about getting fed, because his pups always take care of him. One of them races over and drops a fish at Banjo's feet. The pup scampers off and Dad eats.

Does Banjo's caring family contribute to his long life? "Absolutely," says carnivore curator Tammy Schmidt. "That's part of his secret."

1

The freshwater-loving **AMAZON RIVER DOLPHIN** can be found in the Amazon and Orinoco Rivers in South America. Following a flood, they can swim through parts of forests.

2

DON'T LET THE NICKNAME FOOL YOU: "KILLER WHALES" ARE ACTUALLY DOLPHINS.

3

SOME WILD DOLPHINS **PLAY CATCH WITH COCONUTS.**

4

The SMALLEST DOLPHIN, Hector's dolphin, is only four feet long (1.2 m). It's one of the rarest types, and it is shorter than an orca's dorsal fin.

15 COOL THINGS ABOUT

5

RISSO'S DOLPHINS CAN HOLD THEIR BREATH FOR **30 MINUTES.**

6

Every dolphin has a **SIGNATURE WHISTLE** it uses to identify itself.

7

A dolphin "SLEEPS" for about eight hours a day, although it is never fully unconscious. Only half its brain is asleep at a time!

8

NEWBORN DOLPHINS HAVE A TINY **PATCH OF HAIR** ON THEIR SNOUTS.

9

THE IPAD is the latest high-tech tool researchers are using to help enhance communication between humans and dolphins.

10

Dolphins have a special superpower that makes finding their way underwater easier. They use a type of sonar called echolocation to hunt and navigate.

11

JUST LIKE HUMANS, DOLPHINS GET ONE SET OF TEETH TO LAST A LIFETIME.

DOLPHINS

12

IF A **DOLPHIN BECOMES SICK,** OTHER DOLPHINS WILL TAKE TURNS

PUSHING IT TO THE SURFACE **SO IT** CAN BREATHE.

13

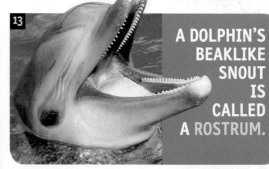

A DOLPHIN'S BEAKLIKE SNOUT IS CALLED A ROSTRUM.

14

A DOLPHIN BREATHES AIR THROUGH A **BLOWHOLE** LOCATED AT THE TOP OF ITS HEAD.

15

A PINK BOTTLENOSE DOLPHIN WAS DISCOVERED IN A LOUISIANA, U.S.A., LAKE.

OCEAN SUPERSTARS

The fascinating lives of 6 sea turtle species

Think all sea turtles are the same? Think again! Each of these species stands out in its own way.

1 GREEN SEA TURTLE: THE NEAT FREAK

In Hawaii, U.S.A., green sea turtles choose a "cleaning station"—a location where groups of cleaner fish groom the turtles by eating ocean gunk, like algae and parasites, off their skin and shells. In Australia, the turtles rub against a favorite sponge or rock to scrub themselves. Neat!

2 KEMP'S RIDLEY: THE LITTLE ONE

They may be the smallest sea turtles, but they're not so tiny: Adults weigh as much as many ten-year-old kids, and their shell is about the size of a car tire. They're speedy, too: It takes them less than an hour to dig a nest, then lay and bury their eggs.

3 OLIVE RIDLEY: THE ULTRA-MOM

Every year, hundreds of thousands of female olive ridley sea turtles take over beaches to lay their eggs and then bury them before disappearing back into the sea. Call it safety in numbers: With thousands of turtles swarming the shoreline, they're sure to overwhelm any predator.

4 LEATHERBACK: THE MEGA-TURTLE

These giants among reptiles have shells about as big as a door and weigh as much as six professional football players! Their size doesn't slow them down, though. A leatherback can swim as fast as a bottlenose dolphin.

5 HAWKSBILL: THE HEARTY EATER

What's the hawksbill's favorite snack? Sponges! These turtles gobble about 1,200 pounds (544 kg) of sponges a year. The turtles can safely eat this sea life, which is toxic to other animals. That means there are plenty of sponges to snack on!

6 LOGGERHEAD: THE TOUGH GUY

The loggerhead sea turtle's powerful jaws can easily crack open the shells of lobsters, conchs, and snails to get at the meat inside. Some loggerheads swim a third of the way around the world to find food.

31

Meet the
PENGUINS

Check out 10 of the world's coolest penguin species.

Rockhopper

Both northern and southern rock-hopper penguins are expert climbers. They use their sharp claws to hop and scramble up steep cliffs to nest. The two species live in the subarctic. Only northern rock-hoppers are endangered.

Little

More than a half million tourists a year watch the nightly parade of these blue-gray, football-size penguins from New Zealand and Aus-tralia returning to their burrows after foraging at sea.

Adélie

Adélie penguins must win a deadly game of freeze tag while crossing thin ice in Antarctica. Leopard seals lurk below, watching for movement. If an Adélie sees a predator, it "freezes" until the danger passes.

Emperor

Emperor penguins are the largest species—as tall as a seven-year-old kid. They can dive 1,853 feet (565 m) straight down and hold their breath underwater for up to 22 minutes.

Galápagos

Instead of fighting frost-bite, these penguins battle sunburn. That's because they live on the Galápagos Islands at the Equator. They shade their feet with their flippers to avoid sunburn.

Gentoo

When a gentoo parent returns from hunting subantarctic seas, it races away from its chicks. But hungry chicks will follow. Once a chick is fed and full, it won't bother chasing its parent anymore.

Royal

Royal penguins spend about four months each year eating and sleeping at sea—somewhere between Australia and Antarctica.

Macaroni

Every October, about 18 million macaroni penguins nest on the hillsides and cliffs of Antarctic and sub-Atlantic shorelines. Macaronis have the largest population of all penguins.

African

The only species that breeds on the coast of Africa, the African penguin faces land predators such as leopards, rats, snakes, and mongooses. It is known for its mating call, which sounds like a braying donkey.

Yellow-eyed

Unlike penguins that nest together in crowded colonies, yellow-eyed penguins hide in coastal forests and shrubland far from any other penguin's nest.

33

5 COOL THINGS ABOUT KOALAS

A koala doesn't look like the kind of creature that keeps campers awake at night or dines on food that would give you a serious stomachache. There's a lot more to these living "teddy bears" than cotton-ball ears and a laid-back lifestyle. Check out five amazing things about these wild, loud, and lovable creatures from Australia.

1. Loudmouths
Imagine a burp so loud it brings you to your knees, followed by a snore that rattles the rafters. Combine them and you have the typical bellow of a koala. Why so noisy? Male koalas grunt with gusto to broadcast their whereabouts to distant females or to scare rivals.

2. Toxic Diet
Koalas eat one to two pounds (450 to 900 g) of eucalyptus leaves each day. The leaves are not only poisonous—they're also tough to digest and provide little nutrition. But koalas have a specially adapted digestive system that extracts every drop of energy from the leaves while neutralizing their toxins.

3. Mistaken Identity
The Europeans who first settled in Australia mistook these tree dwellers for a type of bear, and the name "koala bear" stuck. However, a koala is actually a marsupial—a type of mammal that protects and nurtures its tiny newborns in a pouch.

4. Feisty Guys
A koala may look like a stuffed animal, but you'd be sorry if you tried to cuddle a wild one. Their long, sharp claws—supremely adapted for climbing trees— are used as daggers when two male koalas argue over territory or a mate.

5. Awesome Moms
Born blind, hairless, and no bigger than a jelly bean, a baby koala spends six months sleeping and drinking milk in its mother's pouch. Eventually, it will poke its head out to eat pap—a poopy soup from its mother that builds resistance to eucalyptus poison. When the joey leaves the pouch, the mama koala carries it on her back or belly as she climbs trees and teaches the tiny koala by example.

Snowy Owls

How these birds of prey keep on the move to survive in cold climates

A young male owl began life in the Arctic about five months ago. This winter he flew hundreds of miles south to Logan International Airport near Boston, Massachusetts, U.S.A. His white feathers are tipped with brown stripes, but they'll soon be almost all white. Suddenly, the owl launches, gliding silently toward the water's edge. He stretches out his talons and snatches an unsuspecting duck. Dinner is served.

Raptors on the Move

Snowy owls migrate to and from their Arctic breeding grounds each spring and fall in a quest for food. Logan Airport is a popular winter

WHO'S WHO? ADULT MALES ARE ALL WHITE; FEMALES HAVE STYLISH BROWN-AND-WHITE FEATHERS.

destination for them in the northeastern United States since the habitat looks like a tundra and there's plenty to eat there, too. But not all snowy owls migrate so far south. Some stay in the Arctic, hunt there, and endure the harsh winter in constant darkness. Though temperatures

can plummet to minus 40°F (-40°C) the owls are kept warm by their layers of feathers.

Researchers used to think snowy owls always flew south in the winter, but after tracking the birds with electronic transmitters, they've realized that some stay in the north by the coast, feasting on seabirds.

Tundra Life

In the spring, a female owl migrates to find a good nesting site. She lands on the tundra near Barrow, Alaska, where there's a good supply of small rodents called lemmings to feast on.

WHERE'S DINNER? CHICKS HUDDLE IN THEIR NEST.

By May, the female sits atop a nest of eight eggs, which hatch in mid-June. They snuggle under their mother's wings and against the featherless brood patch on her belly to keep warm. Their father provides food for the whole family. The chicks grow quickly, each eating about two lemmings a day.

When the owlets are about two months old, they learn to fly. By October, the chicks are ready to strike out on their own. Silently, they glide into the darkness to their winter destinations.

FREAKY frogs!

Nearly 6,000 species of frogs hop, burrow, climb, swim, and even soar in exotic ecosystems around the world—and your own neighborhood. Their sometimes startling adaptations make them remarkable survivalists. Here are some frogs whose freakish good looks and bizarre lifestyles will make you become a frog fan.

WARNING LABEL

From the top, the Oriental fire-bellied toad from Korea, China, and southeastern Russia appears to be a mild-mannered frog. If threatened, though, it flashes its brightly colored belly to warn predators, "Look but don't touch." Not only is it toxic, it's also covered with sharp warts.

An amphibian is a **frog**, **toad**, newt, **salamander**, or caecilian.

CLEARLY SEE-THROUGH

From Central and South America, glass frogs are translucent (kind of see-through, like fogged glass). This type of camouflage makes them appear nearly invisible or like a bump on a leaf. Some even have green bones to blend in and trick predators. If you flip over a glass frog, you can see its heart beating through its skin.

FROG-ZILLA!

At 7 pounds (3.2 kg) and with a sitting length of 12.5 inches (31.8 cm), the Goliath frog from Cameroon and Equatorial Guinea is bigger than a Chihuahua. The world's largest frog, it can leap ten times its body length, or about 10 feet (3 m) each hop. Its body and legs can stretch 29.5 inches (75 cm) long, a little longer than a tennis racket.

FLYING FROG

Why hop when you can fly?
These amphibians, which live high
up in the rain forest canopy in Indonesia,
Malaysia, and Thailand, glide from tree to tree to
escape predators or search for food. With its webbed
feet and side skin flaps, this four-inch (10-cm)-long frog can
glide up to 50 feet (15 m). That's like flying from the pitcher's
mound to home plate on a Little League field.

Frogs live on **every** continent **except** Antarctica.

BIG GULP

Go ahead and yell, "Hey, big mouth!" The
Amazon horned frog won't be offended. That's
because its mouth is 1.6 times wider than its
entire body length. It eats anything it can fit
inside that mega-mouth, including rodents,
snakes, lizards, and even other frogs. And it
swallows the prey whole. Sometimes its eyes
are bigger than its stomach. Some Amazon
horned frogs have attempted to eat prey that
was larger than themselves.

KISS ME AND CROAK

A golden poison frog has enough poison on its skin to kill several
men. This tiny toxic frog from Colombia doesn't make its own
poison. It absorbs toxins from the insects that it eats. Unlike most
frogs, it boldly rests out in the open for everyone to see. Its color
warns enemies to leave it alone. Being armed with enough poison
to drop half a football team means there's no need to hide.

BURPING UP BABY

The male Darwin's frog of Argentina and Chile gives
"birth," but in his own weird way. After the female lays
eggs, the male guards them for about 20 days. Then he
swallows them, and the tadpoles grow and morph into
frogs inside his throat pouch. After 50 to 60 days, daddy
belches up more than a dozen baby frogs. Yum!

THE BIGGEST SMALLEST DISCOVERY

In 2009, on the rain forest floor in Papua
New Guinea, scientists discovered the planet's
smallest frog species, known only by its
scientific name, *Paedophryne amauensis*.
How small is it? A couple of them could sit
on a dime and still have room!

Meerkat CITY

Meerkats always have something to do. These mongoose relatives live in busy communities, with no time to sit around being bored. In their family groups of up to 40 members, everyone pitches in to get all the jobs done.

A SENTINEL KEEPS WATCH.

Guards

Meerkats are very territorial. Guards, called sentinels, are always on the lookout for rival meerkats that try to move in on their territory. If a sentinel (left) spots any intruding meerkats, it sends out an alarm call. The whole group gathers together and stands tall to try to scare away the rivals. If that doesn't work, meerkats quickly decide whether to fight or retreat.

Predators such as eagles or jackals rate a different warning call. When the sentinel spots a predator, it lets out an alarm call that sends all the meerkats scurrying into the nearest bolt hole—an underground safety den where the eagle can't follow.

Babysitters

Within a meerkat group, the alpha, or leader, female and the alpha male are usually the only ones that have babies. When their babies are too young to follow along while they search for food, meerkat parents have to go without them. So they leave their pups with babysitters—other adult meerkats in the group. The pups stay inside their family's underground burrow for the first three weeks of life, protected and cared for by the babysitters.

Diggers

Picture yourself looking for a tasty bug to eat (below) when suddenly you hear the alarm call for "eagle." You dash left, you dash right, and you finally find a bolt hole.

Bolt holes provide fast getaways for meerkats in danger. Members of the group cooperate to make sure bolt holes are properly dug out, that nothing is blocking the entry, and that there are enough bolt holes in every area.

Meerkats are built to be superdiggers. All four of their paws have long, sturdy claws that they use like rakes. They dig to find food, such as lizards and other small reptiles, insects and their larvae, and scorpions.

HOME SWEET BURROW

DIGGING FOR FOOD

WILD DOGS OF AFRICA

The puppy-dog eyes and pleading squeals of a five-month-old African wild dog named Cici can mean only one thing: dinnertime. An older sister in Cici's pack responds, dragging over a meaty impala bone. In African wild dog society, puppies have all the power. "It's up to the older siblings to take care of the puppies," says Micaela Gunther, a scientist who studies wild dogs, including Cici's family. "The doting grown-ups even deliver toys, such as a strip of impala skin perfect for puppy tug-of-war." Imagine your big brother or sister working hard to hand you snacks and games while you eat, play, and rest all day.

DOG DAYS

Like wolves, wild dogs live in a pack of up to 15 dogs. Pups stay in the pack for about two years. Then some may break off to start packs of their own, while others stay with their mom and dad.

When the pups are newborn, every member of the pack works together to provide for them. At first the puppies stay near the den, often under the watch of a babysitter while the pack hunts. Returning pack members throw up meat for the pups. Sound gross? Puppies love these leftovers.

PACK ATTACK

By the time the pups are six months old, they join the pack on hunting expeditions. First they learn how to stalk prey, and eventually they participate in the kill. Single 60-pound (27-kg) dogs rarely catch larger prey on their own, but a pack of 20 proves that there really is strength in numbers. Together they can take down a zebra or wildebeest weighing up to 1,000 pounds (454 kg).

Hunting wild dogs often pursue herds of gazelle for miles, fresh dogs trading places with tired ones. Eventually the weakest of the chased animals tires. The dogs surround it and attack from every direction. This teamwork is bred from the pack's intense social bonding, such as the daily greeting ceremonies and puppy play sessions. Team-building is the reason wild dogs spoil the pups, who grow up united and ready to contribute to the strength of the pack.

SUPER SNAKES

Snakes are masters of disguise, skilled hunters, and champion eaters. More than 2,500 species of snakes slither around the world. Check out these surprising facts about snakes.

AMAZON TREE BOA

SNAKES SMELL WITH THEIR TONGUES.

Smell that mouse? A snake uses its tongue to help it smell. It flicks its long, forked tongue to pick up chemical molecules from the air, ground, or water. The tongue carries the smelly molecules back to two small openings—called the Jacobson's organ—in the roof of the snake's mouth. Cells in the Jacobson's organ analyze the scent. *Mmm*, lunch!

SNAKES CHANGE THEIR SKIN.

Snakes literally grow out of their skin. Every few months, most start rubbing against the ground or tree branches. Starting at the mouth, a snake slithers out of its too-tight skin. Like a sock, the skin comes off inside out. *Voilà*—the snake has a fresh, shiny look. Nice makeover.

EMERALD TREE BOA

CONSTRICTORS GIVE WICKED HUGS.

Boas, anacondas, pythons, and other snakes called constrictors are amazing squeezers. This kind of snake wraps its muscular body around a victim and squeezes until the animal suffocates. The twisted talent comes from muscles attached to 200 or more vertebrae in a snake's backbone. (Humans are born with only 33 vertebrae.)

DIONE RAT SNAKE

SOME SNAKES CAN DISAPPEAR.

Snakes are great hunters, but often they're the prey. Birds, raccoons, foxes, and other animals have a taste for snakes. One way to hide: camouflage. Many snakes sport colors and patterns that allow them to blend in with their surroundings. For instance, a green tree python looks like a vine when it coils itself around a branch. A yellow eyelash viper blends in with flowers. And a rainbow boa disappears on gnarled tree stumps.

PUFF ADDER

BRAZILIAN RAINBOW BOA

SNAKE VENOM CAN KILL.

By sinking two hollow, pointy fangs into their prey, many snakes inject venom to paralyze or kill victims before devouring them. Africa's black mamba is thought to be one of the world's deadliest snakes. Up to 14 feet (4.3 m) long and as skinny as a pool cue, the black mamba strikes fast. Two drops of its venom can kill a human. It's a snake to be respected—from a distance.

SNAKES DON'T CHEW.

A snake's lower jawbone is hinged very loosely in back, so the snake can open superwide. The snake's backward-curved teeth are designed to grab prey and move it down its throat. Loosely attached ribs and elastic skin expand as the food moves on down. Boas and other huge snakes can even eat goats and deer. After a big meal, snakes can go weeks without food.

GREEN TREE PYTHON

SEDGE VIPER

SNAKES "SEE" HEAT.

Some snakes—such as pythons, rattlesnakes, and copperheads—can't see well and use other senses to find prey. These creatures have openings called pit holes in front of their eyes. These pits sense the heat given off by warm-blooded prey. The snakes' heat vision allows the vipers to track prey day or night.

5 COOL THINGS ABOUT HARP SEALS

With their irresistible faces and fluffy fur, harp seals are some of the cutest animals around. But their snow-white pelts and icy habitat make harp seals especially vulnerable to hunters, global warming, and other environmental threats. Here's more about harp seals—and why it's extra-important to protect these adorable animals.

1 6,000-MILE JOURNEY

Each year, harp seals migrate more than 6,000 miles (9,600 km), spending summers feeding in northern Arctic coastal waters and heading back south in the fall to breed. They migrate in small groups of up to 20 individuals. By late February, harp seals gather in large herds. As many as one million form an enormous herd found on the floating mass of pack ice in the Gulf of St. Lawrence in Canada. Once breeding season is over, the seals travel back north for the summer.

2 SEE-THROUGH COAT

When a harp seal pup is born, its coat has a yellow tint. But it turns completely white within a couple of days. The fine, silky fur is almost transparent. This allows the pup's skin to absorb the sun's rays, which helps it stay warm. The whitecoats, as they are called, look like this only for about two weeks. Then they molt, or shed, their white fur. Their new coats are gray.

DID YOU KNOW? Harp seals are known as "earless" seals because they don't have external earflaps.

3 HEART TRICK

When a young harp seal sees a polar bear, instinct takes over. The pup can't escape the predator by running away, so it hides—in plain sight. The ball of white fur plays possum. The seal lies motionless with its head tucked into its chubby neck, looking like a heap of snow (below). The pup's heart rate slows from about 80 to 90 beats a minute to only 20 to 30 beats. If the trick works, the bear doesn't see the harp seal and moves on. Then the seal can stretch out and relax. Whew!

4 DEEP DIVERS

It's not unusual for a harp seal to hold its breath for 5 minutes. But when it needs to, the seal can stay underwater for as long as 20 minutes and dive more than 800 feet (244 m) down. That's six times deeper than a scuba diver can go safely. Harp seals can get places fast, too—100 feet (30 m) down in 15 seconds. As the seals zip through the water hunting for fish, they also stay alert for orcas and sharks that might eat *them*.

5 QUICK-CHANGE ARTISTS

By the time a harp seal is 14 months old, it has changed coats—and nicknames—five times. A whitecoat at first, it then becomes a graycoat, a ragged jacket, a beater, and finally a bedlamer. At four years old a harp seal has a silvery gray coat with a few spots—and it's called a spotted harp. Some females look like that the rest of their lives. Males, as well as many females, develop a distinctive black pattern that is shaped like a harp, which explains the name of the species.

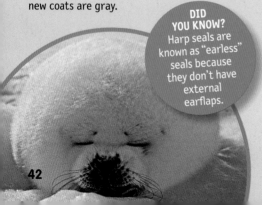

MONKEY TROUBLE

A YOUNG BABOON TAKES A DANGEROUS SWIM.

It's a chilly winter morning in Botswana's Okavango Delta in Africa. A troop of chacma baboons wades across a narrow stream. But an eight-month-old infant named Chobe is left behind. She frantically paces the shore and calls out. The others ignore her as they move through the cold water without her.

Because the baboons' territory is flooded for half of the year, they must cross water all day. They move from island to island to find food and to escape predators such as lions and leopards.

1

DANGEROUS CROSSING

To cross the stream, bigger kid baboons hitch a ride with one of their parents, climbing onto the adult's back. Chobe usually gets a lift across the water with her dad, but today he's gone on ahead. So she has to figure out a way to get across the water and keep up with her troop. A young baboon cannot survive alone in the wild.

2

CAUGHT IN THE CURRENT

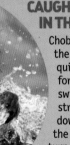

Chobe begins to wade into the cold stream. The water quickly becomes too deep for her, so she starts to swim clumsily. Midway, the strong current drags her downstream, farther from the shore. Her screams turn to gurgles as she starts to swallow water.

4

COMFORT AFTER A CLOSE CALL

Chobe's tiring fast, but just then, her feet find a shallow bank in the stream and she races out of the water. She sits on the shore, shivering. Her mother soon arrives, holds her close, and grooms her. Grooming is a great form of comfort for baboons. In no time, Chobe is running around with the other young baboons.

3

STAYING SAFE WITH DAD

Baboons have to learn to survive on their own, and sometimes that involves dangerous lessons. Chobe got a taste of what it's like to be an independent member of the troop. She decides she isn't quite ready to be a grown-up yet ...so she makes sure to find her father and hop onto his back at the next water crossing.

Animal Rescues

KOALA
QUEENSLAND, AUSTRALIA

Dogs viciously attack a young male koala, biting and shaking him. Somehow the koala escapes and struggles up a tree to seek shelter. Without medical care, he'll die of his wounds.

Home owners finally notice the injured animal and call Moreton Bay Koala Rescue. The rescuers gently place the wounded animal in a large cage and drive him to the Australia Zoo Wildlife Hospital. During the trip, they decide to name the koala Lewis.

RESCUE FROM TREE

GROWING STRONGER
The staff changes Lewis's bandages and cleans his wounds every day. It takes more than three months for the koala's arms and legs to heal. After eight months, Lewis is scaling trees over 60 feet (18 m) tall and gathering his own leaves. He's ready to return to the wild.

BACK TO THE BUSH
Lewis is driven back to the area where he was rescued, and then carried in a cage deep into the bush—far from private property and dogs. After a half-hour hike, the release team opens the cage. At first, Lewis is a bit hesitant. But then he quickly climbs up the tree, without looking back.

DOLPHIN TURKISH COAST

RESCUE FROM POOL

For months two male dolphins, named Tom and Misha, have been attractions in a moneymaking scheme near the coast of Turkey. Tourists pay to swim with the 9-foot (2.7-cm)-long dolphins in a small, 13-foot (4-m)-deep swimming pool.

The business owner neglects them. No one cleans the pool. A thick pile of dolphin waste and uneaten, rotting fish builds up on the bottom, creating a terrible stench. The contaminated water makes the dolphins sick, and the pair rapidly lose weight. The stressed, cooped-up dolphins fight each other. They're only weeks from dying.

HELP ARRIVES
A local organization called the Dolphin Angels hears about the desperate situation and begins a protest campaign. Soon the Born Free Foundation, an animal rights group in England, joins the cause. Once they win custody of Tom and Misha, the rescuers put their plan into action to release the dolphins back to the wild.

AROUND THE WORLD

ELEPHANT
ZAMBIA, AFRICA

In the Kapani Lagoon in Zambia, Africa, a baby elephant playfully rolls around in the sticky mud to chill out. But when it stands up, one of its feet sinks deep into the mud and gets stuck. The terrified baby squeals to its mother. She ignores the muddy danger and tries to yank her calf out with her strong trunk. The mud traps the heavy mother too, swallowing her legs like thick cement. Without help, the two elephants will slowly dehydrate and die in the heat— if the lions and hyenas don't find them first.

HELP ON THE WAY

An employee at a nearby safari lodge hears the animals' cries and sees their dangerous situation. The staff of the lodge alerts the government wildlife department, and help is on the way in the form of heavy rope, lots of manpower, and a tractor!

HELP ARRIVES

BACK TO THE HERD

After many tries the rescuers are able to pull the baby elephant out of the mud using rope and having a good old-fashioned tug-of-war. On the other hand, extracting the mother elephant from the mud pit requires a lot more effort—the rope, the manpower, and the tractor. Free at last, mother and child are happily together again and eager to rejoin the herd.

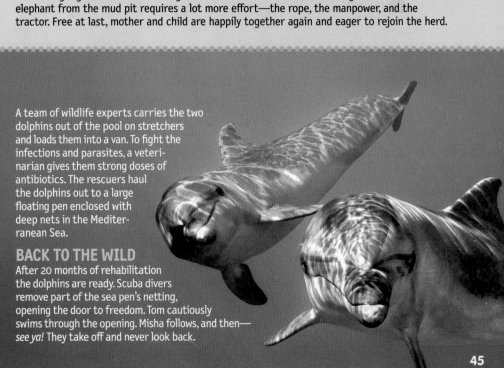

A team of wildlife experts carries the two dolphins out of the pool on stretchers and loads them into a van. To fight the infections and parasites, a veterinarian gives them strong doses of antibiotics. The rescuers haul the dolphins out to a large floating pen enclosed with deep nets in the Mediterranean Sea.

BACK TO THE WILD

After 20 months of rehabilitation the dolphins are ready. Scuba divers remove part of the sea pen's netting, opening the door to freedom. Tom cautiously swims through the opening. Misha follows, and then— *see ya!* They take off and never look back.

ROCK-A-BYE MONKEY

INTAN ENJOYS ACROBATICS.

INTAN CUDDLES WITH HER MOM WHEN SHE'S READY TO REST.

Gleefully vaulting from branch to branch, Intan, a six-week-old monkey, is so daring—and so uncoordinated. She slips, then screams for help while dangling from 60 feet (18 m) up a tree. Mom and other females in the troop rush to her rescue.

Ebony langurs, a kind of monkey, spend most of their lives high in the forest canopy. There they effortlessly leap from tree to tree. But today is Intan's first day in a real tree in a real forest. The troop was just released from captivity into the forest of Bromo Tengger Semeru National Park on the island of Java in Indonesia.

Monkey Business

Illegally captured from the wild and sold as pets, the monkeys in this troop are survivors. The Indonesian Conservation Department rescued them, bringing them to a center where caregivers prepare them for release back into the wild. Little Intan is born while the troop is at the center.

When the monkeys are released, biologists and photographers hide on an observation platform high in a tree to watch them settle in. But the monkeys easily find the observers.

Nice Trip. See You Next Fall!

Intan's mother becomes exasperated as she rescues her baby from climbing predicaments. After a few falls, she carries Intan to the not-so-secret blind, and puts her in photographer Djuna Ivereigh's lap.

Before Ivereigh can move the baby from her lap, Intan leaps up to play with a stick. Chasing it across the platform, Intan accidentally topples over the edge. The humans watch in horror as the baby tumbles 25 feet (8 m) to the ground!

Shrieking langurs rush toward the motionless monkey. Scooping up Intan, Mom gently rocks her baby. Very soon, Intan peeks out, unharmed. She bounds away for more monkey mischief.

The dirty looks the others give Ivereigh suggest their opinion of her babysitting skills. The near-disastrous result may achieve one goal, though: No troop member will ever trust a human with one of its own again.

According to an ancient Indian legend, the Raven turned one out of every ten bears white to remind people of a time when Earth was covered by snow and ice.

Secrets of the Spirit Bear

A rare animal creates a mysterious sight in the forest.

On a cold, rainy October night in the rain forest, a hulking white form with a ghostly glow appears in the distance. No, it's not the ghost of a black bear. It's a spirit bear, also called a Kermode bear, which are black bears with white hair. They live almost exclusively in one place: the Great Bear Rainforest along the coast of British Columbia, Canada. Researchers want to figure out why the bears with white coats have survived here. Fewer than 200 spirit bears call this area home.

WHITE COAT CLUES

For many animals, unusual white coloration can make it hard to survive since they may have trouble hiding from predators. But the Kermode bears' coloring may actually help them survive and give them an edge while catching salmon.

"A white bear blends into the background during the day and is more successful catching fish," explains biologist Thomas Reimchen. "There is an advantage to one bear in some conditions and the other in different conditions."

TALE OF TWO ISLANDS

Canada's Gribbell Island has the highest concentration of Kermode bears, followed by neighboring Princess Royal Island. These isolated islands may be another key to the bears' survival since there's no competition from grizzly bears, and wolves are the only natural threat. The islands' trees provide shelters, and rivers are filled with salmon.

Even though spirit bears have flourished on these islands, new threats such as logging worry scientists and the members of the Native American Gitga'at First Nation, who have lived with and protected spirit bears for centuries. That's why researchers are working hard to understand the biology of the spirit bear. As they do, they can find the best ways to ensure its survival.

BIG CATS

A young male
jaguar

What are big cats? To wildlife experts, they are the four living members of the genus *Panthera*: tigers, lions, leopards, and jaguars. They can all unleash a mighty roar and, as carnivores, they survive solely on the flesh of other animals. Thanks to powerful jaws; long, sharp claws; and daggerlike teeth, big cats are excellent hunters.

WHO'S WHO?

BIG CATS MAY HAVE a lot of features in common, but if you know what to look for, you'll be able to tell who's who in no time.

FUR

TIGERS

Most tigers are orange-colored with vertical black stripes on their bodies. This coloring helps the cats blend in with tall grasses as they sneak up on prey. These markings are like fingerprints: No two stripe patterns are alike.

JAGUARS

A jaguar's coat pattern looks similar to that of a leopard, as both have dark spots called rosettes. The difference? The rosettes on a jaguar's torso have irregularly shaped borders and at least one black dot in the center.

LEOPARDS

A leopard's yellowy coat has dark spots called rosettes on its back and sides. In leopards, the rosettes' edges are smooth and circular. This color combo helps leopards blend into their surroundings.

LIONS

Lions have a light brown, or tawny, coat and a tuft of black hair at the end of their tails. When they reach their prime, most male lions have shaggy manes that help them look larger and more intimidating.

JAGUAR
100 to 250 pounds
(45 TO 113 KG)
5 to 6 feet long
(1.5 TO 1.8 M)

LEOPARD
66 to 176 pounds
(30 TO 80 KG)
4.25 to 6.25 feet long
(1.3 TO 1.9 M)

BENGAL TIGER
240 to 500 pounds
(109 TO 227 KG)
5 to 6 feet long
(1.5 TO 1.8 M)

AFRICAN LION
265 to 420 pounds
(120 TO 191 KG)
4.5 to 6.5 feet long
(1.4 TO 2 M)

49

CHEETAHS: Built for SPEED

This wild cat's body makes it an incredible predator.

Breathing deeply, the cheetah prepares her body for the chase. Head low, eyes focused on an impala, she slowly inches forward. In three seconds this streamlined, superfast cat is sprinting at 60 miles an hour (96 km/h), eyes locked, laserlike, on the fleeing impala.

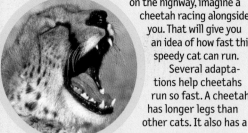

Long, muscular tail for balance in tight turns

The legendary Jamaican runner Usain Bolt is the world's fastest human. Bolt ran 200 meters in 19.19 seconds, about 23 miles an hour (37 km/h), but that's slow compared with the cheetah. Cheetahs can run about three times faster than Bolt. At top speed a sprinting cheetah can reach 70 miles an hour (113 km/h). Next time you're in a car on the highway, imagine a cheetah racing alongside you. That will give you an idea of how fast this speedy cat can run.

Several adaptations help cheetahs run so fast. A cheetah has longer legs than other cats. It also has a

Small, short face with enlarged nostrils to take in lots of air

long, extremely flexible spine. These features work together so a running cheetah can cover up to 23 feet (7 m) in one stride—about the length of five ten-year-olds lying head to feet in a row.

Most other cats can retract their claws when they're not using them. Cheetahs' claws stick out all the time, like dogs' claws. Cheetahs use these strong, blunt claws like an athlete uses cleats on track shoes—to help push off and quickly build up speed. The large center pad on the cheetah's foot is covered with long ridges that act like the treads on a car tire. A sprinting cheetah needs to be able to stop fast, too. It is able to spread its toes wide, and its toe pads are hard and pointed. This helps a cheetah turn quickly

Strong, blunt claws and ridged footpads to grip the ground

and brake suddenly. It can stop in a single stride from a speed of more than 20 miles an hour (32 km/h).

All these body adaptations add up to extraordinary hunting abilities. A cheetah stalks up close to a herd of impalas, then streaks forward with lightning speed. As the herd bolts, the cat singles out one individual and follows its twists and turns precisely. As it closes in on its prey the cheetah strikes out with a forepaw, knocks the animal off its feet, and clamps its jaws over the prey's throat.

Snow Leopard SECRETS

High-tech tools help scientists understand how to save these big cats.

On a cool summer night, a snow leopard curiously sniffs an overhanging boulder for a strong scent sprayed by other cats. He rubs his cheeks on the boulder, scrapes the ground with his hind paws, and then urinates.

This act—called scraping—is how snow leopards communicate with one another. A scrape tells other snow leopards what they're doing and may reveal whether a snow leopard is male or female, has cubs, or is looking for a mate.

Recently, researchers studying the 4,000 to 7,000 snow leopards in the wild have set up motion-activated cameras at scraping sites in an effort to gather more information on these elusive cats and expose new details about how many snow leopards there are, how long they live, and how we can protect them.

Even though snow leopards live in some of the most rugged mountain terrain on Earth, people pose the biggest threat to their survival. Poachers can sell a snow leopard's hide and bones for thousands of dollars. Herders often kill any snow leopard that attacks their livestock. Hunters target ibex, wild sheep, and other animals for food and trophies—removing important snow leopard prey.

Like a snow leopard reality show, the cameras expose everything that happens. The images also help researchers count the number of snow leopards in an area and reveal whether prey animals, livestock, or poachers are nearby.

Other researchers will gently trap the wild cats and put satellite radio collars on them to track where the cats roam and to learn new things about how and where they live. Technology like this is essential to help researchers protect snow leopards in the wild and preserve their habitat.

MARKING TERRITORY

Despite their name, snow leopards are not snow-colored. Their spotted gray or beige fur actually stands out against a snowy background—but blends in with rocks.

TWO CUBS

CHASING DOWN PREY

51

TIGERS in the Snow

These wild cats survive the cold of eastern Russia.

Many Amur tigers have beachfront property—they live in Russian forests on the edge of the Sea of Japan.

Silently moving through the trees, a tigress stalks her prey. Deep snow covers the ground, and with each step the big cat sinks to her belly. She knows the snow will muffle any sounds, so she can sneak up on a wild boar that is rooting around for pine nuts. A few yards away, the tiger pauses, crouches, and then launches her 280-pound (127-kg) body toward her prey. Snow sprays up with each leap as she prepares to pounce on the boar with her plate-size paws. A powdery cloud fills the air. Then the snow settles, revealing the three-foot (0.9-m)-long tail and orange, black, and white body. Now stained red, the tigress grasps the boar in her mouth.

She carries her catch behind some larch trees, and her two cubs join her from a nearby hill. Camouflaged in the trees, they were watching their mother hunt. Soon, they'll start hunting for themselves. But for now, they are content with the meal their mother has provided, followed by a nap.

These Siberian, or Amur, tigers live in the eastern reaches of Russia—farther north than any other tiger subspecies. Thick coats of fur insulate their bodies from the freezing winter temps. In the summer, their coats blend in with the forest, making them nearly impossible to see.

HUNGER GAMES

The tiger trio is among the some 400 Amur tigers that researchers think are left in the wild. As recently as 50 years ago, there were plenty of deer and wild boar, the staples of a tiger's diet. Today, those prey animals are harder to find. People hunt

A TIGER CUB STICKS WITH MOM FOR AT LEAST 18 MONTHS.

them, and logging companies and fires destroy the forest where they live. Some tiger habitat is protected, but the cats wander beyond these safe zones in search of prey. Half of all tiger cubs die young because they are sick, killed by hunters, or orphaned. Cubs that survive leave Mom at about 18 months old, relying on the hunting skills they learned growing up. Sometimes a young male must travel far to find unclaimed land that has enough food. But the odds are that his journey will take him through areas where people live.

TROUBLESHOOTING

It is late winter when the male tiger leaves his mother's care. When he scratches against a tree, he catches his paw on something. He's walked into a wire snare, and the more he moves, the tighter it gets. A little while later, he hears voices. People. They stay behind the trees, and one of them raises a gun. The tiger roars at the sharp pain in his backside, then lies down and falls asleep. He's been shot by a researcher's tranquilizer gun, not a hunter. Unable to find enough food in the snowy forest, this tiger started taking livestock and dogs in a nearby town. Dale Miquelle and his team are called in to fix the problem. "Relocating them gives them a second chance," Miquelle says. Otherwise, the farmer would track down the tiger and shoot him.

The researchers quickly weigh and measure the tranquilized tiger. Then they fit a collar with a radio transmitter around his neck. This will let Miquelle's team keep track of the tiger's whereabouts for at least three years.

NEW TERRITORY

Two hours later, the tiger wakes up in the back of a truck about 150 miles (241 km) from the town. The cage gate opens, and the wild cat leaps out. Unfamiliar with the territory, he searches for signs of other tigers. He comes across a birch tree with a strong odor. Another male sprayed the tree and left scrape marks and urine on the ground to tell others, "Occupied. Keep moving."

The young tiger walks on. Miquelle's team monitors his movements using signals from the radio collar. They hope he can find food, avoid other males, find his own territory, and eventually mate with a local female. The tiger spots a deer ahead. Melting snow drips from the trees, masking his footsteps as he ambushes his prey. His odds just got a little better.

THIS TIGER'S SCRATCHES ON TREES ARE MESSAGES FOR OTHER TIGERS.

In the 1930s, only about 30 Amur tigers were left in the wild.

ICE-COLD WATER QUENCHES THIS TIGER'S THIRST.

Family Pride

Lion cubs grow up strong with help from moms, aunts, and big sisters.

Hidden among tall grass and bushes in Africa, a mother cub rests while her two lion cubs bury their faces in her belly to nurse. At five weeks old, they've eaten only mother's milk since birth. In a couple of weeks they'll start to eat meat, but first they must meet the pride, or family group.

Family First

After their nap, the mother takes the cubs to the woods near a river, where they're greeted by six young cats, the cubs' cousins. More lions lounge nearby. They are familiar with the newcomers because their mom has been wearing their scent when she has returned to the pride for group hunts.

A shaggy mane surrounding a massive male lion's head appears from behind the rock. The pride ruler. The mother lion waits to see if he recognizes her cubs as his offspring. If not, he will kill them on the spot. He pads over to the cubs and sniffs their heads. They bat his nose with tiny paws. He bats back, growling. He finally decides the cubs are his and plops down to rest.

Pride Power

It's time for the lions to eat. Hunting is an organized family affair: It will take several lions to overpower something like a one-ton (907-kg) buffalo bull. While the females fan out and surround a small group of buffalo, the younger cubs quietly watch from a distance.

A lioness sprints toward a bull, and the other lions jump on, digging in their teeth as they pull the bull down. Then the whole pride runs over to claim some meat. The pride's large male chases away the females and eats his fill. When he moves away, the rest of the pride fights over any leftovers. The two cubs gnaw small pieces with their new teeth.

The distracted pride doesn't notice a new male lion approaching. He wants to take over the pride and its territory, so he challenges the pride leader, who is older and weaker. Eventually, the injured old ruler limps away, abandoning the pride. The new male moves to his next victims: the cubs. He wants his own offspring, so these cubs must go. But the older females fight him off, and the twins' mother escapes with her cubs.

Again on the move, the twins stay close to their mother. She and two of her sisters have split from the pride to save their offspring. Even a small group is better protected than a lone lion with cubs, so they're hoping it will be enough to survive.

A MALE LION ACCEPTS HIS OWN CUB AS IT APPROACHES TO PLAY.

SCAN THIS PAGE!
GET BONUS MOBILE CONTENT! Download the free NG Kids scanner app. Directions on inside front cover.

YOUNG LIONS PRACTICE HUNTING SKILLS AS THEY PLAY.

HUNTING IS A GROUP EFFORT, ESPECIALLY WHEN PREY IS AS BIG AS THESE BUFFALO.

BIZARRE Insects

Check out some of the strangest bugs on Earth!

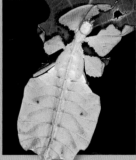

The bright-colored head of the puss moth caterpillar warns predators to stay away. This species, one of the most toxic caterpillars in North America, can spray acid from its head when it is attacked.

puss moth caterpillar

walking leaf

This flat, green insect is a master of disguise: It's common to mistake this bug for an actual leaf, thanks to its large, feathery wings. This clever camouflage provides protection from potential predators.

giraffe-necked weevil

No surprise, this bug gets its name from its extra-long neck. The males have longer necks than females do, which they use to fight other males for mating rights.

thorn bugs

One tiny thorn bug may not be a match for a bigger predator, but when grouped together on a branch, these spiky bugs create a prickly pack no bird wants a bite of!

spiny katydid

This katydid is covered in sharper-than-knives spikes. If a predator attacks, this species springs into action, defending itself by jabbing an enemy with its spiny legs and arms.

cockshafer beetle

The wild, feathery antennae on the male cockshafer may be cool to look at, but they're also helpful tools. They enable the bug to sniff for food and feel out its surrounding environment.

acorn weevil

The acorn weevil's hollow nose is longer than its body, and perfect for drilling through the shells of acorns. A female will feast on the nut by sucking up its rich, fatty liquid, and then lay her eggs in the acorn.

pink grasshopper

Though most grasshoppers are green or brown, some—like this pink nymph—are much brighter. Pink grasshoppers are rare, most likely because they are easy for predators to spot.

man-faced stinkbug

There are more than 4,500 species of stinkbugs world-wide, including this brilliant yellow species, whose shield-shaped body displays a unique pattern resembling a tribal mask. Like all stinkbugs, this species secretes a foul-smelling liquid from scent glands between its legs when it feels threatened.

rhinoceros beetle

Ounce for ounce, this insect, which gets its name from the horn-like structure on the male's head, is considered one of the world's strongest creatures. It is capable of carrying up to 850 times its own body weight.

5 SiLLY Pet Tricks

1 GOAT SKATEBOARDS

Jumping on her skateboard, Happie the goat zips down driveways and cruises along sidewalks. The animal first showed her zeal for wheels when she tried to leap on a bicycle that owner Melody Cooke was riding. Cooke decided to get Happie her very own skateboard and train her to ride. After a lot of practice and goodies, the goat learned some sweet boarding moves: Happie can coast for more than 100 feet (30 m) without stopping. Talk about being on a roll.

2 HORSE PLAYS B-BALL

Before he makes a slam dunk, Amos the miniature horse looks around to see if people are watching. "Amos definitely likes an audience," owner Shelly Mizrahi says. To teach him to "play" basketball, Mizrahi gave Amos carrot slices each time he touched his nose to a hoop set on a short stand. Later Amos learned to pick up a small ball with his teeth and place it in the hoop. Scoring baskets has become the horse's all-time favorite activity. The hoofed athlete once dunked the ball a hundred times in a row. "Amos can also paint and play a xylophone with a mallet," Mizrahi says. "But if I place a paintbrush, a musical instrument, and a basketball in front of him, he always goes for the basketball."

4 PIG JAMS ON HORNS

Why won't you see Jax the cat's paw prints on the floor? Because the kitty can move around on a large, rolling ball! "Jax has always loved perching on narrow surfaces," owner Samantha Martin says. "I thought she'd like even cooler balancing acts." To prepare for the trick, Jax practiced standing on a smaller ball set in a bowl so it couldn't move. Then Martin placed her on a bigger ball at one end of a short track. On the other end were yummy cat treats. The clever kitty quickly figured out that if she inched backward on the ball, she could move it down the track—and get her delicious reward.

CAT WALKS ON BALL 3

Mudslinger the pig could be a real hog when it came to music. He enjoyed creating tunes with horns, and once he got started, he sometimes didn't want to stop. Trainer John Vincent introduced the pig to the horns by tooting some in front of him. After watching his owner, the curious pig tried squeezing the instruments with his mouth to make noise. Whenever he continued, Vincent fed him juicy grapes to keep him motivated. The curly-tailed rock star created new sound patterns whenever he played.

5 MACAW TAKES UP SKIING

Luna the hyacinth macaw loves to fly—down a ski slope! Owner Mark Steiger knew the eight-year-old bird would be a natural skier. "Hyacinth macaws like Luna have strong legs," he says. First, Luna practiced walking while clutching handles on tiny skis with her claws. Then Steiger taught her to slide down a custom-made four-foot (1.2-m)-tall slope on the skis, rewarding the bird with treats at the bottom. The macaw even learned to take a "ski lift" up her slope. With her hardy beak, she grasps onto a metal ring that her owner uses to pull her up the slide. Just before Luna whooshes back down, she leans forward like a competitive skier. "She picked that up all on her own," Steiger says. "Luna's a total pro."

Lifestyles of the

C elebs and royalty aren't the only ones lapping up luxury. With decked-out doghouses, private jets, and cat crowns, the lifestyles of some pets are totally drool-worthy. In 2013, U.S. pet owners spent about $55 billion on their furry companions. "Pets are an important part of the family," says Bob Vetere, associate president of the American Pet Products Association. "Some owners like to shower their animals with nice things."

Loving your pet doesn't have to cost an arm and a paw. Hugs, kisses, snacks, and attention are all your furry friend needs to feel like royalty.

COCO'S LOOKIN' GOOD WITH HER FLASHY LOCKS.

KITTY GLITTER

Like many pampered pets, Coco the cat has all the must-have fashion accessories. When this kitty wants to show off her rock-star style, she slips on a hot-pink wig. For a more elegant look, the feline fashionista dons a faux fur coat and tiara. This kitty is sitting pretty!

CANINE CASTLES

Coco Puff the Yorkshire terrier and Rio the Doberman pinscher love to kick back in their two-bedroom doghouse. Many people are buying custom-made homes like this one for their pets. "Owners want an area where their dogs feel relaxed," says Michelle Pollak of La Petite Maison, which builds luxury pet homes. Fancy doggie digs can have wood floors, bay windows, and balconies. Some are big enough to hold six people!

THIS DOG FEELS RIGHT AT HOME IN HIS POOCH PALACE.

RICH and FURRY

BASED ON A WORK BY THOMAS GAINSBOROUGH CALLED "THE BLUE BOY," THIS PAINTING FEATURES A SERIOUSLY DAPPER-LOOKING KITTY!

▶ JOIN THE CLUB

Frank the bulldog's favorite hangout isn't a dog park—it's a country club! The Club Beverly Hills is an ultra-fancy resort that caters to canines. "Dogs are so excited when they arrive here, they leap out of the car," owner Marjorie Lewis says. Members start their visits by running around a specially made fitness course. To relax, posh pets can soak in a hot tub, get massages, or do yoga with a human instructor.

CATS ON CANVAS ▲

Tiger the tabby's owners wanted more than just photographs of their beloved feline. So they asked an artist to paint a portrait. "Pet paintings are a tribute to the bond people share with their animals," says Rebecca Collins of Art Paw portrait studio. Collins and her team create pet paintings (starting at $135) based on snapshots. They'll even re-create famous works of art and add your pet to the scene.

DOG DOES YOGA!

RICOCHET THE GOLDEN RETRIEVER LIVES THE HIGH LIFE WITH A GOURMET MEAL ON A PLANE.

◀ JET-SET PETS

Beijit the golden retriever travels in style. When she flies on private jets with her owners, they hire a pet flight attendant to care for her. "Our animal customers get majorly pampered," says Carol Martin, owner of Sit 'n Stay Global. The company's pet flight attendants serve fresh-cooked entrées on fine china and give thirsty critters chilled spring water in crystal bowls. After the plane lands, pet flight attendants become pet nannies, caring for their animal clients while the owners go sightseeing. *Bone* voyage!

BEIJIT ENJOYS THE VIEW.

REAL ANIMAL HEROES!

THESE ANIMALS SHOW AMAZING BRAVERY.

DOG SAVES KID FROM TRUCK

Geo the German shepherd mix follows ten-year-old Charlie Riley everywhere. Naturally the pup goes along on family walks.

One day Charlie, his mom, and two younger brothers are standing at a street corner. Geo is sitting at Charlie's side. Suddenly ...

"We hear a roar," Charlie's mother says. An out-of-control pickup jumps the curb. It's heading straight for Charlie!

But Geo makes a flying leap. "He hits me so hard I fall over," Charlie says. The speeding truck slams into Geo instead. They rush an injured Geo to the animal hospital for emergency surgery.

"My dog could have died," Charlie says. And my son could have too, thinks his mother. But he didn't—thanks to Geo.

CAT RESCUES COUPLE

Three years after adopting a stray cat named Tiger, Michelle and Rod Ramsey are in bed with blinding headaches. Suddenly Tiger bursts into their room and howls. When Tiger won't stop, Michelle stumbles down the hall and lets him outside. That's when she sees her older cat staggering and calls the vet. "You have carbon monoxide poisoning," the veterinary assistant says when she hears Michelle slurring. Carbon monoxide is a deadly gas. Invisible and odorless, it's leaking out of the Ramseys' heating system.

Paramedics arrive. An emergency helicopter airlifts the Ramseys to the hospital. They both survive. All thanks to a cat no one else wanted.

BLIND FELINE DEFEATS ROBBER

Homer the blind cat weighs only four pounds. Gwen Cooper adopted the little stray in Miami, Florida, U.S.A., when he was three weeks old. Because of an eye infection that left him blind, he would have been euthanized if she hadn't taken him in.

Homer never lets blindness stop him. "He's a bold little adventurer," Cooper says. "He's fearless." The cat proves this one night when his growling wakes up Cooper. He's never growled before. Surprised, Cooper opens her eyes. A burglar is standing at the foot of her bed! Cooper reaches for her phone to call 911.

"Don't do that!" the intruder says. The sound of his voice pinpoints his exact location, and blind Homer leaps. No match for a snarling cat with extended claws, the would-be robber flees.

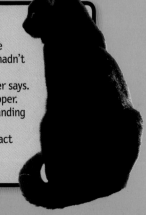

NAUGHTY PETS

CAUGHT ON CAMERA

NAME Lotse

FAVORITE ACTIVITY
Running a shelter for rescued dogs—hot dogs, that is

FAVORITE TOY
Squirting ketchup

PET PEEVE
Hot dog vendors in the park

DON'T WORRY, MY WIENER DOG COUSIN! I'LL SAVE YOU!

TWO-PLY TOILET PAPER IS SO MUCH EASIER TO UNROLL THAN ONE-PLY.

NAME June

FAVORITE ACTIVITY
Redecorating the bathroom

FAVORITE TOY
Rubber ducky

PET PEEVE Wet toilet paper under her claws

NAME Wookie

FAVORITE ACTIVITY
Building an empire of sweets

FAVORITE TOY
Lightsaber cake cutter

PET PEEVE
Wearing a helmet at the dinner table

SEND DOWN THE TUNA! DON'T MAKE ME COME UP THERE.

NAME Fuji

FAVORITE ACTIVITY
Scaling the fridge

FAVORITE TOY Napkin rings

PET PEEVE Being put back down on the floor

IS THIS A MAGNETIC CAKE? BECAUSE MY TONGUE IS FEELING THE FORCE.

PAW ENFORCEMENT

★★★★★★★★★★★★★★★★★★★★★★★★★★★★★

DOGS ON DUTY SNIFF OUT SMUGGLERS.

NON-POISONOUS GOPHER SNAKES **ARE USED FOR TRAINING.**

Walking his beat at the Honolulu International Airport in Hawaii, Taylor stops to observe two women waiting for a flight to the U.S. mainland. Taylor's partner, Inspector Edna Tanaid, has no reason to believe the women might be smugglers, but Taylor smells trouble. He's a skilled, no-nonsense detective that works for the federal government. There's only one thing Taylor likes more than busting smugglers—the mouthwatering flavor of meaty dog treats. Taylor is a beagle mix. And you're in trouble if he sits down next to you and wags his tail so hard it looks ready to fly off.

BUSTED BY A DOG

"Where are your fruits?" Tanaid asks.

"We aren't carrying any," the women reply. Taylor excitedly wags, pants, and aims his sensitive nose back and forth at the women's jacket pockets. Sure enough, they have mangoes in their pockets. Tanaid seizes the contraband, or illegal goods, and gives Taylor some extra petting along with his meaty reward.

Sniffing around may sound like fun—and for Taylor, it is—but it's important work. Mangoes could contain the larvae of the Mediterranean fruit fly, a variety that lives in Hawaii but not in the continental United States. If these fruit flies reach the mainland, they could devastate American crops, costing billions of dollars.

Taylor was born with his great nose, but before putting it to work, he and his canine colleagues get about three months of training at the National Detector Dog Training Center in Georgia. There the new recruits learn the basic scent of contraband and how to find it in bags, boxes, and pockets—an advanced game of hide-and-seek.

CANINES AT WORK

In addition to sniffing around travelers and baggage, dog teams also examine U.S. and international mail, which is a huge job. Janelle Michalesko checks out arriving cargo and mail with her canine partner, Khaz, at JFK Airport in New York City. Khaz is equal parts Chesapeake Bay and Labrador retriever, a big energetic mix that makes him perfect for patrolling long warehouses and inspecting big boxes.

GOOD JOB

Along with the fruits and vegetables they discover, Khaz and Michalesko regularly find mailed meat products that could carry diseases. The handler guesses that it would take her a full day to search a warehouse that Khaz can clear in 15 minutes. Other breeds do different jobs. Tiny, fearless Jack Russell terriers, for instance, are perfect for finding brown tree snakes in cargo leaving Guam, a U.S. island in the Pacific Ocean. If stowaway snakes spread to Hawaii, it could doom the state's rare birds.

SMART PUPS

For sniffing baggage and passengers at airports, beagles are the ideal breed. "They're very friendly and people usually aren't intimidated by them," says Andrew Bateman, a Customs and Border Protection (CBP) handler who, with pup partner Cayenne, guards the Hartsfield-Jackson Atlanta International Airport. Detector dogs don't just smell well; they're trained to smell the difference between contraband and safe snacks.

Someone might assume a dog as valuable as Cayenne was raised in a special kennel and trained from birth. "She was actually found on the side of the road on a highway," Bateman says. All detector dogs that deal with agricultural items were adopted. Many, like Cayenne, are found at animal shelters, while others are donated by owners or breeders.

"I couldn't for the life of me figure out why somebody would give away a dog that's so handsome," says handler Jonathan Saito about his stocky beagle partner, Bruno, a former pound dog. "He's just an incredible dog to work with. We say 'work,' but actually, it's a game for the dogs."

Tanaid agrees. "Taking in one of these dogs and giving it a second chance at doing an important public service is great. And the dogs love what they do."

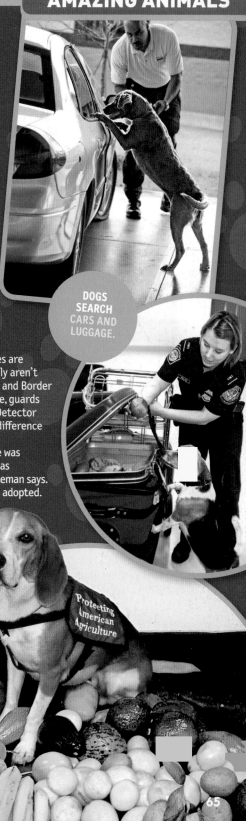

DOGS SEARCH CARS AND LUGGAGE.

IN ONLY TWO DAYS, TAYLOR FOUND ALL THIS.

Protecting American Agriculture

15 Cutest Animals of 2015

From arctic foxes to zebras, baby animals easily qualify as some of the cutest creatures on Earth. Here's NG Kids' roundup of cuddly critters that are sure to make you say *awww*.

1

OUT AND ABOUT

A young Emperor penguin stays fluffy to fight the chill in Antarctica. A chick stays snug in its mother's brood pouch for two months. As it grows older, adults leave chicks in groups called crèches while they go off to fish.

2

BEAR-Y CUTE

Talk about *panda*-monium: A collection of giant panda cubs rests in a crib at a research center in China where they're being bred to help boost the endangered animal's numbers in the wild.

3

REAL TROOPERS

A family—or troop—of ring-tailed lemurs get close and cuddly in a zoo enclosure. In the wild, lemurs live in groups of up to 30 animals. They travel as a pack foraging for food during the day and spend their nights huddled together as they snooze.

4

SUMMER STYLE

Hi, there! This adorable arctic fox pops out of his burrow in Alaska. This animal's thick fur changes color with the seasons, going from grayish brown in the summer to white in the winter.

5

STUCK ON YOU

This itsy-bitsy amphibian may look harmless, but watch out! The Amazon milk frog gets its name from the milky-colored fluid it secretes when threatened. Native to South America, milk frogs spend most of their lives high in the rain forest canopy and hardly ever touch the ground.

6

MUG SHOT

Why so glum? "Grumpy Cat" Tardar Sauce became an Internet sensation after her owner's brother posted a video on YouTube. But this kitty's not really mad: Her frowny face is likely a result of feline dwarfism.

7

FUR BABY

A harp seal pup soaks up the sun on ice off the coast of the Gulf of St. Lawrence in Canada. Born with very little body fat, the pups have thick, white fur that traps heat from the sunlight to keep them warm and snug.

8

PUPPY LOVE

Abandoned by the side of the road as a puppy, Tuna the chiweenie (that's part Chihuahua, part dachshund) was so traumatized, he'd squirm on his belly instead of walking. Now? The puppy is thriving in an adopted home, and pics of his adventures—and his funny outfits—have earned him fans around the world. How's that for a happy ending?

9

SHOW-OFF

Just call him four eyes:
A bespectacled dolphin
steals the show at a water
park in Phuket, Thailand.
Considered one of the
smartest mammals on
the planet, dolphins can
recognize themselves in
a mirror and can hear
sounds underwater that
are 15 miles (24 km) away.

10

HOW *DEER*

Gimme a kiss! A roe deer plants one on her
friend in Olympic National Park, Washington,
U.S.A., as they graze in a spring meadow.
In the wild, fawns stay protected from predators like red foxes and bears by hiding in long
grass until they're ready to join the rest of
the herd—usually at six weeks old.

11

HOOFIN' IT

Catch me if you can! A young zebra flocks in a field of flowers in Namibia, Africa. Speedy zebras, which can walk just 20 minutes after they're born, tend to run in a zigzag pattern to confuse predators.

12

MONKEYING AROUND

A golden snub-nosed monkey perches atop a branch high in the mountains of China. These elusive monkeys travel in groups of up to 400 monkeys. That smushed-in nose isn't just there to look cute: It may also be an adaptation to protect the primates from extremely cold temps.

13

PLAYTIME

Hey mom, wake up! Two polar bear cubs climb on their resting mom in Wapusk National Park in Manitoba, Canada. In the wild, playful polar bear cubs tend to stick by their mama's side for about two years. During that time, she will protect them and teach them how to hunt.

14

STANDOUT

Chameleons usually do a pretty good job of blending into their backgrounds. Not this guy. With its bright blue skin and helmet-shaped head, the panther chameleon definitely stands out. The lizards, which can grow to be as long as a cat, are native to the tropical forests of Madagascar, and are also very popular pets.

15

HEAD COUNT

It's a raccoon totem pole! Three baby raccoons—or kits—create a too-cute tower as they poke their heads out of a tree. After building a den in the hollow of a tree or a burrow, raccoon mamas give birth to litters of about two to five kits. Babies stay with their mom until they are over one year old.

Prehistoric TIME LINE

HUMANS HAVE WALKED on Earth for some 200,000 years, a mere blip in Earth's 4.5-billion-year history. A lot has happened during that time. Earth formed, and oxygen levels rose in the millions of years of the Precambrian time. The productive Paleozoic era gave rise to hard-shelled organisms, vertebrates, amphibians, and reptiles.

Dinosaurs ruled the Earth in the mighty Mesozoic. And 64 million years after dinosaurs became extinct, modern humans emerged in the Cenozoic era. From the first tiny mollusks to the dinosaur giants of the Jurassic and beyond, Earth has seen a lot of transformation.

THE PRECAMBRIAN TIME

4.5 billion to 542 million years ago

- The Earth (and other planets) formed from gas and dust left over from a giant cloud that collapsed to form the sun. The giant cloud's collapse was triggered when nearby stars exploded.
- Low levels of oxygen made Earth a suffocating place.
- Early life-forms appeared.

THE PALEOZOIC ERA

542 million to 251 million years ago

- The first insects and other animals appeared on land.
- 450 million years ago (m.y.a.), the ancestors of sharks began to swim in the oceans.
- 430 m.y.a., plants began to take root on land.
- More than 360 m.y.a., amphibians emerged from the water.
- Slowly the major landmasses began to come together, creating Pangaea, a single supercontinent.
- By 300 m.y.a., reptiles had begun to dominate the land.

What Killed the Dinosaurs?

WAS IT AN ASTEROID, A VOLCANO, OR BOTH? Scientists seeking to explain the disappearance of dinosaurs 65 million years ago believe that a huge impact, such as from an asteroid or comet, a massive bout of volcanic activity, or the combination of the two events might have choked the sky with debris that starved Earth of the sun's energy. The resulting greenhouse gases may have caused the temperature to soar, causing half of the world's species—including the dinosaurs—to die in a mass extinction.

DINO TIMES

THE MESOZOIC ERA

251 million to 65 million years ago

The Mesozoic era, or the age of the reptiles, consisted of three consecutive time periods (shown below). This is when the first dinosaurs began to appear. They would reign supreme for more than 150 million years.

TRIASSIC PERIOD

251 million to 199 million years ago

- Appearance of the first mammals. They were rodent-size.
- The first dinosaur appeared.
- Ferns were the dominant plants on land.
- The giant supercontinent of Pangaea began breaking up toward the end of the Triassic.

JURASSIC PERIOD

199 million to 145 million years ago

- Giant dinosaurs dominated the land.
- Pangaea continued its breakup, and oceans formed in the spaces between the drifting landmasses, allowing sea life, including sharks and marine crocodiles, to thrive.
- Conifer trees spread across the land.

CRETACEOUS PERIOD

145 million to 65 million years ago

- The modern continents developed.
- The largest dinosaurs developed.
- Flowering plants spread across the landscape.
- Mammals flourished, and giant pterosaurs ruled the skies over the small birds.
- Temperatures grew more extreme. Dinosaurs lived in deserts, swamps, and forests from the Antarctic to the Arctic.

THE CENOZOIC ERA—TERTIARY PERIOD

65 million to 2.6 million years ago

- Following the dinosaur extinction, mammals rose as the dominant species.
- Birds continued to flourish.
- Volcanic activity was widespread.
- Temperatures began to cool, eventually ending in an ice age.
- The period ended with land bridges forming, which allowed plants and animals to spread to new areas.

DINO Classification

Classifying dinosaurs and all other living things can be a complicated matter, so scientists have devised a system to help with the process. Dinosaurs are put into groups based on a very large range of characteristics.

Scientists put dinosaurs into two major groups: the bird-hipped ornithischians and the reptile-hipped saurischians.

Ornithischian

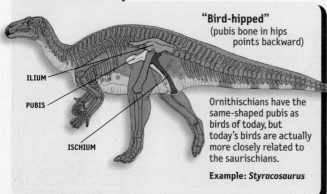

"Bird-hipped"
(pubis bone in hips points backward)

ILIUM

PUBIS

ISCHIUM

Ornithischians have the same-shaped pubis as birds of today, but today's birds are actually more closely related to the saurischians.

Example: *Styracosaurus*

Saurischian

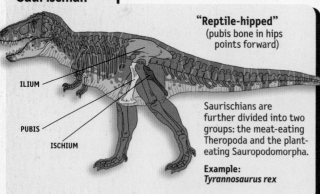

"Reptile-hipped"
(pubis bone in hips points forward)

ILIUM

PUBIS

ISCHIUM

Saurischians are further divided into two groups: the meat-eating Theropoda and the plant-eating Sauropodomorpha.

Example:
Tyrannosaurus rex

Within these two main divisions, dinosaurs are then separated into orders and then families, such as Stegosauria. Like other members of the Stegosauria, *Stegosaurus* had spines and plates along the back, neck, and tail.

SOME DINOSAURS **HAD** 1,000 **TEETH.**

ALL DINOSAURS **WALKED ON THEIR TOES.**

LIKE BABY HUMANS, *PSITTACOSAURUS* CRAWLED BEFORE IT WALKED.

MOST DINOSAURS COULD SWIM.

4 NEWLY DISCOVERED DINOS

Humans have been searching for—and discovering—dinosaur remains for hundreds of years. In that time, at least 1,000 species of dinos have been found all over the world, and thousands more may still be out there waiting to be unearthed. Recent discoveries include the dog-size, 230-million-year-old *Eodromaeus*, found in Argentina and believed to be one of the world's earliest predators. For more exciting dino discoveries, read on.

4 *Xenoceratops foremostensis*
(Ornithischian)

Alien horn-faced

Length: 20 feet (6 m)

Time Range: Late Cretaceous

Where: Alberta, Canada

1 *Nasutoceratops titusi*
(Ornithischian)

Big nose horned face

Length: 15 feet (5 m)

Time Range: Late Cretaceous

Where: Utah, U.S.A.

3 *Nyasasaurus parringtoni*
(Saurischian)

Lake Nyasa lizard

Length: 6.5–10 feet (2–3 m)

Time Range: Early Triassic

Where: Tanzania, Africa

2 *Pegomastax africanus*
(Ornithischian)

Thick jaw from Africa

Length: Less than 2 feet (0.6 m)

Time Range: Early Jurassic

Where: South Africa

OLDEST DINO EVER?

Just when you thought dinos couldn't get any older, the oldest dinosaur (*Nyasasaurus parringtoni*) has been found in Africa. The fossils push back the dawn of the dinosaurs to around 240 million years ago—about 10 to 15 million years earlier than previously thought. But there's not enough information yet to say whether the creature was a true dinosaur or whether it was the dinosaur's closest cousin.

Dynamite DINO AWARDS

Spiky body armor. Razor-sharp teeth. Unimaginable strength. No doubt, all dinos are cool. But whether they were the biggest, the fiercest, or the biggest-brained of the bunch, some stand out more than others. Here are seven of the most amazing dinos ever discovered.

Supersize Appetite

Big Brain

Scientists think that *Tyrannosaurus rex* could gulp down 500 pounds (227 kg) of meat at a time—that's like eating 2,000 hamburger patties in one bite!

Troodon, a meat-eater the size of a man, had a brain as big as an avocado pit—relatively large for a dinosaur of its small stature. Because of its big brain, scientists think *Troodon* may have been the smartest dino and as intelligent as modern birds.

Cool Camo

The birdlike *Sinornithosaurus* had feathers similar to those of modern birds. It may have also had reddish brown, yellow, and black coloring that kept this turkey-size raptor camouflaged as it hunted in the forest.

Heavy-weight

The heaviest of all dinosaurs, *Argentinosaurus* is believed to have weighed 220,000 pounds (99,790 kg)—more than 15 elephants.

Pint-Size Predator

Microraptor zhaoianus, the smallest meat-eating dinosaur, measured just 16 inches (40 cm) tall. With long toe tips for grasping branches, it's thought to be closely related to today's birds.

Built for Speed

Ornithomimids, a group of dinosaurs that resembled ostriches, would have given the world's fastest man a run for his money. Some of these long-limbed, toothless meat-eaters are thought to have clocked speeds of 50 miles an hour (80 km/h).

Super Spines

Known as the "spine lizard," *Spinosaurus* had huge spines sticking out of its back, some taller than a fourth grader! Weighing up to 22 tons (20,000 kg), it may have been the biggest meat-eating dinosaur.

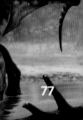

DINOSAUR MYTHS

BUSTED!

CHECK OUT THESE PREHISTORIC PUZZLES.

Some ideas about dinosaurs are just plain wrong, but they still can be hard to get rid of. (Have you heard the one about *Stegosaurus* having a brain in its rump? It didn't.) Here's another myth about *Stegosaurus*, along with more news about other dinos you may know.

THE MYTH

STEGOSAURUS' BRAIN WAS ONLY THE SIZE OF A WALNUT.

WHERE IT PROBABLY CAME FROM

In 1877, a paleontologist named O.C. Marsh studied the first *Stegosaurus* found. He measured plaster casts of the inside of the tiny braincase and announced it had "the smallest brain of any known land vertebrate." Newspapers began trumpeting the tiny brain. Publishers found they could sell books if they included the not-very-smart *Stegosaurus,* saying it had "a brain no larger than a walnut."

WHAT WE KNOW NOW

More than a century later, Ashley Morhardt of Ohio University's WitmerLab wondered if the walnut story was true. Using computers, she produced a digital cast of *Stegosaurus'* brain cavity. She modeled the brain's odd shapes in a software program and figured out each shape's volume. Then she added them up. The brain was really the size of *two* walnuts! "*Stegosaurus* was still probably pretty dumb, though," Morhardt says.

$1 \times 1 = 11$

THE MYTH

DINOSAURS FOUND IN THE "DEATH POSE" DIED IN AGONY.

WHERE IT PROBABLY CAME FROM

Head pulled back upside down over the hips, tail stretched forward. The death pose is common among theropods, which were two-legged, mostly meat-eating dinosaurs. Paleontologists long wondered why. One thought the dinos had died while sleeping. Others believed that they'd been poisoned, suffocated, or died in agony. Or that dead dinos might have become fossilized pretzels as they dried out.

WHAT WE KNOW NOW

What if the dead dinosaurs ended up in a lake or a stream? wondered Alicia Cutler and Brooks Britt of Brigham Young University. To test this idea, they placed dead chickens in buckets of water. The heads swung back almost instantly! In water, the head and neck float. That allows ligaments between the backbones to shorten, pulling the neck into a tight arch. A chicken placed on dry sand didn't take the death pose, even months after drying out.

THE MYTH

ONLY LITTLE DINOSAURS HAD FEATHERS.

WHERE IT PROBABLY CAME FROM

Paleontologists have been finding extremely well-preserved skeletons of small, nonflying feathered dinosaurs in China's Liaoning Province. Scientists think the feathers might have kept them warm or helped attract mates. It seemed only little dinosaurs had feathers. The biggest was *Beipiaosaurus,* which was seven feet (2.1 m) long. Other feathered dinos were pip-squeaks, like *Sinosauropteryx.* But a feathered *Tyrannosaurus rex?* No way!

WHAT WE KNOW NOW

Recently, Chinese and Canadian scientists reported a huge new dinosaur with long feathers covering most of its body. *Yutyrannus* was 30 feet (9.2 m) long and 40 times heavier than *Beipiaosaurus.* And it was a tyrannosaur, three-quarters the length of its ginormous later relative, *T. rex.* So maybe the terrifying Tyrant King was really soft and fluffy.

STUMP YOUR PARENTS

AMAZING ANIMALS QUIZ

Do your parents know all about animals? Find out by testing their smarts on all sorts of species. (All questions are based on information in this chapter.)

ANSWERS BELOW

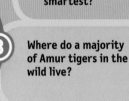

① **True or false?** Glass frogs have black bones.

② **Which dino is believed to have been the smartest?**
- **a.** *T. rex*
- **b.** *Troodon*
- **c.** *Apatosaurus*
- **d.** Barney

③ **Where do a majority of Amur tigers in the wild live?**
- **a.** Russia
- **b.** China
- **c.** Hawaii
- **d.** Antarctica

④ **A snake can smell with its _____.**
- **a.** tongue
- **b.** nose
- **c.** teeth
- **d.** feet

⑤ **What is an extended lion family called?**
- **a.** a team
- **b.** a clan
- **c.** a pride
- **d.** a litter

Not **STUMPED** yet?
Check out the *National Geographic Kids Quiz Whiz* collection for more crazy **ANIMAL** questions!

ANSWERS: 1. False. They have green bones to help them blend in with leaves; 2. b; 3. a; 4. a; 5. c

Wildly Good Animal Reports

beluga whale

Your teacher wants a written report on the beluga whale. Not to worry. Use these organizational tools so you can stay afloat while writing a report.

STEPS TO SUCCESS: Your report will follow the format of a descriptive or expository essay (see p. 117 for "How to Write a Perfect Essay") and should consist of a main idea, followed by supporting details and a conclusion. Use this basic structure for each paragraph as well as the whole report, and you'll be on the right track.

1. Introduction
State your **main idea.**
> *The beluga whale is a common and important species of whale.*

2. Body
Provide **supporting points** for your main idea.
> *The beluga whale is one of the smallest whale species.*
> *It is also known as the "white whale" because of its distinctive coloring.*
> *These whales are common in the Arctic Ocean's coastal waters.*

Then **expand** on those points with further description, explanation, or discussion.
> *The beluga whale is one of the smallest whale species.*
> *Belugas range in size from 13 to 20 feet (4 to 6.1 m) in length.*
> *It is also known as the "white whale" because of its distinctive coloring.*
> *Belugas are born gray or brown. They fade to white at around five years old.*
> *These whales are common in the Arctic Ocean's coastal waters.*
> *Some Arctic belugas migrate south in large herds when sea ice freezes over.*

3. Conclusion
Wrap it up with a **summary** of your whole paper.
> *Because of its unique coloring and unusual features, belugas are among the most familiar and easily distinguishable of all the whales.*

KEY INFORMATION

Here are some things you should consider including in your report:

> What does your animal look like?
> To what other species is it related?
> How does it move?
> Where does it live?
> What does it eat?
> What are its predators?
> How long does it live?
> Is it endangered?
> Why do you find it interesting?

SEPARATE FACT FROM FICTION: Your animal may have been featured in a movie or in myths and legends. Compare and contrast how the animal has been portrayed with how it behaves in reality. For example, penguins can't dance the way they do in *Happy Feet*.

PROOFREAD AND REVISE: As with any great essay, when you're finished, check for misspellings, grammatical mistakes, and punctuation errors. It often helps to have someone else proofread your work, too, as he or she may catch things you have missed. Also, look for ways to make your sentences and paragraphs even better. Add more descriptive language, choosing just the right verbs, adverbs, and adjectives to make your writing come alive.

BE CREATIVE: Use visual aids to make your report come to life. Include an animal photo file with interesting images found in magazines or printed from websites. Or draw your own! You can also build a miniature animal habitat diorama. Use creativity to help communicate your passion for the subject.

THE FINAL RESULT: Put it all together in one final, polished draft. Make it neat and clean, and remember to cite your references.

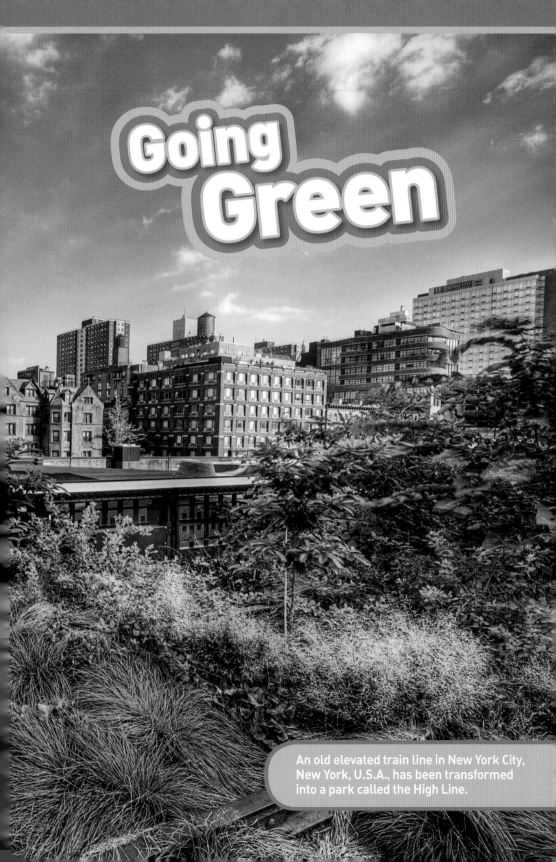

Going Green

An old elevated train line in New York City, New York, U.S.A., has been transformed into a park called the High Line.

1

Putting on a

WARM SWEATER

instead of

TURNING UP THE HEAT

can keep 1,000 pounds (454 kg) of carbon dioxide out of the atmosphere every year.

2

In the U.S. and Great Britain, a **FRUIT OR VEGETABLE TRAVELS** an average of 1,200 miles (1,931 km) from farm to table!

3

EARTH-FRIENDLY
BAMBOO

grows quickly and can be used to make everything from **FLOORS AND CLOTHES TO RADIOS AND EVEN AN IPAD STYLUS (PEN).**

15 COOL THINGS ABOUT

4

REDUCE the number of **VAMPIRE APPLIANCES** in your home. A TV and its remote use more energy while they are off during the day than they do when you watch TV for four hours.

5

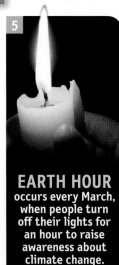

EARTH HOUR occurs every March, when people turn off their lights for an hour to raise awareness about climate change. In 2013, people in 153 countries and territories took part.

6

A DESIGNER HAS CREATED **"LIVING" SHOES** — ONCE YOU HAVE WORN THEM OUT YOU CAN PLANT THEM AND THEY WILL SPROUT FLOWERS.

7

WORLDWIDE, PEOPLE RECYCLE ABOUT ONE-THIRD OF ALL ALUMINUM PRODUCTS. THAT'S **19.8 MILLION TONS** (18 MILLION MT).

8 A year's worth of the **AVERAGE AMERICAN KID'S LAUNDRY** would weigh 500 pounds (227 kg). That's heavier than a gorilla!

9 A designer has created a cell phone with a casing **MADE OUT OF GRASS.** After the life of the phone is over, it decomposes and the keys and screen **CAN BE RECYCLED.**

10 **GO PORTABLE** TO REDUCE YOUR CARBON FOOTPRINT. Laptop computers use **50 TO 90 PERCENT LESS ENERGY** than desktop computers.

11 Carbon dioxide, the gas that makes your soda fizzy, is **ALSO LINKED TO CLIMATE CHANGE.**

GOING GREEN

12 INSTEAD OF GAS-GUZZLING LAWN MOWERS, THE INTERNET COMPANY GOOGLE USES GOATS TO **TRIM ITS LAWN.**

13 AS MUCH AS **90%** of the energy used by standard lightbulbs escapes as heat and is not converted into **USABLE LIGHT.**

14  ELECTRIC CARS COST **TEN CENTS LESS PER MILE** (1.6 km) to drive than a car that runs on gas. A trip between San Francisco and Los Angeles, California, U.S.A., costs $34 less in an **ELECTRIC CAR.**

15 **ONE MILLION PLASTIC BAGS ARE USED EVERY MINUTE.**

WHERE HAVE THE ANIMALS GONE?

All around the world, countless animals are being driven out of their habitats as a result of deforestation, or trees being cut down for lumber or logs or to clear land. Here, you can check out two endangered animals and their fight for survival.

Habitat

SPIDER MONKEY WITH BABY

TWO ADULT SPIDER MONKEYS

BROWN SPIDER MONKEY

A farmer living in South America and deep in one of Colombia's rain forests has spotted a rare species of spider monkey thought to be extinct in the region.

Spider monkeys spend most of their lives high in tree branches. They travel in social groups called troops. A spider monkey swings from branch to branch as easily as you walk from your living room to the kitchen. Its tail has a grip strong enough to support the animal's entire weight, leaving the other four long limbs free to pick tasty nuts, fruits, and leaves.

Hunting and habitat loss have threatened all species of spider monkeys. Some are critically endangered, although those living in national parks are safe from hunters and habitat loss.

Suddenly, you hear whoops and wails. You spot a few dark shapes swinging from the highest branches—brown spider monkeys! "This is the only population found within a national protected area," says Nestor Roncancio, a Wildlife Conservation Society researcher. "It's one of the largest fragments of forest left with good habitat for the species."

Destruction

IBERIAN LYNX

CAPTIVE-BRED LYNX RECEIVES BOTTLE FEEDING

"You need patience, luck, and a guide who knows where to look to see an Iberian lynx in the wild," says Miguel Rodrigues, your local lynx expert. Today you have all three. "There, behind that bush," he says. You grab the binoculars, focus, and spot the hornlike tufts of black fur poking above the leaves. You've caught a glimpse of the world's most endangered cat!

Unfortunately, these cats have nearly vanished from Earth. With less than 300 Iberian lynx left in the wild, they live in just a few pockets of protected forests in Spain and possibly Portugal. Their habitat has been chopped down to make way for farms, tree plantations, cities, dams, and highways.

Scientists took emergency action. They began breeding captive lynx and releasing them in protected areas. The captive-bred lynx have since raised cubs.

You wonder if the lynx you've spotted behind the bush is one of these success stories. With so few of these cats left in the world, you feel lucky to have seen one. "The lynx is a relatively small feline that doesn't need much space," says conservationist Dan Ward. So you hope that humans and these wild cats can be good neighbors.

GLOBAL WARMING

Climate Change, Explained

Fact: The world is getting warmer. The summer of 2013 is tied with 2009 as the world's fifth-warmest summer since records began in 1880. Summer 2013 temperatures were 1.12°F (.62°C) higher than the average summer temperature in the 20th century. This is the direct effect of climate change, which refers not only to the increase in the Earth's average temperature (known as global warming), but also to the long-term effects on winds, rain, and ocean currents. Global warming is the reason glaciers and polar ice sheets are melting—resulting in rising sea levels and shrinking habitats. This makes survival for some animals a big challenge. Warming also means more flooding along the coasts and drought for inland areas.

Why are temperatures climbing?

Some of the recent climate changes can be tied to natural causes—such as changes in the sun's intensity, the unusually warm ocean currents of El Niño, and volcanic activity—but human activities are a major factor as well.

Everyday activities that require burning fossil fuels, such as driving gasoline-powered cars, contribute to global warming. These activities produce greenhouse gases, which enter the atmosphere and trap heat. At the current rate, Earth's global average temperature is projected to rise from 2 to 11.5°F (1 to 6.4°C) by the year 2100, and it will get even warmer after that. And as the climate continues to warm, it will unfortunately continue to affect the environment and our society in many ways.

Polar bear on a piece of melting iceberg

Greenland's Giant Canyon

Think the Grand Canyon in Arizona, U.S.A., is huge? Well, imagine a canyon nearly twice as long! That's just what sits under Greenland's Ice Sheet, a thick layer of frozen water that covers an area about a quarter of the size of the continental United States.

The recently discovered canyon, which runs as deep as a half a mile (800 m) and as long as 466 miles (750 km), was likely part of a massive river system before an ice sheet covered it millions of years ago. Scientists think that water once flowed in the canyon from the interior of Greenland coast and may one day play a major role in transporting meltwater below the ice into the Arctic Ocean.

Rising sea levels

Global warming is taking a toll on Greenland. In 2009, record-high temperatures caused changes in the ice sheet, like the 150-foot (46-m)-deep Birthday Canyon, carved by meltwater. And although the chances of Greenland's entire ice sheet melting are remote, there is enough frozen fresh water there to raise sea levels by about 20 feet (6 m), which would impact coastlines around the world. It's very important for scientists to have a better understanding of what lies beneath the ice so they can predict how water will flow if—or when—things start to melt.

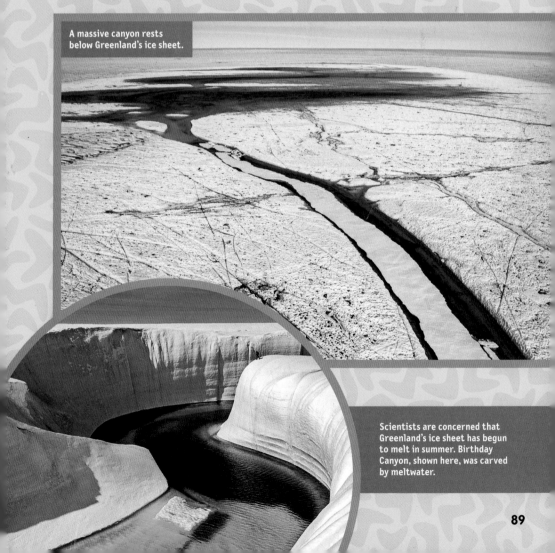

A massive canyon rests below Greenland's ice sheet.

Scientists are concerned that Greenland's ice sheet has begun to melt in summer. Birthday Canyon, shown here, was carved by meltwater.

Pollution
Cleaning Up Our Act

So what's the big deal about a little dirt on the planet? Pollution can affect animals, plants, and people. In fact, some studies show that more people die every year from diseases linked to air pollution than from car accidents. And right now nearly one billion of the world's people don't have access to clean drinking water.

A LITTLE POLLUTION = BIG PROBLEMS

You can probably clean your room in a couple of hours. (At least we hope you can!) But you can't shove air and water pollution under your bed or cram them into the closet. Once released into the environment, pollution—whether it's oil leaking from a boat or chemicals spewing from a factory's smokestack—can have a lasting environmental impact.

KEEP IT CLEAN

It's easy to blame things like big factories for pollution problems. But some of the mess comes from everyday activities. Exhaust fumes from cars and garbage in landfills can seriously trash the Earth's health. We all need to pitch in and do some house-cleaning. It may mean bicycling more and riding in cars less. Or not dumping water-polluting oil or household cleaners down the drain. Look at it this way: Just as with your room, it's always better not to let Earth get messed up in the first place.

SCAN THIS PAGE!
GET BONUS MOBILE CONTENT! Download the free NG Kids scanner app. Directions on inside front cover.

Bottled Up!

Sure, water is good for you. But before you sip, think about how often you use plastic water bottles—and what you're doing with them when you're done. For every six water bottles we use, only one will wind up in a recycling bin. The rest end up in landfills or as litter on land or in rivers, lakes, and oceans, taking many hundreds of years to disintegrate. So, what can you do? Fill up from the tap and drink out of a refillable steel container. And if you do use a plastic bottle, make sure to recycle it.

Declining Biodiversity
Saving All Creatures Great and Small

Earth is home to a huge mix of plants and animals—perhaps 100 million species—and scientists have officially identified and named only about 1.9 million so far! Scientists call this healthy mix biodiversity.

THE BALANCING ACT

The bad news is that half of the planet's plant and animal species may be on the path to extinction, mainly because of human activity. People cut down trees, build roads and houses, pollute rivers, overfish, and overhunt. The good news is that many people care. Scientists and volunteers race against the clock every day, working to save wildlife before time runs out. By building birdhouses, planting trees, and following the rules for hunting and fishing, you can be a positive force for preserving biodiversity, too. Every time you do something to help a species survive, you help our planet to thrive.

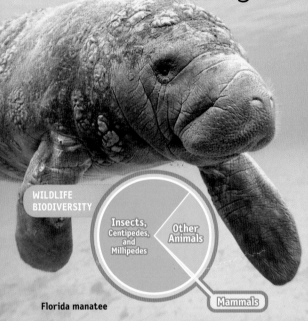

WILDLIFE BIODIVERSITY

Insects, Centipedes, and Millipedes

Other Animals

Mammals

Florida manatee

Habitats Threatened
Living on the Edge

Even though tropical rain forests cover only about 7 percent of the planet's total land surface, they are home to half of all known species of plants and animals. Because people cut down so many trees for lumber and firewood and clear so much land for farms, hundreds of thousands of acres of rain forest disappear every year.

SHARING THE LAND

Wetlands are also important feeding and breeding grounds. People have drained many wetlands, turning them into farm fields or sites for industries. More than half the world's wetlands have disappeared within the past century, squeezing wildlife out. Balancing the needs of humans and animals is the key to lessening habitat destruction.

Toucan

Bet you didn't know

6 FUN FACTS about **GOING GREEN**

1 You can **create electricity** out of both **cow manure** and **elephant dung.**

2 Some **cars** can run on **used french-fry oil.**

3 A **newly invented lightbulb** has to be **changed only once** every 20 years!

4 **A cyclist** invented a **bike helmet** made from **recycled newspapers.**

5 It can take up to **200 years** for an aluminum can to **decompose.**

6 **A wind farm** in Texas, U.S.A., with more than **600 turbines** provides power to 265,000 homes.

GREEN inventions

BACK VIEW

ELECTRIC TRICYCLE

Imagine if your bicycle had all the features of a car, right down to a windshield wiper, a trunk for stashing your stuff, and even a motor. The Emcycle encloses the rider in a rain-shielding shell complete with locking doors and three wheels so it won't topple over at stop signs. As with a bicycle, you pedal the Emcycle and steer with handlebars. But pedaling also charges an electric motor that boosts your speed to 40 miles an hour (64 km/h). "That makes you feel like Superman—it amplifies your pedal power two to three times," inventor Michael Scholey says. A dashboard on the handlebars features battery and speed displays, plus controls for the turn signals, heater, and headlights. You can even add a radio and cup holder. Talk about riding in style.

MUSICAL SHOWER

You love singing in the shower, but your family doesn't seem to appreciate your, um, talent. Here's a way to quiet the unappreciative booing—and help protect the planet. The H₂O Shower Powered Radio, which runs on energy created by the flow of water, drowns out your shower voice. To set it up, attach the radio to the base of the showerhead. When you turn on the shower, water runs through the radio, rotates a tiny turbine (similar to a waterwheel), and creates energy to power the radio. The device can even store enough juice to keep playing for up to an hour, post-shower. Rock on.

WET RADIO

8 FUN WAYS to Get Outside

Staying inside all day? Snooze! It's time to step outside and explore the world around you. Here's a roundup of eight activities that will get you outdoors and keep you energized.

1 TAKE A HIKE!

Immerse yourself in the great outdoors by hiking. Organize your family and friends for a walk in your local park, or hit some mountain trails for a challenging and scenic route. Don't forget to pack snacks and water to stay fueled while you walk.

2 PICK IT UP

Grab some gloves and a trash bag, then hit your local park creek to pick up trash. You'll get some fresh air and exercise—and help the environment, too.

3 DESIGN YOUR OWN HEADLAMP

Color-coordinate your camping gear by going online and designing your own headlamp. Princeton Tec Spectrum lets you choose your own look for everything from the headlamp's body to the battery door.

Check out the Get Outside Guide for more ideas!

④ STARGAZING!

On a clear night you can really see, well, forever! Take an evening stroll in your neighborhood to explore the starry skies. Enhance your view with a smart-phone app offering a 3-D map of the stars, constellations, and galaxies.

⑤ THE AMAZING RACE

Get into the competitive spirit by organizing an obstacle race with your neighborhood pals. Set up a series of silly—but safe—stunts (Think: jumping rope, crossing the monkey bars, and hula-hooping), then see who can get through it the fastest. Ready? Go!

⑥ LIGHT UP THE SOCCER FIELD

Have an electrifying game of soccer—literally! By kicking the SOCCKET ball you can create enough energy to light an LED lamp for several hours.

⑦ INDOOR PICNIC

Bring the outdoors inside with the PicNYC Table. Its aluminum tabletop frame forms a deep area for growing a lush lawn where you can picnic. You can even sprout an herb garden instead of grass!

Rainy Day Fun

⑧ GET GROWING

You don't need a huge patch of land to grow a garden. Select a small square of backyard or even a flowerpot on your balcony, plant some seeds, water them daily, then watch your blooms blossom!

World Energy & Minerals

Almost everything people do—from cooking to powering the International Space Station—requires energy. But energy comes in different forms. Traditional energy sources, still used by many people in the developing world, include burning dried animal dung and wood. Industrialized countries and urban centers around the world rely on coal, oil, and natural gas—called fossil fuels because they formed from decayed plant and animal material accumulated from long ago. Fossil fuel deposits, either in the ground or under the ocean floor, are unevenly distributed on Earth, and only some countries can afford to buy them. Fossil fuels are also not renewable, meaning they will run out one day. And unless we find other ways to create energy, we'll be stuck. Without energy we won't be able to drive cars, use lights, or send emails to friends.

TAKING A TOLL

Environmentally speaking, burning fossil fuels isn't necessarily the best choice, either: Carbon dioxide from the burning of fossil fuels, as well as other emissions, are contributing to global warming. Concerned scientists are looking at new ways to harness renewable, alternative sources of energy, such as water, wind, and sun.

DIGGING FOR FOSSIL FUELS

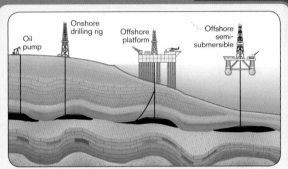

This illustration shows some of the different kinds of onshore and offshore drilling equipment. The type of drilling equipment used depends on whether the oil or natural gas is in the ground or under the ocean.

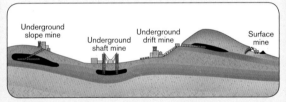

The mining of coal made the industrial revolution possible, and coal still provides a major energy source. Work that people once did using picks and shovels is now done with mechanized equipment. This diagram shows some kinds of coal mines currently in use.

CHINA'S POLLUTION PROBLEM

On any given day, a dense cloud of smog hovers over Beijing and other parts of China, an obvious sign of the country's environmental crisis. Now, the Chinese government is trying to curb the pollution by taking steps to limit the use of coal, including a ban on the construction of coal-fired power plants in certain regions. Experts hope this move will encourage the use of natural gas and nuclear power and eventually improve the country's air quality. Whether China will ever be smog free is unknown, but this is a positive step toward solving the country's pollution problem, one plant at a time.

Alternative Power

WIND
Strong winds blowing through the mountains in California (U.S.A.) spin windmill blades on an energy farm, powering giant turbines that generate electricity for the state.

HYDROELECTRIC
Hydroelectric plants, such as this one at Santiago del Estero in Argentina, use dams to harness running water to generate clean, renewable energy.

GEOTHERMAL
Geothermal power, from groundwater heated by molten rock, provides energy for this power plant in Iceland. Swimmers enjoy the warm waters of a lake created by the power plant.

SOLAR
Solar panels on Samso Island in Denmark capture and store energy from the sun, an environmentally friendly alternative to fossil fuels.

BIODIESEL
This Aero L-29 Delfin, nicknamed BioJet 1, was the first jet aircraft powered by 100 percent biodiesel fuel. Biodiesel—which can be made from vegetable oil, animal fats, or french-fry grease—is cleaner and emits fewer pollutants than fossil fuels do into the air.

97

STUMP YOUR PARENTS

GOING GREEN QUIZ

How much do your parents know about protecting the planet? Find out with this quiz.

ANSWERS BELOW

① About how many Iberian lynx are left in the wild?
a. 3
b. 30
c. 300
d. 300,000

② **True or false?** You can create electricity out of both cow manure and elephant dung.

③ Where have scientists recently discovered a giant canyon?
a. under Greenland's ice sheet
b. on the moon
c. in the Atlantic Ocean
d. in Antarctica

④ How can you promote biodiversity?
a. follow hunting and fishing rules
b. build a birdhouse
c. plant a tree
d. all of the above

⑤ What's the biggest threat to the future of brown spider monkeys living in South America?
a. drought
b. cold temperatures
c. lack of bananas
d. hunting and habitat loss

Not **STUMPED** yet?
Check out the *National Geographic Kids Quiz Whiz* collection for more crazy **ENVIRONMENT** questions!

ANSWERS:
1. c; 2. True; 3. a; 4. d; 5. d

Write a Letter That Gets Results

Knowing how to write a good letter is a useful skill. It will come in handy anytime you want to persuade someone to understand your point of view. Whether you're emailing your congressperson or writing a letter for a school project or to your grandma, a great letter will help you get your message across. Most important, a well-written letter leaves a good impression.

Check out the example below for the elements of a good letter.

Your address

Date

Salutation
Always use "Dear" followed by the person's name; use Mr., Mrs., Ms., or Dr. as appropriate.

Introductory paragraph
Give the reason you're writing the letter.

Body
The longest part of the letter, which provides evidence that supports your position. Be persuasive!

Closing paragraph
Sum up your argument.

Complimentary closing
Sign off with "Sincerely" or "Thank you."

Your signature

Abby Jones
1204 Green Street
Los Angeles, CA 90045

March 31, 2015

Dear Mr. School Superintendent,

I am writing to you about how much excess energy our school uses and to offer a solution.

Every day, we leave the computers on in the classroom, the TVs are plugged in all the time, and the lights are on all day. All of this adds up to a lot of wasted energy, which is not only harmful for the Earth, as it increases the amount of harmful greenhouse gas emissions into the environment, but is also costly to the school. In fact, I read that schools spend more on energy bills than on computers and textbooks combined!

I am suggesting that we start an Energy Patrol to monitor the use of lighting, air-conditioning, heating, and other energy systems within our school. My idea is to have a group of students dedicated to figuring out ways we can cut back on our energy use in the school. We can do room checks, provide reminders to students and teachers to turn off lights and computers, replace old lightbulbs with energy-efficient products, and even reward the classrooms that do the most to save energy.

Above all, I think our school could help the environment tremendously by cutting back on how much energy we use. Let's see an Energy Patrol at our school soon. Thank you.

Sincerely,

Abby Jones

Abby Jones

COMPLIMENTARY CLOSINGS

Sincerely, Sincerely yours,
Thank you, Regards,
Best wishes, Respectfully,

99

With the Matterhorn looming in the background, an Alpine climber scales the cold, icy north face of Obergabelhorn above Zermatt, Switzerland.

Awesome Adventure

DARE to EXPLORE

Do you have what it takes to be a great explorer? Read these stories of four famous adventurers, and see how you can get started on the exploration path.

KAKANI KATIJA
Biological Oceanographer

WANT TO BE A BIOLOGICAL OCEANOGRAPHER?
STUDY: Mathematics, physics, and marine biology
WATCH: *NOVA* and *Nature* on PBS
READ: *Twenty Thousand Leagues Under the Sea* by Jules Verne

"Never stop learning. Learn as much as you can and never close yourself off to any opportunity."

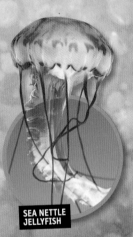

SEA NETTLE JELLYFISH

"My team and I plunged into the water. We couldn't turn on any bright lights until we reached our destination nearly a hundred feet (30 m) down, or the jellies would be scared off. So we dived through the sea in darkness. Finally we made it to our site. I switched on an underwater lamp and panned it around me. Jellyfish were everywhere! It was incredible.

"My job is to watch how marine animals move through the water—many glide along with amazing efficiency. Then I think about how to design underwater vehicles that move in the same way. This may help us invent submarines that whisk you to the deepest parts of the ocean. Our oceans are so important and we've explored only a sliver of them. There's much more to see."

A GROUP OF JELLYFISH IS CALLED A SMACK.

BRADY BARR
Herpetologist

WANT TO BE A HERPETOLOGIST?
STUDY: Biology, anatomy, and ecology
WATCH: *Dangerous Encounters With Brady Barr* on Nat Geo WILD
READ: *Crocodile Encounters!* by Brady Barr

"Learn everything you can about the animals you're interested in, have a passion, and stay true to your hopes and dreams."

A herpetologist is a scientist who studies reptiles and amphibians.

"If you want to catch a one-ton (907-kg) crocodile, sometimes you just have to jump on its back and ride it out. I don't always do things the normal way—I've caught a croc with a ball of string, tracked great white sharks with remote-controlled helicopters, and even dressed up as a hippo, a crocodile, and a baboon to get closer to animals.

"Once I climbed down a croc burrow in Costa Rica thinking the sides of the burrow were just mud walls. But then I realized they weren't walls at all. They were actually crocs covered in mud, and I realized this when they suddenly opened their eyes!

"I'm scared every single day, but being afraid keeps me safe. You make one mistake and you could lose a part of your body. But don't ever let anyone tell you that you can't do something."

REAL-LIFE CROC

A CROCODILE CAN'T STICK OUT ITS TONGUE.

GERLINDE KALTENBRUNNER
Mountain Climber

WANT TO BE A MOUNTAIN CLIMBER?
STUDY: Geography, geology, and meteorology
WATCH: Nat Geo Adventure's *First Ascent*
READ: *Climbing Everest: Tales of Triumph and Tragedy on the World's Highest Mountain* by Audrey Salkeld

"Your passion doesn't have to be mountaineering—it could be art or playing an instrument— but it's important to always feel your passion from the inside."

KALTENBRUNNER ON K2

NATIONAL GEOGRAPHIC KIDS
SCANNER

SCAN THIS PAGE!
GET BONUS MOBILE CONTENT! Download the free NG Kids scanner app. Directions on inside front cover.

"Early one morning while climbing Dhaulagiri I, a mountain in Nepal, my tent was swept down by an avalanche when I was still inside it. I tumbled about 130 feet (40 m) downhill. I couldn't tell what was happening and when it stopped, I was buried in the snow and wasn't even able to tell if I was up or down. Thankfully, after an hour of digging and climbing, I was able to reach the surface and climb out of the snow.
"There are many challenges in mountain climbing. But climbing is not all about the danger. When I reach the top of a mountain, it's always a very calm, quiet moment for me, when I can say 'thank you' to the universe for allowing me to have the experience."

MOUNT EVEREST WAS ONCE KNOWN AS "PEAK 15."

BARRINGTON IRVING
Pilot

WANT TO BE A PILOT?

STUDY: Algebra, chemistry, biology, and geography

WATCH: *Flight Simulator* or *X-Plane*

READ: *Popular Science* and *Popular Mechanics* to keep up with technology

THE PILOT FUELS HIS AIRPLANE.

IRVING IN THE COCKPIT

"You have to have confidence. **If you don't believe, no one else will.** Confidence will always keep you going."

"**I** was flying from Saudi Arabia to Egypt when a wall of sand suddenly rose up in front of the plane. As I flew into the sandstorm, grains began seeping into the cockpit through vents. All I could do was hope that none of it got into the engine turbochargers, which would have been disastrous. Luckily I made it through the storm unharmed.

"My trip around the world took 97 days and included 145 hours of flying. Sometimes I flew more than 12 hours in a row before making a stop. And there were times after landing when I had to crawl from the plane on my elbows because I lost my leg strength during the long flight.

"But being a pilot is totally worth it. You have the opportunity to explore the world from amazing heights."

THE FIRST AIRPLANE FLIGHT LASTED 12 SECONDS.

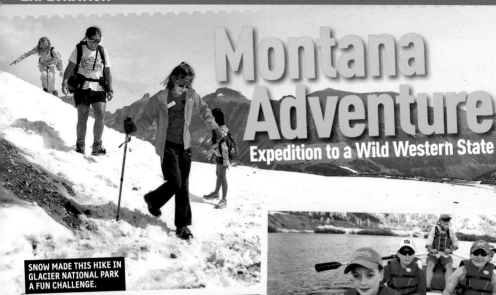

SNOW MADE THIS HIKE IN GLACIER NATIONAL PARK A FUN CHALLENGE.

Montana Adventure
Expedition to a Wild Western State

PADDLING DOWN THE MISSOURI RIVER

S potting a grizzly bear, uncovering dinosaur fossils, hiking, and floating down the Missouri River are just a few of the wild adventures that 15 young explorers experienced in Montana, U.S.A., after winning the Hands-On Explorer Challenge (HOEC), an essay and photo competition.

While exploring northwestern Montana, the winners walked in the footsteps of Lewis and Clark's historic expedition along the Missouri River, played in snow (yes, in July!), saw mountain goats and bighorn sheep, and dug for dinosaur bones and other prehistoric fossils, all while taking photographs of their adventures. They even watched a huge grizzly bear on the shore of St. Mary Lake. "We were on a boat, so we were able to do it safely," says Ben Zino, 11, of Salisbury, North Carolina. "It was awesome!"

On a visit to an Indian Reservation, team members played traditional Blackfeet games, learned a few words in the Blackfoot language, and peered over a 50-foot (15-m)-cliff that was used long ago as a buffalo jump. "Blackfeet and other Native Americans used to hunt buffalo by herding them off a cliff," says Jackson Jacobs, 9, of Hillsboro, Tennessee. "They used every part of the buffalo they killed for things such as clothes, cooking pots, food, and shelter."

HOEC team members were on the move all day, every day. "We did so many cool things on this expedition that I can't pick a favorite," says Emily Marshall, 10, of Ashburn, Virginia. "I loved it all!"

Glacier National Park

MONTANA

UNITED STATES

A GRIZZLY BEAR SIGHTING FROM THE SAFETY OF A BOAT

CAREFULLY LOOKING OVER THE EDGE OF AN OLD BUFFALO JUMP

MYSTERY IN THE SKIES

What happened to Amelia Earhart?

PILOT AMELIA EARHART AND HER COPILOT FRED NOONAN REVIEW A FLIGHT CHART.

A Lockheed Electra airplane took off into the sky over the Pacific, with no sign of trouble ahead. At the controls was famous American pilot Amelia Earhart, the first woman to fly solo across the Atlantic Ocean. Alongside her sat Fred Noonan. Together, they planned to fly 2,556 miles (4,113 km) from the island nation of Papua New Guinea to Howland Island in the South Pacific Ocean, the third-to-last leg in a trip around the world. The date was July 2, 1937. That was the last time anyone ever saw them.

Earhart's disappearance remains a mystery. Now, more than 75 years later, new research is shedding light on what may have happened during that fateful flight.

SPLASH AND SINK

The most widely accepted explanation for what happened to Earhart is that her plane crashed into the ocean. According to a U.S. Coast Guard boat keeping radio communication with the Electra during the flight, Earhart said she was searching for the island but could not find it—and that she was running low on fuel. No underwater wreckage has been found, but searches continue. A recent expedition used a deep-sea sonar system to scan a wide area around which the Electra likely went down, but it did not find any sign of a plane.

CRASH LANDING

Others think the Electra landed on the remote Pacific atoll Nikumaroro and that Earhart and Noonan lived as castaways. Newly discovered evidence found on Nikumaroro—such as fragments of glass made in the U.S. and a cosmetics jar—have caused speculation that Earhart lived there for an unknown amount of time before she died. But despite multiple expeditions to the island, no plane or other conclusive evidence has been found.

LEGACY

Other less likely theories—including one claiming that Earhart acted as a spy during World War II and then changed her identity—are still floating around, offering extra ideas for what happened. As the search for answers continues, one thing remains certain: Amelia Earhart will always be one of the most celebrated aviators in history.

SECRETS OF THE

DARING SCIENTISTS SEARCH FOR

A bizarre world lies under the sparkling Atlantic Ocean off the islands of the Bahamas, a world few have seen. Here, a system of super-deep underwater caves called blue holes contain odd-looking creatures, six-story-high rock formations, and even ancient human remains. Scuba-diving scientists must dodge whirl-pools and squeeze through narrow tunnels to study blue holes—but their risky expeditions uncover amazing secrets.

CREATURE FEATURE

FANGED CRUSTACEAN

WEIRD WATER

NEON PINK CAVE WATER!

Dive about 30 feet (9 m) into some blue holes, and the water turns pink. It looks nice—but it's poison-ous. Because of a weak current here, rainwater and salt water mix in a way that traps a layer of toxic gas where pink bacteria thrive. To avoid getting ill, divers do not linger here.

In other blue holes, ocean tides can whip up whirlpools that look like giant bathtub drains. Scientists must circle carefully, or else risk being sucked in.

Farther down, the caves become dark and twisty. Anthropologist and National Geographic explorer Kenny Broad and his team have found many odd species here, including a tiny, transparent crustacean that is venomous (above).

Blue holes also contain fossils of animals—even birds. During the last ice age, these areas were dry and made perfect perches for the fliers. In one watery cave, a 12,000-year-old owl's nest was found surrounded by lizard bones—leftovers from the owl's meals.

BLUE HOLES

CLUES ABOUT UNDERWATER CAVES.

HOW BLUE HOLES FORMED

During past ice ages—the most recent about 18,000 years ago—water levels dropped and new land was exposed. Rain ate away at the land, forming holes that became deep caves. The caves filled with water after sea levels rose again. The deepest known blue hole is about 660 feet (200 m) deep.

BONE-CHILLING DISCOVERY

The most amazing find in the blue holes? Human skeletons. Scientists were able to trace the remains back 1,400 years to the time of the Lucayans—the first people believed to live in the Bahamas. No one is sure how the bones ended up in the submerged caves. But the team thinks the Lucayans might have used these areas as burial sites for their dead. With more investigation, the mystery of the skeletons may soon be solved. But scientists believe that other secrets are waiting to be uncovered in blue holes. "There are hundreds left that no human has seen," Broad says. "It's a whole other world for exploration."

A BLUE HOLE OFF BELIZE

1 YOU CAN START A FIRE WITH THE BATTERY OF A CELL PHONE, STEEL WOOL, AND DRY STICKS.

2 Wireless operators aboard the *Titanic* called for help using SOS in 1912.

TITANIC
·19· ·12·
LONDON

3 Some people say TWINKIES are the best food for a survival kit because they never seem to spoil, but their shelf life is only 45 days.

4 DRINKING SALT WATER IS WORSE THAN NOT DRINKING ANY WATER AT ALL. SALT WATER ACTUALLY DEHYDRATES YOU.

15 COOL THINGS ABOUT

5 EATING INSECTS has helped people survive in the wilderness. Insects are a good source of protein and fat.

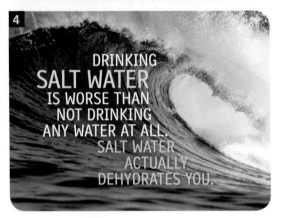

6 Detrás de los 33 atrapados en la mina
San José

Thirty-three men in Chile were stuck in a mine for 69 days— the longest anyone has ever been trapped underground. They all survived.

7

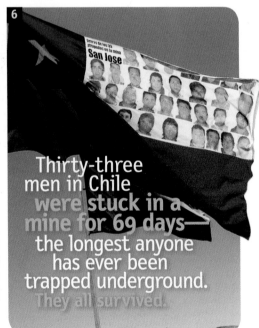

SOS

THE SIGNAL FOR SOS, WHICH CAN BE USED AS A VISUAL OR AUDIO CALL FOR HELP, IS THREE SHORT, THREE LONG, AND THEN THREE SHORT SIGNALS.

8 YOU LOSE **10** PERCENT OF YOUR BODY HEAT THROUGH YOUR HEAD.

9 The best way to **SURVIVE A TORNADO** if you're outside and nowhere near a shelter is to flatten yourself on the ground like a pancake.

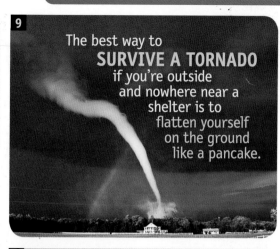

10 A New York, U.S.A., man **was stuck in an elevator** for 41 hours.

11 PEOPLE HAVE BEEN POISONED BY SNAKE VENOM EVEN AFTER THE SNAKE IS DEAD.

SURVIVAL

12 PUNCHING OR KICKING **A SHARK** IN ITS MOST SENSITIVE AREAS—NOSE, EYES, AND GILLS—CAN SEND IT SWIMMING THE OTHER DIRECTION IN THE MIDDLE OF AN ATTACK.

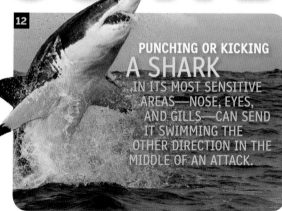

13 It takes ten minutes to lose feeling in your arms and legs after falling through ice into water.

DANGER THIN ICE

14 Some lizards' tails are constructed to break off easily so they can escape in an attack. **Usually a new tail is regenerated in a few months.**

15 THE INTERNATIONAL **SIGN OF DISTRESS** WHEN USING FIRE IS TO BUILD THREE FIRES IN A TRIANGLE.

SURVIVAL STORY

ORANGUTAN
TO THE RESCUE

After getting lost in the rain forest, National Geographic explorer Agustín Fuentes receives some very unlikely help. Read on to find out how Fuentes found his way home.

All Agustín Fuentes wanted to do was find the rare maroon leaf monkey. He'd been spending some time at Camp Leakey, an orangutan research camp on Borneo, a large, mountainous island in southeast Asia, and he got the urge to take a day trip into the dense rain forest to seek one out. So he packed up his compass, headlamp, and small backpack, and off he went.

After four hours of following marked trails, Fuentes thought he caught a glimpse of a maroon leaf monkey. But then it scampered away into the rain forest. He had a decision to make: Should he stay on the trails and hope he sees the monkey again? Or should he follow it?

"I took a risk and went off trail," Fuentes says.

Bad move. Forty-five minutes later, Fuentes found himself deep in the rain forest, with no maroon leaf monkey in sight. He used his compass to make a guess as to which direction he was heading and kept walking.

"Another 30 minutes passed, and I began to get a little nervous," says Fuentes. "Darkness was coming on quickly."

Fuentes tried to find comfort in the fact that he was in a place where another human had likely never been. As he looked around the rain forest, there was so much to admire.

"At one point, I spotted a shimmering metallic blue pool in an opening. I moved closer, and the blue image vibrated. Suddenly, hundreds of blue butterflies took flight before me," he says. "They had been feasting on wild pig droppings on the ground a few feet away."

Pulling out his compass, Fuentes headed south, thinking he'd eventually hit the river, if not a trail first. It paid off. After about 20 minutes, he saw an unmarked trail. Seconds later, he heard a rustling. He shone his headlight toward the sound. It was an orangutan! And not just any orangutan: Fuentes recognized right away that she was one of the tribe being rehabilitated at camp.

"We looked at each other, and she held out her hand to me." he says. "Then she led me, hand-in-hand, to camp. Just like me, she was heading back for the evening."

HOW TO
SURVIVE A
KILLER BEE ATTACK!

1 Buzz Off
Killer bees—or Africanized honey bees—only attack when their hive is being threatened. If you see several bees buzzing near you, a hive is probably close by. Heed their "back off" attitude and slowly walk away.

2 Don't Join the Swat Team
Your first instinct might be to start swatting and slapping the bees. But that just makes the buzzers angry. Loud noises have the same effect, so don't start screaming, either. Just get away.

3 Don't Play Hide-and-Seek
Hives are often near water, but don't even think about outlasting the bees underwater. They'll hover and attack when you come up for air, even if you try to swim for it.

4 Make Like Speedy Gonzalez
Killer bees will chase you, but they'll give up when you're far enough away from the hive (usually about 200 yards [183 m]). Take off running and don't stop until the buzzing does.

5 Create a Cover-Up
Killer bees often go for the face and throat, which are the most dangerous places to be stung. While you're on the run, protect your face and neck with your hands, or pull your shirt over your head.

HOW TO SURVIVE A
BEE STING!

1. De-Sting Yourself
First, get inside or to a cool place. Then, remove the stinger by scraping a fingernail over the area, like you would to get a splinter out. Do not squeeze the stinger or use tweezers unless you absolutely can't get it out any other way.

2. Put It on Ice
Wash the area with soap and water and apply a cool compress to reduce swelling. Continue icing the spot for 20 minutes every hour. Place a washcloth or towel between the ice and your skin.

3. Treat It Right
With a parent's permission, take an antihistamine and gently rub a hydrocortisone cream on the sting site.

4. Hands Off
Make sure you don't scratch the sting. You'll just increase the pain and swelling.

5. Recognize Danger
If you experience severe burning and itching, swelling of the throat and/or mouth, difficulty breathing, weakness, or nausea, or if you already know you are allergic to bees, get to an emergency room immediately.

113

EXTREME
ACTION SPORTS

Forget soccer and softball: Some athletes go above and beyond when it comes to their sport of choice. These activities take a ton of skill—and plenty of guts, too. Here's a roundup of some *extreme*-ly out-there sports!

BASE JUMPING

SPECIAL GEAR
Parachute

WHY IT'S EXTREME
Instead of leaping from an airplane, BASE jumpers parachute from fixed objects, including buildings (B), antennas (A), spans (S), such as bridges, and Earth's formations (E).

EXTREME IRONING

SPECIAL GEAR
Iron, ironing board, and wrinkled clothes

WHY IT'S EXTREME
Thrill-seekers iron their laundry while performing an extreme sport, like riding on a moving car or scuba diving.

SNOWKITING

SPECIAL GEAR
Skis, large kite

WHY IT'S EXTREME
Skiers use large kites to propel themselves across snow and ice—and off mountains.

STILT JUMPING

SPECIAL GEAR
Jumping stilts

WHY IT'S EXTREME
Stride up to nine feet (2.7 m) with these spring-loaded stilts that you can walk, jump, and jog in.

FLARE SURFING

SPECIAL GEAR
Surfboard, flares

WHY IT'S EXTREME
Surfers create a fiery display while they ride the waves by attaching flares to the backs of their boards.

UNDERWATER HOCKEY

SPECIAL GEAR
Hockey puck, stick, swimming pool

WHY IT'S EXTREME
Players hold their breath as they dive to the bottom of the pool to go after the puck and push it to the goal.

STUMP YOUR PARENTS

AWESOME ADVENTURE QUIZ
See if your parents are up to speed by quizzing their knowledge on all things adventure.
ANSWERS BELOW

1 What is a possible theory explaining Amelia Earhart's disappearance?
a. Her plane crashed into the ocean.
b. She landed on a remote island and lived as a castaway.
c. She changed her identity.
d. All of the above.

2 **True or false?** If you're stung by a bee, you should remove the stinger as soon as you can.

3 What does a herpetologist study?
a. insects and spiders
b. plants
c. reptiles and amphibians
d. pets

4 What is a blue hole?
a. a canyon made of blue rocks
b. a superdeep underwater cave
c. the entrance to the Smurfs' underground village
d. a mountain lake

5 What does "BASE" in BASE jumping stand for?
a. Be A Smart Eagle
b. Bravery, Agility, Speed, and Energy
c. Buildings, Antennas, Spans, and Earth's formations
d. It doesn't stand for anything

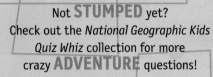

Not STUMPED yet?
Check out the *National Geographic Kids Quiz Whiz* collection for more crazy ADVENTURE questions!

ANSWERS:
1. d; 2. True; 3. c; 4. b; 5. c

116

How to Write a Perfect Essay

Need to write an essay? Does the assignment feel as big as climbing Mount Everest? Fear not. You're up to the challenge! The following step-by-step tips will help you with this monumental task.

1 **BRAINSTORM.** Sometimes the subject matter of your essay is assigned to you, sometimes it's not. Either way, you have to decide what you want to say. Start by brainstorming some ideas, writing down any thoughts you have about the subject. Then read over everything you've come up with and consider which idea you think is the strongest. Ask yourself what you want to write about the most. Keep in mind the goal of your essay. Can you achieve the goal of the assignment with this topic? If so, you're good to go.

2 **WRITE A TOPIC SENTENCE.** This is the main idea of your essay, a statement of your thoughts on the subject. Again, consider the goal of your essay. Think of the topic sentence as an introduction that tells your reader what the rest of your essay will be about.

3 **OUTLINE YOUR IDEAS.** Once you have a good topic sentence, then you need to support that main idea with more detailed information, facts, thoughts, and examples. These supporting points answer one question about your topic sentence—"Why?" This is where research and perhaps more brainstorming come in. Then organize these points in the way you think makes the most sense, probably in order of importance. Now you have an outline for your essay.

4 **ON YOUR MARK, GET SET, WRITE!** Follow your outline, using each of your supporting points as the topic sentence of its own paragraph. Use descriptive words to get your ideas across to the reader. Go into detail, using specific information to tell your story or make your point. Stay on track, making sure that everything you include is somehow related to the main idea of your essay. Use transitions to make your writing flow.

5 **WRAP IT UP.** Finish your essay with a conclusion that summarizes your entire essay and restates your main idea.

6 **PROOFREAD AND REVISE.** Check for errors in spelling, capitalization, punctuation, and grammar. Look for ways to make your writing clear, understandable, and interesting. Use descriptive verbs, adjectives, or adverbs when possible. It also helps to have someone else read your work to point out things you might have missed. Then make the necessary corrections and changes in a second draft. Repeat this revision process once more to make your final draft as good as you can.

Super
Science

Traffic jam? No problem! Scientists at a Dutch corporation have created **PAL-V ONE**, a flying car with a short takeoff and landing capability so it can take to the air from almost anywhere.

THE UNIVERSE BEGAN WITH A BIG BANG

Clear your mind for a minute and try to imagine this: All the things you see in the universe today—all the stars, galaxies, and planets—are not yet out there. Everything that now exists is concentrated in a single, incredibly hot, dense state that scientists call a singularity. Then, suddenly, the basic elements that make up the universe flash into existence. Scientists say that actually happened about 13.7 billion years ago, in the moment we call the big bang.

For centuries scientists, religious scholars, poets, and philosophers have wondered how the universe came to be. Was it always there? Will it always be the same, or will it change? If it had a beginning, will it someday end, or will it go on forever?

These are huge questions. But today, because of recent observations of space and what it's made of, we think we may have some of the answers. Everything we can see or detect around us in the universe began with the big bang. We know the big bang created not only matter but also space itself. And scientists think that in the very distant future, stars will run out of fuel and burn out. Once again the universe will become dark.

POWERFUL PARTICLE

It's just one tiny particle, but without it the world as we know it would not exist. That's what scientists are saying after the recent discovery of the Higgs boson particle, a subatomic speck related to the Higgs field, which is thought to give mass to everything around us. Without the Higgs boson, all the atoms created in the big bang would have zipped around the cosmos too quickly to collect into stars and planets. So you can think of it as a building block of the universe—and of us!

EARLY LIFE ON EARTH

About 3.5 billion years ago
Earth was covered by one gigantic
reddish ocean. The color came
from hydrocarbons.
   The first life-forms on Earth
were Archaea that were able
to live without oxygen. They
released large amounts of methane gas into an atmosphere that
would have been poisonous to us.

About 3 billion years ago
erupting volcanoes linked together
to form larger landmasses. And a
new form of life appeared—
cyanobacteria, the first living
things that used energy from
the sun.

Some 2 billion years ago
the cyanobacteria algae filled
the air with oxygen, killing off
the methane-producing Archaea.
Colored pools of greenish brown
plant life floated on the oceans.
The oxygen revolution that would
someday make human life possible
was now under way.

About 530 million years ago
the Cambrian explosion occurred.
It's called an explosion because
it's the time when most major
animal groups first appeared in
our fossil records. Back then,
Earth was made up of swamps,
seas, a few active volcanoes, and
oceans teeming with strange life.

More than 450 million years ago
life began moving from the oceans
onto dry land. About 200 million
years later dinosaurs began to
appear. They would dominate
life on Earth for more than 150
million years.

PLANETS

CERES

MARS

EARTH

VENUS

MERCURY

JUPITER

SUN

MERCURY
Average distance from the sun:
    35,980,000 miles (57,900,000 km)
Position from the sun in orbit: first
Equatorial diameter: 3,030 miles (4,878 km)
Length of day: 59 Earth days
Length of year: 88 Earth days
Surface temperatures: -300°F (-184°C)
    to 800°F (427°C)
Known moons: 0
Fun fact: Mercury is home to one of the
    largest craters in the solar system.

VENUS
Average distance from the sun:
    67,230,000 miles (108,200,000 km)
Position from the sun in orbit: second
Equatorial diameter: 7,520 miles (12,100 km)
Length of day: 243 Earth days
Length of year: 225 Earth days
Average surface temperature: 864°F (462°C)
Known moons: 0
Fun fact: It never rains on Venus.

EARTH
Average distance from the sun:
    93,000,000 miles (149,600,000 km)
Position from the sun in orbit: third
Equatorial diameter: 7,900 miles (12,750 km)
Length of day: 24 hours
Length of year: 365 days
Surface temperatures: -126°F (-88°C)
    to 136°F (58°C)
Known moons: 1
Fun fact: Earth traveled more than 5,000
    miles (8,047 km) in the past 5 minutes.

MARS
Average distance from the sun:
    141,633,000 miles (227,936,000 km)
Position from the sun in orbit: fourth
Equatorial diameter: 4,221 miles (6,794 km)
Length of day: 25 Earth hours
Length of year: 1.88 Earth years
Surface temperatures: -270°F (-168°C)
    to 80°F (27°C)
Known moons: 2
Fun fact: Iron-rich soil gives Mars its
    reddish appearance.

This artwork shows the 13 planets and dwarf planets. The relative sizes and positions of the planets are shown but not the relative distances between them.

SATURN

URANUS

NEPTUNE

PLUTO

HAUMEA

MAKEMAKE

ERIS

JUPITER

Average distance from the sun:
  483,682,000 miles (778,412,000 km)
Position from the sun in orbit: sixth
Equatorial diameter: 88,840 miles (142,980 km)
Length of day: 9.9 Earth hours
Length of year: 11.9 Earth years
Average surface temperature: -235°F (-148°C)
Known moons: 67*
Fun fact: Europa, one of Jupiter's many moons, is thought to have an ocean that's ten times deeper than any sea on Earth.

SATURN

Average distance from the sun:
  890,800,000 miles (1,433,500,000 km)
Position from the sun in orbit: seventh
Equatorial diameter: 74,900 miles (120,540 km)
Length of day: 10.7 Earth hours
Length of year: 29.46 Earth years
Average surface temperature: -218°F (-139°C)
Known moons: at least 62*
Fun fact: Scientists believe that Saturn's rings will eventually disappear.

*Includes provisional moons, which await confirmation and naming from the International Astronomical Union.

URANUS

Average distance from the sun:
  1,784,000,000 miles (2,870,970,000 km)
Position from the sun in orbit: eighth
Equatorial diameter: 31,760 miles (51,120 km)
Length of day: 17.2 Earth hours
Length of year: 84 Earth years
Average surface temperature: -323°F (-197°C)
Known moons: 27
Fun fact: Summer on Uranus lasts 42 years.

NEPTUNE

Average distance from the sun:
  2,795,000,000 miles (4,498,250,000 km)
Position from the sun in orbit: ninth
Equatorial diameter: 30,775 miles (49,528 km)
Length of day: 16 Earth hours
Length of year: 164.8 Earth years
Average surface temperature: -353°F (-214°C)
Known moons: 13
Fun fact: Large, dark spots on Neptune's surface are believed to be enormous storms.

For information about dwarf planets—Ceres, Pluto, Haumea, Makemake, and Eris—see p. 124.

DWARF PLANETS

Haumea

Eris

Thanks to advanced technology, astronomers have been spotting many never-before-seen celestial bodies with their telescopes. One new discovery? A population of icy objects orbiting the sun beyond Pluto. The largest, like Pluto itself, are classified as dwarf planets. Smaller than the moon but still massive enough to pull themselves into a ball, dwarf planets nevertheless lack the gravitational "oomph" to clear their neighborhood of other sizable objects. So, while larger, more massive planets pretty much have their orbits to themselves, dwarf planets orbit the sun in swarms that include other dwarf planets as well as smaller chunks of rock or ice.

So far, astronomers have identified five dwarf planets: Ceres (which circles the sun in the asteroid belt between Mars and Jupiter), Pluto, Haumea, Makemake, and Eris. Astronomers are studying hundreds of newly found objects in the frigid outer solar system, trying to figure out just how big they are. As time and technology advance, the family of known dwarf planets will surely continue to grow.

CERES
Position from the sun in orbit: fifth
Length of day: 9.1 Earth hours
Length of year: 4.6 Earth years
Known moons: 0

PLUTO
Position from the sun in orbit: tenth
Length of day: 6.4 Earth days
Length of year: 248 Earth years
Known moons: 5*

HAUMEA
Position from the sun in orbit: eleventh
Length of day: 3.9 Earth hours
Length of year: 282 Earth years
Known moons: 2

MAKEMAKE
Position from the sun in orbit: twelfth
Length of day: 22.5 Earth hours
Length of year: 305 Earth years
Known moons: 0

ERIS
Position from the sun in orbit: thirteenth
Length of day: 25.9 Earth hours
Length of year: 561 Earth years
Known moons: 1

*Includes provisional moons.

SUPER SUN!

THE SUN IS 99.8 PERCENT OF ALL THE MASS IN OUR SOLAR SYSTEM.

The SUN'S surface is 9,932°F! (5,500°C)

THERE IS real gold in the SUN.

Even from 93 million miles (150 million km) away, the sun's rays are powerful enough to provide the energy needed for life to flourish on Earth. This 4.6-billion-year-old star is the anchor of our solar system and accounts for 99 percent of the matter in the solar system. What else makes the sun so special? For starters, it's larger than one million Earths and is the biggest object in our solar system. The sun also converts about four million tons (3,628,739 MT) of matter to energy every second, helping to make life possible here on Earth. Now that's *sun*-sational!

Storms on the Sun!

Solar flares are ten million times more powerful than a volcanic eruption on Earth.

With the help of specialized equipment, scientists have observed solar flares—or bursts of magnetic energy that explode from the sun's surface as a result of storms on the sun. Solar storms occur on a cycle of about 11 years, with 2013 being the most recent active year for these types of events. And while most solar storms will not impact the Earth, the fiercer the flare, the more we may potentially feel its effects, as it could disrupt power grids or interfere with GPS navigation systems. Solar storms can also trigger stronger-than-usual auroras, light shows that can be seen on Earth.

Some solar storms travel at speeds of THREE MILLION MILES AN HOUR (4.8 million kph).

Solar storm

Sky Calendar
2015

Jupiter

Leonid meteor shower

Partial solar eclipse

January 3–4 Quadrantids Meteor Shower Peak. A nearly full moon will affect visibility this year, but several bright meteors can still be spotted.

February 6 Jupiter at Opposition. The giant planet is at its closest approach to Earth.

February 22 Conjunction of Venus and Mars. Visible in the west just after sunset, these two bright planets will be unusually close together.

April 4 Total Lunar Eclipse. Visible in most of North America, South America, eastern Asia, and Australia.

May 23 Saturn at Opposition. The best time to view the ringed planet. It makes its closest approach to Earth.

August 12–13 Perseids Meteor Shower Peak. One of the best! Up to 60 meteors per hour. Best viewing is in the direction of the constellation Perseus.

September 1 Neptune at Opposition. The blue planet will be at its closest approach to Earth. Because Neptune is so far away, binoculars or a telescope are necessary for viewing. Unless you have a very powerful telescope, Neptune will appear as a small blue dot.

September 28 Total Lunar Eclipse. Visible throughout most of North America, South America, Europe, Africa, and western Asia.

October 21–22 Orionids Meteor Shower Peak. View up to 20 meteors per hour. Look toward the constellation Orion for the best show.

October 28 Conjunction of Venus, Mars, and Jupiter. Visible in the east just before sunrise, these three planets will be unusually close together, forming a triangle.

November 17–18 Leonid Meteor Shower Peak. View up to 15 meteors per hour.

December 7 Conjunction of Moon and Venus. Look east just before sunrise to view Venus unusually close to the crescent moon.

December 13–14 Geminids Meteor Shower Peak. A spectacular show! Up to 120 multi-colored meteors per hour.

Dates may vary slightly depending on your location. Check with a local planetarium for the best viewing time in your area.

DESTINATION SPACE

LAVA PLANET

You open your spacecraft door and step out at the edge of an ocean. Except this is not a normal seashore—it's made of lava. You're on a planet 489 light-years (the distance light travels in one year) from Earth, far outside your solar system. To explore this lava planet, named CoRoT-7b, you wear a heatproof spacesuit. It's 3,990°F (2,199°C) here—hot enough to vaporize a human.

Like Earth, CoRoT-7b is made largely of rock. But since the lava planet is so hot, the rock melts, forming a red-orange lava ocean that covers almost half the planet. The intense heat vaporizes the liquid rock, turning it into rock gas, which rises above the ocean and forms clouds, just as water does on Earth. As you stare into the sky, you see clouds moving toward you.

Suddenly, pebbles start falling from the cloudy sky. The gas rock condensed and now it's raining rocks! You jump inside your spacecraft and speed away from this extreme planet. Clearly it's no place for a vacation!

Destination
The planet CoRoT-7b

Location
The constellation Monoceros

Distance
489 light-years from Earth

Time to reach
13.3 million years

Weather
Sunny and 3,990°F with a chance of rock rain

Half the planet always faces its sun.

Half the planet always faces away from its sun.

Scientists have discovered three other lava planets like CoRoT-7b.

The lava ocean on CoRoT-7b is 28 miles (45 km) deep.

EYE ON THE SKY
Watch the night sky for the meteor showers. Sometimes called shooting stars, meteors are space rocks that burn up in Earth's atmosphere.

Viewed from Earth, the brightest objects in the sky are the sun, the moon, and Venus.

127

⑤ Freaky Places in Space

THE MOON AND MARS might sound like exciting destinations for an expedition. But some places in space are even more exciting—and weirder—than you've ever imagined. Most of them would squash, freeze, or blow apart a human visitor. But if you could survive the trip, what would these places be like? Blast off to five of the freakiest places in the galaxy to find out.

SUNNY SPOT

Your first expedition is to Kepler-16b, a planet 200 light-years from Earth. (One light-year is almost six trillion miles [9.5 trillion km]!) You arrive at dawn as a bright sun spreads light across the planet's surface. Then things get even stranger: A second sun, small and red, joins the first in the sky.

Kepler-16b, discovered in 2011, is the first confirmed planet ever found that orbits two suns. The suns spin around each other as the planet circles them both every 41 days. Kepler-16b is no place for humans. It has a surface made of gas, and temperatures that drop to minus 100°F (-73°C). "It's like a nippy winter in Antarctica," says Laurance Doyle, one of the scientists who discovered the planet.

OCEAN VIEW

Some of the galaxy's strangest places are right here in our own solar system. To travel to Europa, one of Jupiter's moons, you take off in a different kind of spaceship—one that carries a submarine. Europa looks like a gray ball of string. But scientists are quite sure that beneath its crust of about ten-mile (16-km)-thick ice, this moon has a giant ocean. One day they hope to send a spacecraft to Europa that would break through the ice and launch a submarine into the ocean below. The submarine would search for the weird creatures that might live in this wild place.

WHAT IS LIFE?

This seems like such an easy question to answer. Everybody knows that singing birds are alive and rocks are not. But when we start studying bacteria and other microscopic creatures, things get more complicated.

SO WHAT EXACTLY IS LIFE?

Most scientists agree that something is alive if it can do the following: reproduce; grow in size to become more complex in structure; take in nutrients to survive; give off waste products; and respond to external stimuli, such as increased sunlight or changes in temperature.

KINDS OF LIFE

Biologists classify living organisms by how they get their energy. Organisms such as algae, green plants, and some bacteria use sunlight as an energy source. Animals (like humans), fungi, and some Archaea use chemicals to provide energy. When we eat food, chemical reactions within our digestive system turn our food into fuel.

Living things inhabit land, sea, and air. In fact, life also thrives deep beneath the oceans, embedded in rocks miles below the Earth's crust, in ice, and in other extreme environments. The life-forms that thrive in these challenging environments are called extremophiles. Some of these draw directly upon the chemicals surrounding them for energy. Since these are very different forms of life than what we're used to, we may not think of them as alive, but they are.

HOW IT ALL WORKS

To try and understand how a living organism works, it helps to look at one example of its simplest form—the single-celled bacterium called *Streptococcus*. There are many kinds of these tiny organisms, and some are responsible for human illnesses. What makes us sick or uncomfortable are the toxins the bacteria give off in our bodies.

A single *Streptococcus* bacterium is so small that at least 500 of them could fit on the dot above the letter *i*. These bacteria are some of the simplest forms of life we know. They have no moving parts, no lungs, no brain, no heart, no liver, and no leaves or fruit. Yet this life-form reproduces. It grows in size by producing long chain structures, takes in nutrients, and gives off waste products. This tiny life-form is alive, just as you are alive.

What makes something alive is a question scientists grapple with when they study viruses, such as the ones that cause the common cold and smallpox. They can grow and reproduce within host cells, such as those that make up your body. Because viruses lack cells and cannot metabolize nutrients for energy or reproduce without a host, scientists ask if they are indeed alive. And don't go looking for them without a strong microscope—viruses are a hundred times smaller than bacteria.

Scientists think life began on Earth some 3.9 to 4.1 billion years ago, but no fossils exist from that time. The earliest fossils ever found are from the primitive life that existed 3.6 billion years ago. Other life-forms, some of which are shown below, soon followed. Scientists continue to study how life evolved on Earth and whether it is possible that life exists on other planets.

MICROSCOPIC ORGANISMS*

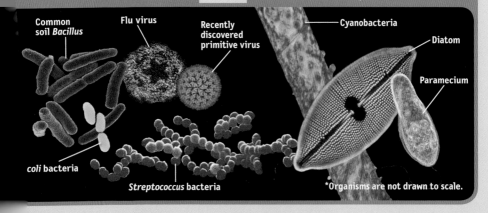

Common soil *Bacillus*

Flu virus

Recently discovered primitive virus

Cyanobacteria

Diatom

Paramecium

coli bacteria

Streptococcus bacteria

*Organisms are not drawn to scale.

3 ALL NIGHT, ALL DAY

Your visit to a red dwarf planet is filled with extremes because it doesn't rotate like Earth does. It's so close to its sun—a small, red star called a red dwarf—that the sun's gravity holds it locked in place. This means that the planet doesn't have days and nights. Instead, one side is always facing the blazing sun, and the other side is always dark. The planet's locked position creates strange weather. An almost continuous hurricane swirls at the point closest to the red dwarf. Streamers from the storm cascade toward the dark side of the planet.

RED DWA

SMOOTH STAR

The surface of the neutron star you're looking a
smoother than glass. Neutron stars are born wh
star runs out of fuel and its core collapses. The
star's gravity pulls so tightly that everything—
dust—is flattened. An earthling wouldn't stand
of survival, so you observe the star from the sa
your spacecraft.

You watch as a star-quake shakes the grour
creating a mountain—just as earthquakes hav
Earth. But here, the mountain rises and vanish
instant, sucked toward the star's
center by the extreme
gravity. The ground
is weirdly smooth
once again.

5 FIREWORKS AND STARDUST

Your last expedition brings you close to a supernova, an exploding star. You watch from your spacecraft as violent nuclear reactions blow apart the star from the inside out. You see an explosion as bright as billions of suns put together. Then, like an immense firework, a colorful wave of gas and dust blasts outward.

The gas and dust hold the ingredients to build everything—from planets to oceans to people. When the universe began, its primary elements were hydrogen and helium. All the rest, from carbon to iron, were created in the interior of stars. The explosion blew these elements far into space, spreading the ingredients for life across the galaxy.

The Three Domains of Life

Biologists divide all living organisms into three domains: Bacteria, Archaea, and Eukarya. Archaean and Bacterial cells do not have nuclei; they are so different from each other that they belong to different domains. Since human cells have a nucleus, humans belong to the Eukarya domain.

1 BACTERIA

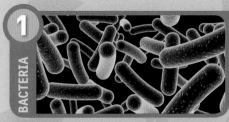

Domain Bacteria: These single-celled microorganisms are found almost everywhere in the world. Bacteria are small and do not have nuclei. They can be shaped like rods, spirals, or spheres. Some of them are helpful to humans, and some are harmful.

2 ARCHAEA

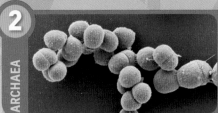

Domain Archaea: These single-celled microorganisms are often found in extremely hostile environments. Like Bacteria, Archaea do not have nuclei, but they have some genes in common with Eukarya. For this reason, scientists think the Archaea living today most closely resemble the earliest forms of life on Earth.

3 EUKARYA

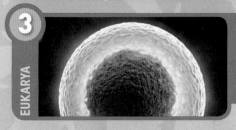

Domain Eukarya: This diverse group of life-forms is more complicated than Bacteria and Archaea, as Eukarya have one or more cells with nuclei. These are the tiny cells that make up your whole body. Eukarya are divided into four groups: fungi, protists, plants, and animals.

FYI

What is a domain? Scientifically speaking, a domain is a major taxonomic division into which natural objects are classified (see p. 20 for "What Is Taxonomy?").

FUNGI

Kingdom Fungi (about 100,000 species): Mainly multicellular organisms, fungi cannot make their own food. Mushrooms and yeast are fungi.

PROTISTS

Protists (about 250,000 species): Once considered a kingdom, this group is a "grab bag" that includes unicellular and multicellular organisms of great variety.

PLANTS

Kingdom Plantae (about 300,000 species): Plants are multicellular, and many can make their own food using photosynthesis (see p. 216 for "Photosynthesis").

ANIMALS

Kingdom Animalia (about 1,000,000 species): Most animals, which are multicellular, have their own organ systems. Animals do not make their own food.

Your Amazing
eyes

Discover the magic of your body's built-in cameras.

You carry around a pair of cameras in your head so incredible they can work in bright sunshine or at night. Only about an inch (2.5 cm) in diameter, they can bring you the image of a tiny ant or a twinkling star trillions of miles (km) away. They can change focus almost instantly and stay focused even when you're shaking your head or jumping up and down. These cameras are your eyes.

A CRUCIAL PART OF YOUR EYE IS AS FLIMSY AS A WET TISSUE.

A dragonfly darts toward your head! Light bounces off the insect, enters your eye, passes through your pupil (the black circle in the middle of your iris), and goes to the lens. The lens focuses the light onto your retina—a thin lining on the back of your eye that is vital but is as flimsy as a wet tissue. Your retina acts like film in a camera, capturing the picture of this dragonfly. The picture is sent to your brain, which instantly sends you a single command—*duck!*

YOU BLINK MORE THAN 10,000 TIMES A DAY.

Your body has many ways to protect and care for your eyes. Each eye sits on a cushion of fat, almost completely surrounded by protective bone. Your eyebrows help prevent sweat from dripping into your eyes. Your eyelashes help keep dust and other small particles out. Your eyelids act as built-in windshield wipers, spreading tear fluid with every blink to keep your eyes moist and wash

away bacteria and other particles. And if anything ever gets too close to your eyes, your eyelids slam shut with incredible speed—in two-fifths of a second—to protect them!

YOUR EYES SEE EVERYTHING UPSIDE DOWN AND BACKWARD!

As amazing as your eyes are, the images they send your brain are a little quirky: They're upside down, backward, and two-dimensional! Your brain automatically flips the images from your retinas right side up and combines the images from each eye into a three-dimensional picture. There is a small area of each retina, called a blind spot, that can't record what you're seeing. Luckily your brain makes adjustments for this, too.

YOUR PUPILS CHANGE SIZE WHENEVER THE LIGHT CHANGES.

Your black pupils may be small, but they have an important job—they grow or shrink to allow just the right amount of light to enter your eyes to let you see.

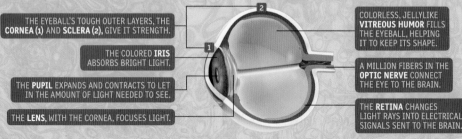

THE EYEBALL'S TOUGH OUTER LAYERS, THE **CORNEA (1)** AND **SCLERA (2)**, GIVE IT STRENGTH.

THE COLORED **IRIS** ABSORBS BRIGHT LIGHT.

THE **PUPIL** EXPANDS AND CONTRACTS TO LET IN THE AMOUNT OF LIGHT NEEDED TO SEE.

THE **LENS**, WITH THE CORNEA, FOCUSES LIGHT.

COLORLESS, JELLYLIKE **VITREOUS HUMOR** FILLS THE EYEBALL, HELPING IT TO KEEP ITS SHAPE.

A MILLION FIBERS IN THE **OPTIC NERVE** CONNECT THE EYE TO THE BRAIN.

THE **RETINA** CHANGES LIGHT RAYS INTO ELECTRICAL SIGNALS SENT TO THE BRAIN.

Your Amazing **heart**

YOUR HEART has the power to lift a 3,000-pound (1,360-kg) car, the strength to pump 2,000 gallons (7,570 L) of blood twice around the world in a day, and the stamina to never take a break. And, oh yeah, it keeps you alive, too!

Here are three more heart-pumping facts about this awesome organ.

Your heart beats 100,000 times daily. And each of these little pitter-patters you feel is actually your heart filling with blood, squeezing, then forcing the blood out and throughout your body. This is done with enough power to pump blood to every cell, delivering oxygen and removing carbon dioxide waste.

Thanks to your heart, blood constantly circulates throughout your body to keep you healthy. And every day, your heart pumps more than 2,000 gallons (7,570 L) of blood through 60,000 miles (96,000 km) of blood vessels—a distance greater than two trips around the world.

#1 One heartbeat is so powerful that it could shoot water six feet (1.8 m) into the air!

#2 Blood travels 60,000 miles (96,000 km) through your body every day.

#3 You have at least four quarts (3.8 L) of blood in your body.

During its endless journeys to and from your heart, the several quarts of blood in your body travel through three types of vessels: arteries, veins, and capillaries. Most arteries carry oxygen-rich blood away from your heart. Veins deliver oxygen-depleted blood back toward your heart. And tiny capillaries connect arteries and veins, forming a vast network in your tissues and reaching every cell in your body. These fragile vessels are so narrow that the microscopic blood cells have to pass through them single file.

Heart **Parts**

AORTA
PULMONARY ARTERY

RIGHT ATRIUM
LEFT ATRIUM
RIGHT VENTRICLE
LEFT VENTRICLE

Your Amazing
brain

Inside your body's supercomputer

You carry around a three-pound (1.4-kg) mass of wrinkly material in your head that controls every single thing you will ever do. From enabling you to think, learn, create, and feel emotions to controlling every blink, breath, and heartbeat—this fantastic control center is your brain. It is a structure so amazing that a famous scientist once called it the "most complex thing we have yet discovered in our universe."

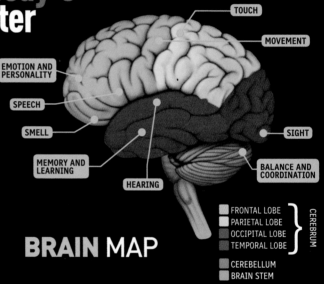

TOUCH

MOVEMENT

EMOTION AND PERSONALITY

SPEECH

SMELL

SIGHT

MEMORY AND LEARNING

HEARING

BALANCE AND COORDINATION

FRONTAL LOBE
PARIETAL LOBE
OCCIPITAL LOBE
TEMPORAL LOBE

CEREBRUM

CEREBELLUM
BRAIN STEM

BRAIN MAP

THE BIG QUESTION

WHAT TAKES UP TWO-THIRDS OF YOUR BRAIN'S WEIGHT AND ALLOWS YOU TO SWIM, EAT, AND SPEAK?

Answer: The huge hunk of your brain called the cerebrum. It's definitely the biggest part of the brain. The four lobes of the cerebrum house the centers for memory, the senses, movement, and emotion, among other things.

The cerebrum is made up of two hemispheres—the right and the left. Each side controls the muscles of the opposite side of the body.

Bet you didn't know

6 mind-bending facts about the brain

1 **Your brain** generates **enough electricity** to power a **lightbulb.**

2 **Each minute,** about **750 milliliters—or two soda cans—of blood** travel through the **brain.**

3 **Eating chocolate** releases chemicals in the **brain** that make us **happy.**

4 **Exercise can** make **your brain** more **active.**

5 It would take close to **3,000** years to count **the neurons,** or nerve cells, **in your brain.**

6 Pressing your **tongue** to the roof of your mouth **eases "brain freeze."**

That's GROSS!

WHO NEEDS SLOBBERING ZOMBIES AND SLIMY MONSTERS THIS HALLOWEEN? THE BACTERIA LIVING INSIDE YOUR BODY ARE ICKY ENOUGH.

Don't panic, but you're outnumbered by alien life-forms. They look like hairy hot dogs, spiky blobs, and oozing spirals, and they're crawling across—and deep inside—your body right this very minute. They're bacteria!

Your body is built of trillions of itty-bitty living blobs, called cells, that work together to do amazing things, such as hold in your organs or help beat your brother at *Super Mario Kart*. But for every cell you call your own, about ten foreign bacteria are clustering around or near it. You can't see these hitchhikers, but you sure can smell a lot of them. Like any living thing, bacteria

eat, reproduce, die, and create waste. A lot of this waste is the source of your body odor, bad breath, and torturous toots. In other words, some bacteria can make your life stink!

If the thought of being a human-shaped planet for microscopic inhabitants makes you queasy, relax. Most of your body's microbes have been harmlessly hanging out in your body for years and are essential for good health. And just like a fingerprint, your bacteria make you who you are, because no two people host the same mix of microorganisms. But that doesn't make things any less disgusting!

Little Monsters

Meet four famous bacteria that call your body "home sweet home..."

1 ACTINOMYCES VISCOSUS

When your dentist breaks out the power tools to jackhammer the brownish coat of slime known as plaque from your teeth, she's really attacking these mouth-dwelling bacteria.

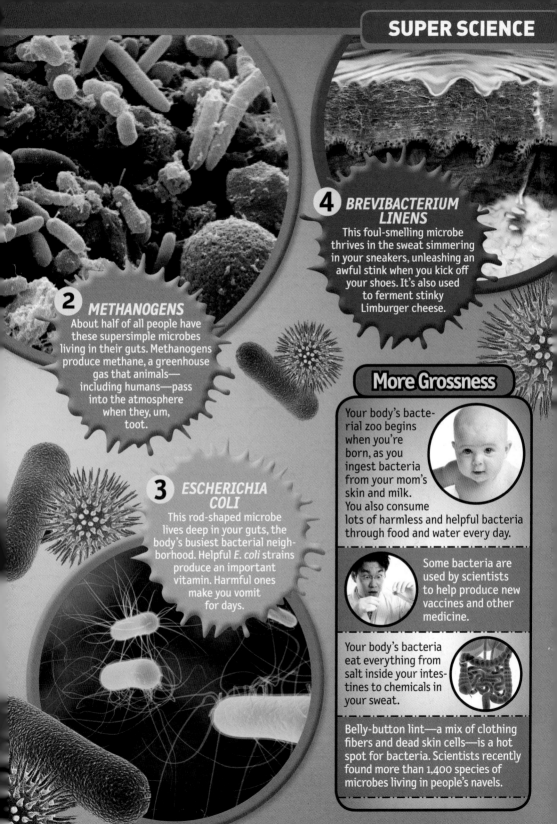

4 BREVIBACTERIUM LINENS

This foul-smelling microbe thrives in the sweat simmering in your sneakers, unleashing an awful stink when you kick off your shoes. It's also used to ferment stinky Limburger cheese.

2 METHANOGENS

About half of all people have these supersimple microbes living in their guts. Methanogens produce methane, a greenhouse gas that animals— including humans—pass into the atmosphere when they, um, toot.

3 ESCHERICHIA COLI

This rod-shaped microbe lives deep in your guts, the body's busiest bacterial neighborhood. Helpful *E. coli* strains produce an important vitamin. Harmful ones make you vomit for days.

More Grossness

Your body's bacterial zoo begins when you're born, as you ingest bacteria from your mom's skin and milk. You also consume lots of harmless and helpful bacteria through food and water every day.

Some bacteria are used by scientists to help produce new vaccines and other medicine.

Your body's bacteria eat everything from salt inside your intestines to chemicals in your sweat.

Belly-button lint—a mix of clothing fibers and dead skin cells—is a hot spot for bacteria. Scientists recently found more than 1,400 species of microbes living in people's navels.

All About YOU

What Your BIRTH ORDER Says About YOU

Whether you're the oldest, the youngest, or an only child, your birth order can shape your personality. "Your position in the family line makes a big impact on the person you are now—and who you'll grow up to be," says psychologist Kevin Leman, author of *The Birth Order Book*. Here's what your sibling status may say about you.

IF YOU'RE THE OLDEST, YOU . . .

are well organized and reliable, excel in school, and have a knack for computers. You're a natural-born leader and like to be in charge of projects, although you don't like big changes. Many firstborns go on to become entertainers.

Celeb matches:
Taylor Swift, Justin Bieber

IF YOU'RE A MULTIPLE . . .

the same birth-order rules apply. If you're a twin or triplet and were born first, your personality is probably like an oldest child's. If you were born last, your personality is probably like a youngest child's. This is usually true even if you have siblings in addition to your twin or triplets.

Celeb matches: Dylan and Cole Sprouse (Dylan's older by 15 minutes.)

IF THESE PERSONALITY PROFILES DON'T MATCH YOURS, THAT'S OK. THIS IS JUST FOR FUN!

IF YOU'RE THE YOUNGEST, YOU . . .

are good at reading people's emotions and understanding how to act accordingly. You aren't scared to say what you think and therefore often get what you want. You love attention and may be the class clown—you could grow up to be a famous comedian.

Celeb matches:
Jack Black, Ariana Grande

IF YOU'RE IN THE MIDDLE, YOU . . .

have a lot of friends and try to resolve fights rather than start them. Always thinking of better ways to do things, you're likely to start a business, such as a lawn-mowing service or lemonade stand. Middle children often become successful business leaders.

Celeb matches:
Donald Trump,
Jennifer Lopez

IF YOU'RE AN ONLY CHILD, YOU . . .

rely on your imagination to keep things interesting. An independent person, you're comfortable talking to new people. You're hardworking and goal-oriented, and you like doing things right the first time around. You may become a professional athlete or government leader.

Celeb matches:
Maria Sharapova,
Selena Gomez

Awful Afflictions DILEMMA

Would you rather SUFFER FROM a SNEEZING SPREE that never ceases, or GET A CASE OF the HICCUPS that lasts forever?

IF YOU CHOOSE SNEEZING:

You're wise not to stifle a sneeze. It's an important bodily function for blasting boogers and other debris from your air passages. But while a lone sneeze is essential, a long fit can be exhausting. Each ahh-choo involves a mini-workout of the muscles in your face, throat, chest, and abdomen, all working together to expel foreign particles from your nose and mouth at nearly 100 mph (161 kph). Now imagine the ordeal of Donna Griffiths, a 12-year-old English girl who suffered from a sneezing spree that lasted more than 977 days!

IF YOU CHOOSE HICCUPS:

Never-ending hiccups might seem less annoying than ceaseless sneezing, but consider the life-disrupting consequences of well-meaning friends offering a "cure." Iowa, U.S.A., farmer Charles Osborne hiccuped every day for nearly 70 years (doctors think he damaged the hiccup-controlling part of his brain after straining to lift a heavyweight hog). Before he passed away in 1991, Osborne received thousands of letters with homemade remedies. One buddy even fired a double-barreled shotgun just out of sight, hoping to scare away the hiccups.

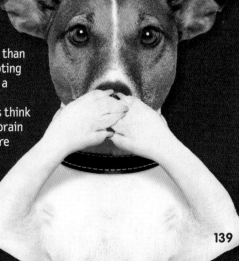

Continents on the Move

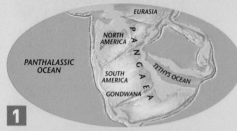

1

PANGAEA About 240 million years ago, Earth's landmasses were joined together in one supercontinent that extended from Pole to Pole.

2

BREAKUP By 94 million years ago, Pangaea had broken apart into landmasses that would become today's continents. Dinosaurs roamed Earth during a period of warmer climates.

3

EXTINCTION About 65 million years ago, an asteroid smashed into Earth, creating the Gulf of Mexico. This impact may have resulted in the extinction of half the world's species, including the dinosaurs. This was one of several major mass extinctions.

4

ICE AGE By 18,000 years ago, the continents had drifted close to their present positions, but most far northern and far southern lands were buried beneath huge glaciers.

A LOOK INSIDE

The distance from Earth's surface to its center is 3,963 miles (6,378 km) at the Equator. There are four layers: a thin, rigid crust; the rocky mantle; the outer core, which is a layer of molten iron; and finally the inner core, which is believed to be solid iron.

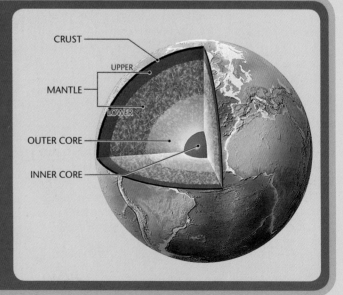

ROCK STARS

The world is full of rocks—some big, some small, some formed deep beneath the Earth, and some formed at the surface. While they may look similar, not all rocks are created equal. Look closely, and you'll see differences between every boulder, stone, and pebble. Here's more about the three top varieties of rocks.

Igneous

Named for the Greek word meaning "from fire," igneous rocks form when hot, molten liquid called magma cools. Pools of magma form deep underground and slowly work their way to the Earth's surface. If they make it all the way, the liquid rock erupts and is called lava. As the layers of lava build up they form a mountain called a volcano. Typical igneous rocks include obsidian, basalt, and pumice, which is so chock-full of gas bubbles that it actually floats in water.

OBSIDIAN   PUMICE

Metamorphic

Metamorphic rocks are the masters of change! These rocks were once igneous or sedimentary, but thanks to intense heat and pressure deep within the Earth, they have undergone a total transformation from their original form. These rocks never truly melt; instead, the heat twists and bends them until their shapes substantially change. Metamorphic rocks include slate as well as marble, which is used for buildings, monuments, and sculptures.

MARBLE   SLATE

Sedimentary

When wind, water, and ice constantly wear away and weather rocks, smaller pieces called sediment are left behind. These are sedimentary rocks, also known as gravel, sand, silt, and clay. As water flows downhill it carries the sedimentary grains into lakes and oceans, where they get deposited. As the loose sediment piles up, the grains eventually get compacted or cemented back together again. The result is new sedimentary rock. Sandstone, limestone, and shale are sedimentary rocks that have formed this way.

SANDSTONE

NATIONAL GEOGRAPHIC KIDS

SCANNER

SCAN THIS PAGE!
GET BONUS MOBILE CONTENT! Download the free NG Kids scanner app. Directions on inside front cover.

1 The Chol Indians of Mexico believe *crystals* have magical powers.

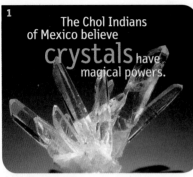

2 Legend says that the mineral aquamarine was found in the treasure chests of mermaids. Sailors wore it for **good luck.**

4 Egypt's PYRAMIDS AT GIZA AND THE SPHINX are made of limestone, a rock that consists mostly of calcite. That's a mineral formed by the remains of tiny sea creatures.

3 INVENTED IN 1839, THE FIRST SUCCESSFUL *cameras used silver* TO HELP PROCESS PHOTOGRAPHS.

15 COOL THINGS ABOUT

5 *Salt* was once considered so valuable that ancient Roman soldiers were paid partly in the mineral **instead of money.**

6 THE HOPE DIAMOND IS VALUED AT MORE THAN $200 MILLION. ITS FORMER OWNER DONATED THE *45.5-carat gemstone* TO THE SMITHSONIAN INSTITUTION IN 1958— AND SENT IT BY REGULAR MAIL.

7 Natural ice formations, such as ICEBERGS AND ICICLES, are considered minerals.

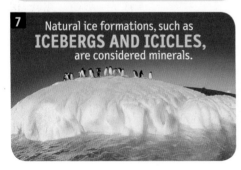

8 The brightly colored rock called **opal** is Australia's national gemstone.

9 The huge ROCK STATUES on Easter Island off Chile were carved from compacted volcanic ash called tuff.

10 FLUORITE CAN GLOW UNDER ULTRA-VIOLET LIGHT.

11 SAPPHIRES AND **RUBIES** ARE THE SAME MINERAL: CORUNDUM.

ROCKS AND MINERALS

12 The gold burial mask of **KING TUT** is decorated with blue rocks called lapis lazuli and the minerals turquoise, carnelian, and quartz.

12

13 THE **HOBA METEORITE** WEIGHS ABOUT 66 TONS (60 MT). THE OUTER SPACE ROCK CONTAINS MINERALS RARELY FOUND ON EARTH'S SURFACE

14 Ancient humans chipped away at **flint** to make **arrowheads** and other **sharp weapons** and **tools.**

15 THERE ARE MORE THAN **4,000** KNOWN MINERALS.

Kaboom!

How demolition experts bring down buildings

1 BEFORE

TEXAS STADIUM

2 EXPLODING!

3 AFTER

Deafening explosions and fiery flashes raced in waves around Texas Stadium. Concrete supports fell like trees, and the steel beams across the top of the building crashed to the ground. Soon a large dust cloud hovered over the rubble. The football arena was gone.

For nearly 40 years, the Dallas Cowboys played home football games at Texas Stadium in Irving. But after the team moved to the new Cowboys Stadium in 2009, the old stadium was no longer needed. So city officials planned to demolish it.

When a structure isn't useful anymore, sometimes the best way to bring it down is also dramatic to watch. Teams of experts can use carefully timed explosions to make a building, bridge, or other structure collapse in a matter of seconds. Let's take a look behind the scenes of the stadium's spectacular demolition.

CONTROLLED DESTRUCTION

The first step to figuring out the most efficient way to demolish Texas Stadium was to study its original plans. Demolition experts take advantage of gravity as much as possible, using the weight of the building to help it collapse. An initial team took out parts of the structure such as walls and ramps so that the whole building perched only on its basic supports, particularly at the lower level of the structure.

EXPLOSIVE SITUATION

Texas Stadium had 12 concrete support structures, called abutments, which circled the outside of the building and held up the roof's six steel beams, called trusses. The team planning the explosion did test blasts to figure out how much dynamite was needed to bring these supports down in the safest way possible. The demolition crew then drilled 3,300 holes into the concrete supports where they placed sticks of dynamite. Special explosives called linear-shaped charges, equipped with a fast-burning, fuse-like cord, cut through the steel in the roof trusses. The charges were linked together so that the concrete supports holding up each of the six trusses exploded at exactly the same time. If they didn't, the roof trusses might not fall to the ground.

SO LONG, STADIUM

After six months of planning, it was time for the explosion. Police and firefighters stopped traffic on highways surrounding Texas Stadium. People gathered at a safe distance to watch. After a countdown, the press of a button set off the series of explosions that, in 60 seconds, left nothing but a massive pile of rubble.

DEMOLITION IN CHINA

1 BEFORE

A BRIDGE IN CHINA WAS DEMOLISHED IN MUCH THE SAME WAY AS TEXAS STADIUM.

2 EXPLODING!

3 AFTER

CRASH AND BURN

PREP TIME FOR TEXAS STADIUM DEMOLITION	NUMBER OF HOLES FOR EXPLOSIVES	TIME TO LOAD EXPLOSIVES	POUNDS OF EXPLOSIVES more than	TIME TO BRING DOWN TEXAS STADIUM	COST OF DEMOLITION
6 months	3,300	5 days	2,000 (907 kg)	60 seconds	$6 million

COOL inventions

WAY UP!

WALL WALKER

It took a radioactive arachnid's bite to turn Peter Parker into Spider-Man, but engineering students at Utah State University have devised an easier way to gain wall-climbing superpowers. Their Personnel Vacuum Assisted Climber enables its wearer to crawl up walls, even on the roughest surfaces. The climber straps on a backpack equipped with powerful vacuum motors. The motors connect to two handheld suction units that stick to the wall when the motors are engaged. Fast climbers could scramble to the Empire State Building's observation deck in about half an hour. They'll want to take the elevator back down, though—the prototype's battery lasts only 30 minutes!

VACUUM POWER

PUSH FOR PIZZA

Your belly's grumbling but the refrigerator is bare. Don't panic! Just push the button inside the box-shaped magnet on your fridge and—*mamma mia!*—a piping-hot pizza arrives at your door in 30 minutes. It might seem magical, but the V.I.P. Fridge Magnet actually contains a transmitter that enables your cell phone to place an order with the local pizzeria. Right now, this amazing magnet is available only to customers of Red Tomato Pizza in the United Arab Emirates, but its inventors predict it will catch on elsewhere. Pizza party, anyone?

ORDER BUTTON

Push for hunger

Hello, I'm a charging port

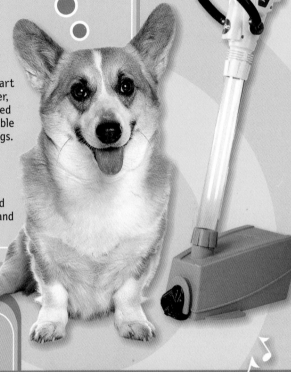

THIS IS ONE VACUUM I'M NOT SCARED OF.

SUPER
SCOOPER

Scooping up after your dog is a dirty job. Leave it to a kid to help invent a device that takes out the grossest part of this chore. Together with his father, nine-year-old Connor Reynolds created the Pooch Power Shovel, a rechargeable vacuum that picks up piles left by dogs. The unit's powerful motor whisks pieces straight into a biodegradable bag, saving you from any close encounters. When the bag's full, just toss it out and replace it. You'll spend less time fetching Fido's "presents" and more time playing fetch!

BIKE RADIO

As much as you might like to rock out while you ride, wearing headphones on a bicycle is just too risky. Soundmatters' handlebar-mounted speakers make your music collection good to go. Just link these rechargeable wireless speakers to a portable music player (such as an iPod touch, iPhone, or Android phone), then enjoy loud-and-clear playback of your favorite road-tripping tunes. The speakers are good for five hours on a single charge, so chances are you'll run out of energy before they do.

Get Ready for ROBOTS

THIS COOL 'DROID COULD SOON BE A PART OF YOUR FAMILY.

School's out. It's been a long day, so you head home to relax. You're greeted by a pal who's happy to see you, listens to you talk about your day, and reminds you to text your cousin happy birthday. And that's before he helps you with your homework.

This is your future, and it all starts with a knee-high robot called NAO (pronounced NOW), which may be available by the year 2040. Representing the new generation of self-guided robots, these 'bots can sense, think, and act. Other robots might do two out of the three. For example, a robot might sense things using cameras and think using computers, but with no arms, wheels, or claws, it can't act. Other robots can move and sense things, but can't think for themselves. But NAO can do it all.

Teams of NAO robots play in the RoboCup, a yearly soccer competition among these self-guided robots.

ROBOT PERSONALITY

"You can program your computer to give NAO what could be called personality," says Natanel Dukan of Aldebaran Robotics, the French company that built NAO. The robot has cute, childlike features—a high voice, a small body, big eyes, and a large head. "These are things that are known to have an emotional appeal to people," robot expert Dan Kara says. NAO's friendly design helps in one of NAO's main functions—to teach people how useful personal robots can be. Someday one may help you ace a test!

3 COOL THINGS ABOUT GPS

Thanks to GPS, you may never get lost—or lose anything—again! Short for *global positioning system,* this superhelpful technology relies on satellites in space to collect and plot your position. You can use that info for everything from finding a friend's house to tracking down your dog. Here are some cool ways GPS can help you!

Left on Interstate
1/2 mi
1:30
15.5 mi
eta 1:45 pm
menu
GPS

1. Find Your Pets

Forget hanging flyers around your neighborhood: When your pet goes missing, just check your phone! Thanks to GPS tracking devices that attach to your dog or cat's collar, you can find out exactly where your pet is from your phone or computer. Some products even send text messages to you if your pet wanders too far from home.

2. Locate Lost Items

Can't find your smartphone? You may be able to locate it with the help of GPS. Many laptops, mobile phones, and tablets are equipped with a built-in GPS receiver that can send out signals to show you its approximate location on a map.

3. Predict the Weather

Knowing the forecast for tomorrow is one thing. But what about the weather tomorrow exactly at 2:55 p.m.? Meteorologists and geodesists are drawing on data from GPS satellites, including atmospheric temperatures, to help generate more accurate—and up-to-the-minute—weather forecasts. How cool!

How GPS Works

A system of about 30 satellites is orbiting 12,550 miles (20,200 km) above the Earth, traveling at speeds of about 8,500 miles (13,800 km) an hour. As they orbit, the satellites transmit signals to GPS receivers on Earth. Once your GPS receiver picks up radio signals from at least four of these satellites, it can calculate their coordinates to pinpoint your exact position on Earth.

GPS units use satellites to determine your location.

ANIMAL KILLERS

BUSTED!

The cool science behind solving wildlife mysteries

FINGERPRINT

Like detectives, scientists at the U.S. National Fish and Wildlife Service (FWS) Forensics Laboratory examine evidence left behind at crime scenes to help solve mysteries. Here's how they use cutting-edge technology to help solve crimes against animals—and catch the crooks!

THE VICTIMS: ELK
THE CRIME SCENE: COLORADO
THE EVIDENCE: FINGERPRINT

STICKY FINGERS

To passersby, the man was enjoying a campout. But he was really illegally sneaking into reserved hunting grounds to kill elk for their prized antlers. Instead of the permitted bow and arrow, he was using a gun.

The hunter couldn't move the large antler racks home during hunting season, so he wrapped them in duct tape and hid them in tree branches. He'd return for them after hunting season.

But the suspect left something else behind. After wardens found one of the racks, FWS lab technicians discovered a fingerprint on the duct tape. No two people have the same fingerprints. So the scientists searched a database, which matched the print with the suspect. They could confidently point their finger at the hunter, who pleaded guilty and went to jail.

BULLET
CRIME SCENE EVIDENCE

THE VICTIMS: TIGERS
THE CRIME SCENE: ILLINOIS
THE EVIDENCE: BULLET

SMOKING GUN

In an abandoned warehouse, two men shot and killed two endangered tigers that they had bought at a roadside zoo. They hoped to sell the hides, skulls, and meat. But the suspects did a sloppy cleanup job. When an undercover agent from the FWS bought a full-body tiger-skin rug from the ringleader, she found a bullet in the tiger's skull.

A gun leaves a pattern of marks on the bullet it fires, which can match it back to that particular weapon. At a lab, scientists fired a test round of bullets from the ringleader's gun and then used a microscope to compare the marks from the test round with the bullet they found. They matched. Now the ringleader is locked up—instead of the tigers that would have been his next victims.

MICROSCOPE

MEATBALLS

THE VICTIMS: FOX, COYOTE, BIRDS
THE CRIME SCENE: IDAHO
THE EVIDENCE: DNA

DNA
CRIME SCENE EVIDENCE

BAD MEAT

The meatball trail stretched two miles (3.2 km) in the snow. What should have been a tasty treat for any animal was actually poisoned with a pesticide. FWS agents found the bodies of a fox, coyote, and three magpies that had died after eating the tainted meat. Based on a tip that someone was using poisoned meatballs to kill wolves, agents searched a man's garage. They discovered a bloodstained tool and a bottle containing pesticide, which was identified as the same poison in the meatballs. All the agents had to do was prove the man made the meatballs, then they would know he had also tried to kill endangered wolves.

A geneticist gathered DNA samples from a meatball and from the tool. Found in the body's cells, DNA determines the traits of all living things. And no two living things have the same DNA. The DNA samples from the meatball and the tool matched, which proved the man had made the poisoned meatballs. The trail of evidence led straight to the killer.

STUMP YOUR PARENTS

SUPER SCIENCE QUIZ

Are your dad and mom mad about science? See how much they really know about the subject with this quiz! ANSWERS BELOW

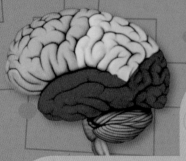

1 **True or false?** There is real gold in the sun.

2 **How many carats is the Hope Diamond?**
a. 91.6
b. 12.4
c. 45.5
d. three bunches

3 **Your brain generates enough electricity to power which household object?**
a. TV
b. refrigerator
c. microwave
d. lightbulb

4 **Which one of the following is considered to be a mineral?**
a. quartz
b. ruby
c. iceberg
d. all of the above

5 **What is the planet CoRoT-7b made of?**
a. ice
b. lava
c. gas
d. chocolate

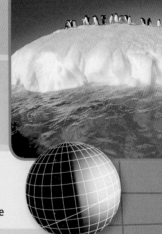

Not **STUMPED** yet?
Check out the *National Geographic Kids Quiz Whiz* collection for more crazy **SCIENCE** questions!

Research Like a Pro

There is so much information on the Internet. How do you find what you need and make sure it's accurate?

Be Specific

To come up with the most effective key-words—words that describe what you want to know more about—write down what you're looking for in the form of a question, and then circle the most important words in that sentence. Those are the keywords to use in your search. And for best results use words that are specific rather than general.

Research

Research on the Internet involves "looking up" information using a search engine (see list below). Type one or two keywords, and the search engine will provide a list of websites that contain information related to your topic.

Use Trustworthy Sources

When conducting Internet research, be sure the website you use is reliable and the information it provides can be trusted. Sites produced by well-known, established organizations, companies, publications, educational institutions, or the government are your best bets.

Don't Copy

Avoid Internet plagiarism. Take careful notes and cite the websites you use to conduct research.

HELPFUL AND SAFE SEARCH ENGINES FOR KIDS

Google Safe Search	squirrelnet.com/search/Google_SafeSearch.asp
Yahoo! Kids	kids.yahoo.com
SuperKids	super-kids.com
Ask Kids	askkids.com
Kids Click	kidsclick.org
AOL Kids	kids.aol.com

FUN and GAMES

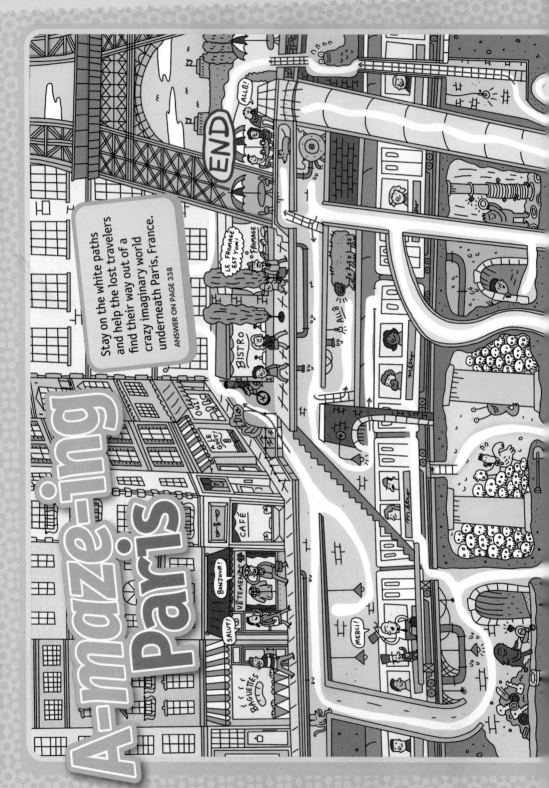

A-maze-ing Paris

Stay on the white paths and help the lost travelers find their way out of a crazy imaginary world underneath Paris, France.

ANSWER ON PAGE 338

Color Café

Some items in this scene have mysteriously changed color. Find at least 12 things that are the wrong color.

ANSWERS ON PAGE 338

Funny Fill-In
Power Plant

Ask a friend to give you words to fill in the blanks in this story without showing it to him or her. Then read it out loud for a laugh.

For our first field trip of the year, my class went to the arboretum to see all the

_____ plants. We dropped our _____ _____ lunches and followed
   adjective   adjective   noun

a(n) _____ through a(n) _____ forest, making sure not to _____
    type of job   adjective   verb

anything. But then I saw a rare _____ _____-eating plant that was as tall
                          color   insect

as a(n) _____ . I leaned in to _____ one of its flowers when I heard a
      noun   verb

_____ . "_____ !" I shouted. My _____ sandwich
  sound   silly expression   something gross

was being devoured by the plant! Still hungry, the plant reached out with its _____
                                       large number

vines. I started to _____ for help. But then the plant _____ into
        verb   past-tense verb

my _____ , pulled out a(n) _____ , and put it in its _____ .
   noun   favorite food   body part

Now that's what I call plant food!

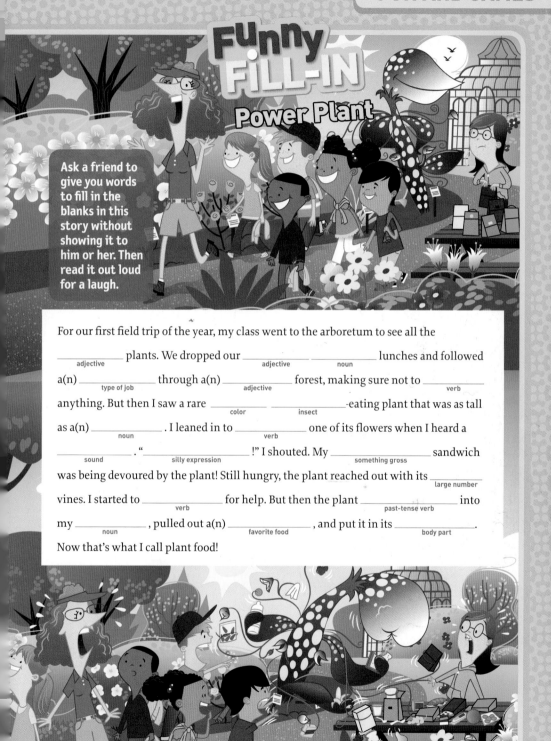

SIGNS
OF THE TIMES

Seeing isn't always believing.
Two of these funny signs are
not real. Can you figure out
which two are fake?

ANSWER ON
PAGE 338

1

POLE 440 mi
BURLINGTON 113
MEXICO CITY 225 mi
MONTREAL 185 mi
KABUL 6576 mi
LONDON 3313 miles
PUTNEY 7 mi
BOSTON 97 mi
BURPING FALLS 16 mi
PARIS 3481 mi
ROME 4150
DUBLIN 3020 mi
MOSCOW 4504 miles

2

FOOT WEARING
NOT ALLOWED

3

Weigh Togo
Road

4

DANG
All Area Beyond
Sign is Closed Because
Of Bear Danger

5

Zzyzx Rd

6

MULE
PARKING
ONLY
NO
MOTORIZED
VEHICLES
ALLOWED

Windy Jumble

A powerful wind has whipped through this neighborhood park. Some visitors' belongings have blown away and ended up with someone else. Figure out which items belong to the people listed on the right. Fill in the correct letter next to the names. We've done the first one for you.

ANSWERS ON PAGE 338

A Eleanor
____ Sam
____ Nicole
____ Steve
____ Carlos

____ Zak
____ Ava
____ Jill
____ Isabel
____ Daniel

161

COLOR YOUR WORLD

These photographs show close-up views of rainbow-colored objects. Unscramble the letters to identify what's in each picture.
Bonus: Use the highlighted letters to solve the puzzle below. ANSWERS ON PAGE 338

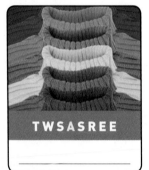

TWSASREE

_____

NBRWAOI

_____

ILPNRSKSE

_____

OODCLER ILSNECP

_____

LRBUEALM

_____

HOUSETRTBSHO

_____

RICCELOI

_____

ELOSTW

_____

AESHFRTE

_____

HINT: Leprechaun or not, anyone would be happy to find this under a rainbow.

ANSWER: ___ ___ ___ ___ ___ ___ G ___ ___ ___

162

Cheetah

Just Joking

KNOCK, KNOCK.
Who's there?
Aardvark.
Aardvark who?
Aardvark a million miles for you!

Q What did the **0** say to the **8**?

A Nice belt.

TOURIST: I'd like to purchase a ticket to the moon, please.
TOUR GUIDE: Sorry, sir. The moon is full tonight.

TONGUE TWISTER!
Say this fast three times:
Shelly is a selfish shellfish.

HA HA HA!

LARRY? ARE YOU IN THERE?

ANIMAL JAM

Twinkle Toes

BONUS: Find 12 hearts in the scene.

In February, the *Animal Jam* crew meets at the dance club to celebrate a holiday called Friendship Festival. Can you guess what each character is thinking? Fill in the number that matches the correct animal.

1. "Put your hands in the air like you just don't care!"
2. "Robots have nothing on me."
3. "Let's do the bunny hop!"
4. "Aloha! Let's hula!"
5. "My moves really pack in the crowds."
6. "Too much dancing—time for a catnap."
7. "It's time for the fox trot!"

ANSWERS ON PAGE 338

EXPLORE!

NATIONAL GEOGRAPHIC KIDS' virtual world online: AnimalJam.com

Enter the special code NGK2015 for a bonus!

The Funnies

"HE'D MAKE A FANTASTIC OUTFIELDER, COACH. HE'S GREAT AT CATCHING FLIES!"

"YOU'RE RIGHT. FROM UP HERE THEY ALL DO LOOK LIKE ANTS. HEY, I'M GETTING HUNGRY!"

"MAN, THIS BACKPACK GETS HEAVIER AND HEAVIER EVERY DAY."

"WHATEVER YOU DO, DON'T EVER CHALLENGE HIM TO A STARING CONTEST!"

"YOU KNOW, HALF THE FOOD THEY SPRINKLE IN HERE IS FOR ME!"

Funny FILL-IN
Spray 'n' Wash

Ask a friend to give you words to fill in the blanks in this story without showing it to him or her. Then read it out loud for a laugh.

CAR WASH! DONATIONS ACCEPTED

This weekend, my mother, sister, and I _____ our _____
                                        past-tense verb   adjective
_____ to a car wash. As a(n) _____ waved us in, we heard a(n)
type of transportation   type of job
_____ . A huge _____ was _____ cars! "_____!"
funny sound   animal   verb ending in –ing   exclamation
we yelled. Using its _____ , it wiped the back of the _____ in front of us.
                      body part   noun
_____ dripped from a(n) _____ strapped to its hoof as it sprayed
something gross   noun
_____ with its trunk. Then the creature _____ the cars with its ears.
noun   past-tense verb
Everyone was covered in _____ . Who knows where that _____
                         type of liquid   same animal
came from—but our car has never been so _____ !
                                          adjective

In Plane Sight

Can you name 10 items at this air show that rhyme with the word "plane"?

ANSWERS ON PAGE 338

AIR SHOW TODAY

Can you find the sky path that leads to the lost kite? Some paths may take you through grass, kites, clouds, and trees. ANSWERS ON PAGE 338

FINISH!

START

What in the World?

RAIN FOREST ROUNDUP

These photographs show close-up views of animals that live in the rain forest. Unscramble the letters to identify what's in each picture. **Bonus:** Use the highlighted letters to solve the puzzle below. ANSWERS ON PAGE 338

GRFO

_____

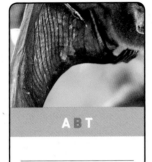

ABT

_____

OTSHL

_____

RGAAUJ

_____

PREVI

_____

ARPHNIA

_____

SPAGSREHROP

_____

IRAPT

_____

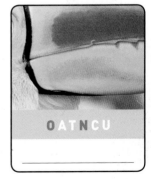

OATNCU

_____

HINT: Where would you go to buy bananas from a loud primate?

ANSWER: __ H W __ R M __ K Y __ S __ E

171

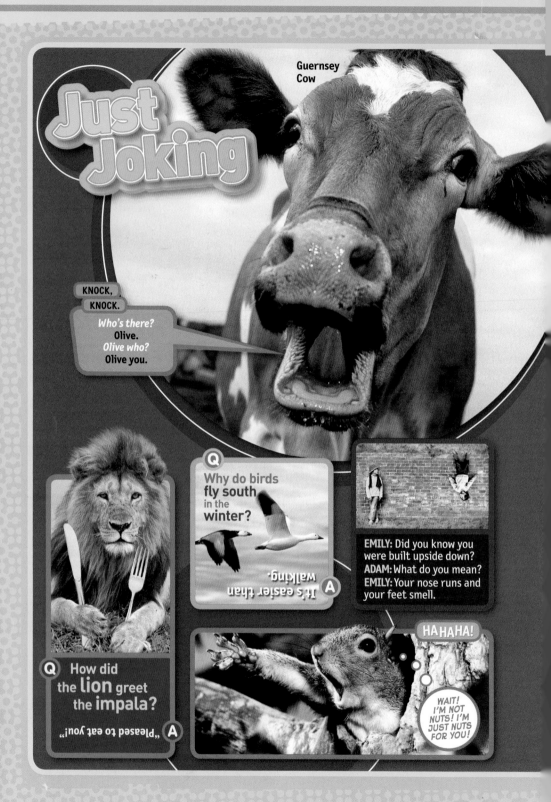

Just Joking

Guernsey Cow

KNOCK, KNOCK.

Who's there?
Olive.
Olive who?
Olive you.

Q Why do birds **fly south** in the **winter?**

A It's easier than walking.

EMILY: Did you know you were built upside down?
ADAM: What do you mean?
EMILY: Your nose runs and your feet smell.

Q How did the **lion** greet the **impala?**

A "Pleased to eat you!"

HA HA HA!

WAIT! I'M NOT NUTS! I'M JUST NUTS FOR YOU!

Funny Fill-In
Ka-ching!

Ask a friend to give you words to fill in the blanks in this story without showing it to him or her. Then read it out loud for a laugh.

_____! I just received _____ billion dollars from my _____
(silly expression)   (large number)   (adjective)

great-great-great-great-aunt for my birthday. I know exactly what I'll do with the _____.
(noun)

First I'll buy the _____. Maybe I could hire _____ to be my
(favorite sports team)   (famous athlete)

_____! I'm going to have all my _____ made of _____
(type of job)   (article of clothing, plural)   (noun, plural)

and build a roller coaster in my new _____. I'll ride a (n) _____
(room of a house)   (verb ending in –ing)

_____ to school—no more bus rides for me. And now I can get
(type of transportation)

_____ a(n) _____ like she always wanted. I think I'll even _____
(female friend's name)   (noun)   (verb)

a charity to save the _____. I'm so rich, I can give my *parents* an allowance.
(animal, plural)

173

Cormorant fishermen light lanterns for night fishing on the Li River in Xingping, China. Instead of nets or lines, cormorant birds are used to catch fish.

Culture Connection

20 CELEBRATIONS

① CHINESE NEW YEAR
February 19
Also called Lunar New Year, this holiday marks the new year according to the lunar calendar. Families celebrate with parades, feasts, and fireworks. Young people may receive gifts of money in red envelopes.

② HOLI
March 6
This festival in India celebrates spring and marks the triumph of good over evil. People cover one another with powdered paint, called *gulal*, and douse one another with buckets of colored water.

③ NYEPI
March 21
A national day of silence, this Hindu holiday marks Lunar New Year in Bali, Indonesia, and encourages meditation and reflection. Those who follow traditional customs do not talk, use electricity, travel, or eat for 24 hours.

④ QINGMING FESTIVAL
April 5
Also known as "grave sweeping day," this Chinese celebration calls on people to return to the graves of their deceased loved ones. There, they tidy up the grave, as well as light firecrackers, burn fake money, and leave food as an offer to the spirits.

⑤ EASTER
April 5
A Christian holiday that honors the resurrection of Jesus Christ, Easter is celebrated by giving baskets filled with gifts, decorated eggs, or candy to children.

⑥ VESAK DAY
May
Buddhists around the world observe Buddha's Birthday with special rituals including chanting and prayer, candlelight processions, and meditation.

⑦ BERMUDA DAY
May 25
The first day of the year that Bermudians take a dip in the ocean. It is also traditionally the first day on which Bermuda shorts are worn as business attire. To celebrate the holiday, there is a parade in Hamilton, and a road race from the west end of the island into Hamilton.

⑧ RAMADAN AND EID AL-FITR
June 18*–July 18**
A Muslim religious holiday, Ramadan is a month long, ending in the Eid Al-Fitr celebration. Observers fast during this month— eating only after sunset. Muslims pray for forgiveness and hope to purify themselves through observance.

⑨ ST. JOHN'S NIGHT
June 21
In Poland, people celebrate the longest day of the year—also known as the summer solstice—with rituals including making bonfires, floating flower wreaths down a stream, and releasing thousands of paper lanterns into the night sky.

⑩ BASTILLE DAY
July 14
The French call this day *La Fête Nationale*, or the celebration of the start of the French Revolution in 1789. In Paris, fireworks light up the night skies while dance parties spill into the streets.

*Begins at sundown.
**Dates may vary slightly by location.

Around the World

11 MELON DAY
August 9
Since 1994, people in the Asian nation Turkmenistan have taken a day—aptly named Melon Day—to celebrate the country's sweet muskmelons.

12 NAG PANCHAMI
August 19
In Nepal and India, Hindus worship snakes—and keep evil spirits out of their homes—by sticking images of serpents on their doors and making offerings to the revered reptiles.

13 ROSH HASHANAH
September 13*–15
A Jewish religious holiday marking the beginning of a new year on the Hebrew calendar. Celebrations include prayer, ritual foods, and a day of rest.

14 OKTOBERFEST
September 19–October 4
Originally celebrating the marriage of Bavarian royalty back in 1810, Oktoberfest is now a mega-festival celebrated all over the world. People enjoy food, drink, music, and merriment.

15 SUKKOT
September 27*–October 4
A Jewish holiday celebrating the fall harvest, when people build (and, often, eat and sleep) in outdoor temporary huts called Sukkahs.

16 GUY FAWKES DAY
November 5
Over 400 years ago, a man named Guy Fawkes plotted with other conspirators to blow up the British Parliament. He failed, and Brits still celebrate his demise by lighting bonfires and setting off fireworks.

17 DIWALI
November 11–15
India's largest and most important holiday. People light their homes with clay lamps to symbolize the inner light that protects against spiritual darkness.

18 HANUKKAH
December 6*–14
This Jewish holiday is eight days long. It commemorates the rededication of the Temple in Jerusalem. Hanukkah celebrations include the lighting of menorah candles for eight days and the exchange of gifts.

19 CHRISTMAS DAY
December 25

A Christian holiday marking the birth of Jesus Christ, Christmas is usually celebrated by decorating trees, exchanging presents, and having festive gatherings.

20 BOXING DAY
December 26
Some people think this national holiday in Great Britain, Australia, Canada, and New Zealand was initially designated as a day to box up donations for the poor. Today? It's all about shopping, parties, and playing soccer.

What's Your Chinese Horoscope?
Locate your birth year to find out.

In Chinese astrology the zodiac runs on a 12-year cycle, based on the lunar calendar. Each year corresponds to one of 12 animals, each representing one of 12 personality types. Read on to find out which animal year you were born in and what that might say about you.

RAT
1972, '84, '96, 2008
Say cheese! You're attractive, charming, and creative. When you get mad, you can have really sharp teeth!

RABBIT
1975, '87, '99, 2011
Your ambition and talent make you jump at opportunity. You also keep your ears open for gossip.

HORSE
1966, '78, '90, 2002, '14
Being happy is your "mane" goal. And while you're smart and hardworking, your teacher may ride you for talking too much.

ROOSTER
1969, '81, '93, 2005
You crow about your adventures, but inside you're really shy. You're thoughtful, capable, brave, and talented.

OX
1973, '85, '97, 2009
You're smart, patient, and as strong as an ... well, you know what. Though you're a leader, you never brag.

DRAGON
1976, '88, 2000, '12
You're on fire! Health, energy, honesty, and bravery make you a living legend.

SHEEP
1967, '79, '91, 2003, '15
Gentle as a lamb, you're also artistic, compassionate, and wise. You're often shy.

DOG
1970, '82, '94, 2006
Often the leader of the pack, you're loyal and honest. You can also keep a secret.

TIGER
1974, '86, '98, 2010
You may be a nice person, but no one should ever enter your room without asking—you might attack!

SNAKE
1977, '89, 2001, '13
You may not speak often, but you're very smart. You always seem to have a stash of cash.

MONKEY
1968, '80, '92, 2004
No "monkey see, monkey do" for you. You're a clever problem-solver with an excellent memory.

PIG
1971, '83, '95, 2007
Even though you're courageous, honest, and kind, you never hog all the attention.

ANNIVERSARIES

Annual	1 year
Biennial	2 years
Triennial	3 years
Quadrennial	4 years
Quinquennial	5 years
Sexennial	6 years
Septennial	7 years
Octennial	8 years
Novennial	9 years
Decennial	10 years
Undecennial	11 years
Duodecennial	12 years
Tredecennial	13 years
Quattuordecennial	14 years
Quindecennial	15 years
Vigintennial or vicennial	20 years
Semicentennial or quinquagenary	50 years
Semisesquicentennial	75 years
Centennial	100 years
Quasquicentennial	125 years
Sesquicentennial	150 years
Demisemiseptcentennial or quartoseptcentennial	175 years
Bicentennial	200 years
Semiquincentennial	250 years
Tercentennial or tricentennial	300 years
Semiseptcentennial	350 years
Quadricentennial or quatercentenary	400 years
Quincentennial	500 years
Sexcentennial	600 years
Septicentennial or septuacentennial	700 years
Octocentennial	800 years
Nonacentennial	900 years
Millennial	1,000 years
Bimillennial	2,000 years

2015 CALENDAR

JANUARY

S	M	T	W	T	F	S
				1	2	3
4	5	6	7	8	9	10
11	12	13	14	15	16	17
18	19	20	21	22	23	24
25	26	27	28	29	30	31

FEBRUARY

S	M	T	W	T	F	S
1	2	3	4	5	6	7
8	9	10	11	12	13	14
15	16	17	18	19	20	21
22	23	24	25	26	27	28

MARCH

S	M	T	W	T	F	S
1	2	3	4	5	6	7
8	9	10	11	12	13	14
15	16	17	18	19	20	21
22	23	24	25	26	27	28
29	30	31				

APRIL

S	M	T	W	T	F	S
			1	2	3	4
5	6	7	8	9	10	11
12	13	14	15	16	17	18
19	20	21	22	23	24	25
26	27	28	29	30		

MAY

S	M	T	W	T	F	S
					1	2
3	4	5	6	7	8	9
10	11	12	13	14	15	16
17	18	19	20	21	22	23
24	25	26	27	28	29	30
31						

JUNE

S	M	T	W	T	F	S
	1	2	3	4	5	6
7	8	9	10	11	12	13
14	15	16	17	18	19	20
21	22	23	24	25	26	27
28	29	30				

JULY

S	M	T	W	T	F	S
			1	2	3	4
5	6	7	8	9	10	11
12	13	14	15	16	17	18
19	20	21	22	23	24	25
26	27	28	29	30	31	

AUGUST

S	M	T	W	T	F	S
						1
2	3	4	5	6	7	8
9	10	11	12	13	14	15
16	17	18	19	20	21	22
23	24	25	26	27	28	29
30	31					

SEPTEMBER

S	M	T	W	T	F	S
		1	2	3	4	5
6	7	8	9	10	11	12
13	14	15	16	17	18	19
20	21	22	23	24	25	26
27	28	29	30			

OCTOBER

S	M	T	W	T	F	S
				1	2	3
4	5	6	7	8	9	10
11	12	13	14	15	16	17
18	19	20	21	22	23	24
25	26	27	28	29	30	31

NOVEMBER

S	M	T	W	T	F	S
1	2	3	4	5	6	7
8	9	10	11	12	13	14
15	16	17	18	19	20	21
22	23	24	25	26	27	28
29	30					

DECEMBER

S	M	T	W	T	F	S
		1	2	3	4	5
6	7	8	9	10	11	12
13	14	15	16	17	18	19
20	21	22	23	24	25	26
27	28	29	30	31		

HALLOWEEN PET PARADE

Some of the sweetest Halloween goodies come wrapped . . . in fur! Millions of pets will wear a disguise for the holiday. Check out these fetching trick-or-treaters.

These pets like wearing costumes, but yours may not. Never force your pet to do something it does not want to do.

I AM ONE CLASSY KITTY.

"MEOW." UM, I MEAN "RIBBIT."

ELROY THE CAT SHOWS SOME STYLE DRESSED AS THE MAD HATTER FROM *ALICE'S ADVENTURES IN WONDERLAND.*

ROSIE THE KITTEN HOPS INTO HAL-LOWEEN WITH HER FROG COSTUME.

TIME FOR MY CLOSE-UP.

DUTCHESS THE STANDARD POODLE SPORTS A PINK FROCK AND SHADES.

FETCHING COSTUMES

What were the HOTTEST pet costumes last Halloween? Take a look at some of the trendiest disguises.

1. pumpkin	4. bee
2. devil	5. cat
3. hot dog	6. witch

SCAN THIS PAGE!
GET BONUS MOBILE CONTENT! Download the free NG Kids scanner app. Directions on inside front cover.

NATIONAL GEOGRAPHIC KiDS
SCANNER

Cool Carvings

Show your pumpkin's true personality with these wacky designs. Use a child-safe carving tool or ask an adult for help.

Express Yourself!

Let your jack-o'-lantern tell the world how it feels with emoticon smileys. It'll make your friends LOL!

Ahoy, Matey!

Pumpkins can wear costumes, too. Hats, inexpensive jewelry, and other accessories can create a pirate, cowboy, or even a baseball player.

Spell It Out

Who says a jack-o'-lantern needs a face? Carve spooky messages into your pumpkins instead.

Stack 'Em Up

Build a snowman by placing the biggest pumpkin at the bottom and the smallest one on top. Slant the knife when you cut off the tops, creating a ledge to support another pumpkin.

CREATE THE PERFECT DESIGN

Before you start cutting, sketch your design on white paper. Tape the paper to your pumpkin where you want the design to be. Punch along the lines of the sketch with a pin, poking through the paper and into the pumpkin. Then carve along the dotted lines you've made on the pumpkin.

1
IN SPAIN, EATING **TWELVE GRAPES** AT THE STROKE OF MIDNIGHT ON NEW YEAR'S DAY BRINGS GOOD LUCK.

2
Believe it or not, in several cultures it's considered **good luck to be POOPED ON** by a bird.

3
IN ENGLAND, FINDING A SPIDER IN YOUR WEDDING DRESS IS CONSIDERED GOOD LUCK.

4
IN GERMANY, IT'S GOOD LUCK TO **TOUCH** A CHIMNEY SWEEP'S BRUSH.

15 COOL THINGS ABOUT

5
Many people believe **CROSSING THEIR FINGERS** brings good luck.

6
AROUND THE WORLD, PEOPLE BELIEVE **LADYBUGS** ARE A SIGN OF GOOD LUCK.

7
EIGHT IS A LUCKY NUMBER IN CHINA: MORE THAN 300,000 COUPLES IN CHINA **GOT MARRIED ON 8/08/08.**

8
WEARING **YELLOW UNDERWEAR** ON NEW YEAR'S DAY IN PERU IS CONSIDERED LUCKY.

9

FOR MORE THAN **2,600 YEARS,** PEOPLE IN WESTERN EUROPE HAVE CONSIDERED **THE FEET OF RABBITS TO BE LUCKY.**

10

THE PHRASE "**BREAK A LEG**" IS SUPPOSED TO BRING GOOD LUCK TO PERFORMERS ABOUT TO GO ONSTAGE.

11

Four-leaf clovers are considered LUCKY, but perhaps the most lucky clover is the WORLD RECORD HOLDER for **most leaves, 56.**

LUCK

12

7

MANY CULTURES CONSIDER THE NUMBER 7 TO BE LUCKY: IN THE UNITED STATES, THE AVERAGE NUMBER OF WEDDINGS TRIPLED ON 7/07/07.

13

IN THE U.S. SOUTH, EATING BLACK-EYED PEAS ON NEW YEAR'S DAY IS BELIEVED TO BRING GOOD LUCK.

14

WHILE CAMPAIGNING FOR PRESIDENT OF THE UNITED STATES, BARACK OBAMA CARRIED A SOLDIER'S BRACELET, A GAMBLER'S LUCKY TOKEN, AND SEVERAL TINY RELIGIOUS ICONS FOR GOOD LUCK.

15

Hanging a horseshoe over a door is believed to bring good luck in the United States.

CHEETAH

WHISKERS CAN BE TRICKY.

The most useful tools? "A fine paintbrush and a steady hand," Daniele says. "My favorite is a cheetah because it was my first and brought me luck."

THE REAL ANIMAL CHEETAHS NEED TO DRINK ONLY ONCE EVERY THREE TO FOUR DAYS.

HANDIMALS

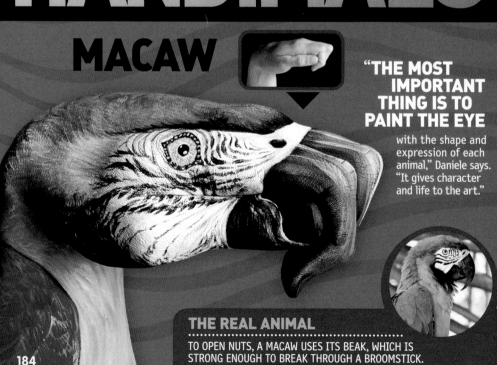

MACAW

"THE MOST IMPORTANT THING IS TO PAINT THE EYE

with the shape and expression of each animal," Daniele says. "It gives character and life to the art."

THE REAL ANIMAL
TO OPEN NUTS, A MACAW USES ITS BEAK, WHICH IS STRONG ENOUGH TO BREAK THROUGH A BROOMSTICK.

184

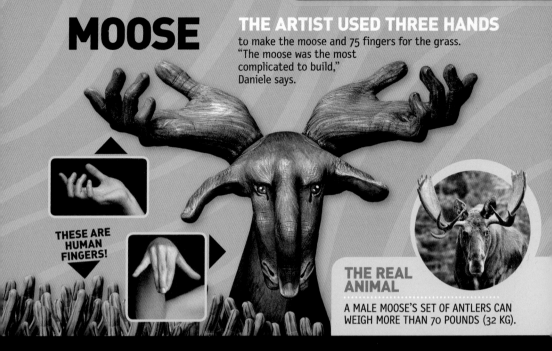

MOOSE

THE ARTIST USED THREE HANDS to make the moose and 75 fingers for the grass. "The moose was the most complicated to build," Daniele says.

THESE ARE HUMAN FINGERS!

THE REAL ANIMAL

A MALE MOOSE'S SET OF ANTLERS CAN WEIGH MORE THAN 70 POUNDS (32 KG).

CHECK OUT THESE WILD HANDMADE CREATIONS.

What do you get when you cross a human hand with an animal? A "handimal"! Artist Guido Daniele, who lives in Milan, Italy, positions people's hands into animal shapes, and then paints them to create realistic works of art. He paints the animals onto the hands of models—usually his son or daughter. Check out these "handimals" and some of the secrets to Daniele's art. In this case, it's OK to "handle" the animals!

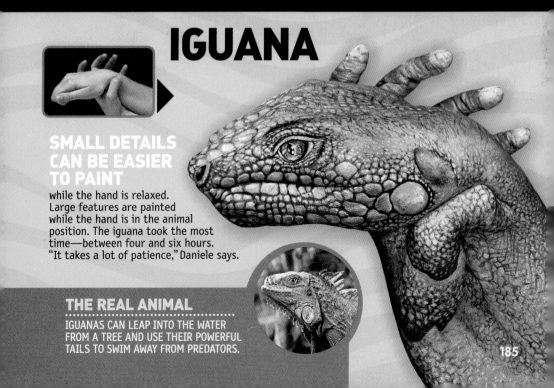

IGUANA

SMALL DETAILS CAN BE EASIER TO PAINT

while the hand is relaxed. Large features are painted while the hand is in the animal position. The iguana took the most time—between four and six hours. "It takes a lot of patience," Daniele says.

THE REAL ANIMAL

IGUANAS CAN LEAP INTO THE WATER FROM A TREE AND USE THEIR POWERFUL TAILS TO SWIM AWAY FROM PREDATORS.

185

Food That Fools You

SOAPY ORANGE JUICE

Bubbles in freshly poured juice disappear quickly. To keep this OJ looking fresh for the photo shoot, stylists created long-lasting bubbles by mixing two drops of soap with some juice in a separate container. These were then added on top of the drink with a spoon.

PIN THE BLUEBERRY ON THE PANCAKE

The fruit on top of this stack won't be rolling away anytime soon. A pin was pushed through each berry and into the pancakes to hold it in place. Some stylists use toothpicks to help position food, such as olives in a salad.

FRUIT COLORING

Sliced strawberries often have bright white insides that don't photograph well. To make the fruit camera-ready, stylists brush red food coloring over the white areas with a small paintbrush. White spots on a strawberry's skin can be colored with dabs of lipstick.

SNIP 'N' SPRAY

Your hair isn't the only thing that sometimes needs a trim. If a pancake isn't perfectly round, stylists will snip it into shape with scissors. A flapjack stack might also be coated with a spray people normally use to protect furniture from stains. The spray keeps the syrup from soaking in.

Your tummy may be rumbling, but if you sink your teeth into *this* chow, you'll get a surprise. The breakfast items are filled with dish soap, pins, cardboard, and other things you would never eat.

Even an amazing dish will start to look bad or lose shape if left out for too long. So food stylists and photographers have some pretty unappetizing techniques to make food appear tasty for things such as ads and cookbooks. A rolled-up tortilla might be glued so it doesn't unfold during a shoot. Or lemon juice could be added to a banana to keep it from turning brown. Feast your eyes on more secrets of food styling.

GOT GLUE?

This bowl isn't really brimming with cereal. A circular piece of cardboard was fitted inside the dish near the rim. That way, cereal pieces couldn't sink to the bottom. A thin layer of glue and flakes were added on top of the cardboard. Why glue? Unlike milk, glue won't make flakes soggy.

SIZZLING SYRUP

Stylists wanted to make this maple syrup look really thick. So before it was drizzled onto the pancakes, the syrup was heated in a saucepan to about 270°F (132°C). (That's more than twice as hot as warm syrup you'd eat.) As the temperature rose, water evaporated and the syrup thickened.

SHAPIN' BACON

To give bacon a wavy shape, stylists first mold a sheet of tinfoil into rows of ridges and fit the strips of raw meat over the foil. They then roast the bacon in an oven. As the meat cooks, its shape hardens.

187

CHEW ON THIS

TACOS!

The word "taco" hasn't always been on restaurant menus. In the 18th century, "tacos" were charges of gunpowder wrapped in paper used by Mexican miners. The wrap concept stuck when cooks started calling tortillas stuffed with meat and beans "tacos." Chow down on more filling facts.

People in the United States spend more money on **SALSA** than on ketchup.

Made from avocado, **GUACAMOLE** comes from the Aztec word *ahuacamolli* (ah-wah-kah-MOH-lee), or avocado sauce.

Natural **CHEDDAR CHEESE** has an almost white color. The bright orange color you see in grocery store cheddar comes from food coloring.

One type of **BLACK BEAN** tastes like mushrooms.

Crunchy corn **TACO** shells have been in U.S. cookbooks only since 1939. But soft tortillas have been around since the 13th century.

MAKE YOUR OWN TACOS

Tacos are crunchy sandwiches—the tortilla is like the bread, which you can stuff with anything you want! Get a parent's help to create a yummy taco.

1 Warm a skillet over medium heat. Cook 1½ pounds (680 g) ground beef or turkey for 6 to 8 minutes.

2 Add 1 teaspoon (5 mL) of cumin and ¾ teaspoon (4 mL) of salt. Stir occasionally for 2 to 3 minutes.

3 Fill 8 taco shells with the meat and top with 1 diced avocado, sour cream, and salsa.

4 Sprinkle with cheddar cheese.

MUSHROOMS are some seriously freaky fungi. They've been grown in caves and buried in, um, excrement, and some even glow in the dark.

PIZZA!
Pizza may have originated 2,000 years ago when the ancient Greeks prepared round, flat breads covered with oil, herbs, and spices. In 1830, chefs in Naples, Italy, cooked their crust in an oven lined with rocks from a nearby volcano. Some say that could have been the first pizzeria. The restaurant is still open today. Gobble up these other tasty tidbits.

People in the United States eat about 250 million pounds (113 million kg) of **PEPPERONI** a year, more than any other pizza topping.

BELL PEPPERS are fruits, not vegetables.

Most **CHEESE** is made from cow's, goat's, or sheep's milk. The traditional way to make mozzarella is from water buffalo's milk.

TOMATOES can be red, orange, yellow, green, purple, and even striped.

MAKE YOUR OWN PIZZA

Created in Naples, Italy, the Margherita pizza represents the colors in the Italian flag: red tomatoes, green basil, and white cheese. **Get a parent's help to make your own.**

1 Bake premade pizza dough at 450°F (232°C) for about 5 minutes. Brush the crust lightly with olive oil.

2 Top dough with 4 or 5 thin tomato slices, and a pinch each of dried oregano, salt, and pepper. Sprinkle 1 cup (240 mL) of shredded mozzarella on top.

3 Bake until golden for 10 to 12 minutes. Sprinkle ½ cup (120 mL) of chopped fresh basil over the top.

12 Ways to Say Happy Birthday

1 **ARABIC** Eid milaad sa'eed
2 **FRENCH (CANADA)** Bonne Fête
3 **GERMAN** Alles Gute zum Geburtstag
4 **GREEK** Hronia polla
5 **HAWAIIAN** Hauʻoli La Hanau
6 **HEBREW** Yom Huledet Sameakh
7 **HINDI** Janmadin mubarak ho
8 **MANDARIN** Shengrì kuàilè
9 **RUSSIAN** S dniom rojdeniya
10 **SPANISH** ¡Feliz cumpleaños!
11 **SWAHILI** Nakutakia mema kwa siku yako ya kuzaliwa!
12 **TURKISH** Dogum günün kutlu olsun

LANGUAGES IN PERIL

TODAY, there are more than 7,000 languages spoken on Earth. But by 2100, more than half of those may disappear. In fact, experts say one language dies every two weeks, due to the increasing dominance of larger languages, such as English, Spanish, and Mandarin. So what can be done to keep dialects from disappearing? Efforts like National Geographic's Enduring Voices Project are now tracking down and documenting the world's most threatened indigenous languages, such as Tofa, spoken by only 30 people in Siberia, and Magati Ke, from Aboriginal Australia. The hope is to preserve these languages— and the cultures they belong to.

10 LEADING LANGUAGES

Approximate population of first-language speakers (in millions)

Rank	Language	Speakers
1.	Chinese*	1,213
2.	Spanish	329
3.	English	328
4.	Arabic	221
5.	Hindi	182
6.	Bengali	181
7.	Portuguese	178
8.	Russian	144
9.	Japanese	122
10.	German	90

Some languages have only a few hundred speakers, while Chinese has some one billion two hundred thirteen million native speakers worldwide. That's more than triple the next largest group of language speakers. Colonial expansion, trade, and migration account for the spread of the other most widely spoken languages. With growing use of the Internet, English is becoming the language of the technology age.

*Includes all forms of the language.

Bet you didn't know

6 **page-turning facts about books**

1 *Percy Jackson and the Olympians* **began as a bedtime** story for author **Rick Riordan's son.**

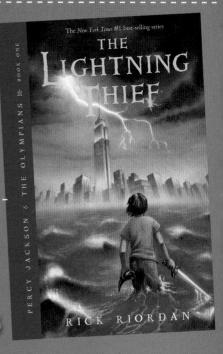

The New York Times #1 best-selling series

THE **LIGHTNING THIEF**

PERCY JACKSON & THE OLYMPIANS ☆ BOOK ONE

RICK RIORDAN

2 In L. Frank Baum's *The Wonderful Wizard of Oz* Dorothy's **shoes** are described as **silver.**

3 **Each book** in R.L. Stine's *Goosebumps* series took about **8 days** to **write.**

4 *Treasure Island* was **inspired by a map** that author **Robert Louis Stevenson** drew with his **12-year-old** stepson.

5 In an early version, **Roald Dahl's** *James and the Giant Peach* featured a giant **cherry.**

6 **J.K. Rowling** considered calling the **final** *Harry Potter* book *Harry Potter and the Elder Wand.*

MONEY Around the World!

THE GREEK GODDESS ATHENA AND HER **SACRED OWL** APPEARED ON COINS MINTED OVER 2,000 YEARS AGO.

A CAMBODIAN LEADER **ONCE ABOLISHED THE USE OF MONEY.**

THE SOUTHERN CROSS CONSTELLATION APPEARS ON **BRAZILIAN COINS.**

BOTSWANA'S CURRENCY IS NAMED *PULA*, OR **RAIN**, WHICH IS VALUABLE IN THIS DESERT NATION.

THIS WILL BUY YOU A LOT OF DOG TREATS.

BELGIUM ISSUED A COIN FEATURING **THE CARTOON HERO TINTIN** AND HIS DOG, **SNOWY.**

FIBERS FROM THE ABACA PLANT, A CLOSE RELATIVE OF THE BANANA PLANT, ARE USED IN **JAPANESE BANKNOTES.**

IN THE NETHERLANDS IN 1636, **TULIPS** WERE SO VALUABLE THAT SOME COST AS MUCH AS **A HOUSE.**

CANADIAN BANKNOTES COME WITH **RAISED DOT PATTERNS** FOR VISUALLY IMPAIRED PEOPLE.

IN INDIA, THE SLANG TERM FOR THE AMOUNT OF **100,000** RUPEES IS *PETI*, OR SUITCASE. YOU MIGHT NEED ONE TO CARRY THAT MUCH MONEY!

DIAMOND JUBILEE
1952 - 2012

The **PERTH MINT** in Australia recently minted a 2.2-pound (1-kg) solid-gold coin worth **$62,950.**

Peru's currency is named the NUEVO SOL, which is Spanish for "NEW SUN."

A MINT ERROR ADDED AN EXTRA HUMP to the bison on some of the **2005 KANSAS STATE, USA, QUARTERS.**

IT'S GONNA BE HARD FITTING ME INTO A WALLET.

A Korean artist is known for his "moneygami"— origami made out of banknotes.

USING A METAL DETECTOR, TWO ENGLISH MEN UNCOVERED 206 ROMAN COINS DATING BACK **2,200 YEARS.**

A 1922 German banknote is called the **"VAMPIRE NOTE"** because some claim that a vampire is biting the neck of the worker on the bill.

Reichsbanknote
Zehntausend Mark

VAMPIRE BITE?

THE U.S. MINT employs full-time sculptors to create models FOR COINS.

The U.S. Bureau of Engraving and Printing uses **8.5 TONS** (7.7 MT) **OF INK** each day to print money.

KING TUT appears on the Egyptian one-pound coin.

MONEY TIP!

ANYTIME YOU BUY SOMETHING ON SALE, PUT **WHAT YOU SAVED IN YOUR PIGGY BANK.**

MYTHOLOGY

GREEK

EGYPTIAN

The ancient Greeks believed that many gods and goddesses ruled the universe. According to this mythology, the Olympians lived high atop Greece's Mount Olympus. Each of these 12 principal gods and goddesses had a unique personality that corresponded to particular aspects of life, such as love or death.

Egyptian mythology is based on a creation myth that tells of an egg that appeared on the ocean. When the egg hatched, out came Ra, the sun god. As a result, ancient Egyptians became worshippers of the sun and of the nine original deities, most of whom were the children and grandchildren of Ra.

THE OLYMPIANS

Aphrodite was the goddess of love and beauty.

Apollo, Zeus's son, was the god of the sun, music, and healing. Artemis was his twin.

Ares, Zeus's son, was the god of war.

Artemis, Zeus's daughter and Apollo's twin, was the goddess of the hunt and of childbirth.

Athena, born from the forehead of Zeus, was the goddess of wisdom and crafts.

Demeter was the goddess of fertility and nature.

Hades, Zeus's brother, was the god of the under-world and the dead.

Hephaestus, the son of Hera, was the god of fire.

Hera, the wife and older sister of Zeus, was the goddess of women and marriage.

Hermes, Zeus's son, was the messenger of the gods.

Poseidon, the brother of Zeus, was the god of the sea and earthquakes.

Zeus was the most powerful of the gods and the top Olympian. He wielded a thunderbolt and was the god of the sky and thunder.

THE NINE DEITIES

Geb, son of Shu and Tefnut, was the god of the Earth.

Isis (Ast), daughter of Geb and Nut, was the goddess of fertility and motherhood.

Nephthys (Nebet-Hut), daughter of Geb and Nut, was protector of the dead.

Nut, daughter of Shu and Tefnut, was the goddess of the sky.

Osiris (Usir), son of Geb and Nut, was the god of the afterlife.

Ra (Re), the sun god, is generally viewed as the creator. He represents life and health.

Seth (Set), son of Geb and Nut, was the god of the desert and chaos.

Shu, son of Ra, was the god of air.

Tefnut, daughter of Ra, was the goddess of rain.

All cultures around the world have unique legends and traditions that have been passed down over generations. Many myths refer to gods or supernatural heroes who are responsible for occurrences in the world. For example, Norse mythology tells of the red-bearded Thor, the god of thunder, who is responsible for creating lightning and thunderstorms. And many creation myths, especially from some of North America's native cultures, tell of an earth-diver represented as an animal that brings a piece of sand or mud up from the deep sea. From this tiny piece of earth, the entire world takes shape.

NORSE

ROMAN

Norse mythology originated in Scandinavia, in northern Europe. It was complete with gods and goddesses who lived in a heavenly place called Asgard that could be reached only by crossing a rainbow bridge.

While Norse mythology is lesser known, we use it every day. Most days of the week are named after Norse gods, including some of these major deities.

NORSE GODS

Balder was the god of light and beauty.

Freya was the goddess of love, beauty, and fertility.

Frigg, for whom Friday was named, was the queen of Asgard. She was the goddess of marriage, motherhood, and the home.

Heimdall was the watchman of the rainbow bridge and the guardian of the gods.

Hel, the daughter of Loki, was the goddess of death.

Loki, a shape-shifter, was a trickster who helped the gods—and caused them problems.

Skadi was the goddess of winter and of the hunt. She is often represented as "The Snow Queen."

Thor, for whom Thursday was named, was the god of thunder and lightning.

Tyr, for whom Tuesday was named, was the god of the sky and war.

Wodan, for whom Wednesday was named, was the god of war, wisdom, death, and magic.

Much of Roman mythology was adopted from Greek mythology, but the Romans also developed a lot of original myths as well. The gods of Roman mythology lived everywhere, and each had a role to play. There were thousands of Roman gods, but here are a few of the stars of Roman myths.

ANCIENT ROMAN GODS

Ceres was the goddess of the harvest and motherly love.

Diana, daughter of Jupiter, was the goddess of hunting and the moon.

Juno, Jupiter's wife, was the goddess of women and fertility.

Jupiter, the patron of Rome and master of the gods, was the god of the sky.

Mars, the son of Jupiter and Juno, was the god of war.

Mercury, the son of Jupiter, was the messenger of the gods and the god of travelers.

Minerva was the goddess of wisdom, learning, and the arts and crafts.

Neptune, the brother of Jupiter, was the god of the sea.

Venus was the goddess of love and beauty.

Vesta was the goddess of fire and the hearth. She was one of the most important of the Roman deities.

World Religions

A round the world, religion takes many forms. Some belief systems, such as Christianity, Islam, and Judaism, are monotheistic, meaning that followers believe in just one supreme being. Others, like Hinduism, Shintoism, and most native belief systems, are polytheistic, meaning that many of their followers believe in multiple gods.

All of the major religions have their origins in Asia, but they have spread around the world. Christianity, with the largest number of followers, has three divisions—Roman Catholic, Eastern Orthodox, and Protestant. Islam, with about one-fifth of all believers, has two main divisions—Sunni and Shiite. Hinduism and Buddhism account for almost another one-fifth of believers. Judaism, dating back some 4,000 years, has more than 13 million followers, less than one percent of all believers.

CHRISTIANITY

Based on the teachings of Jesus Christ, a Jew born some 2,000 years ago in the area of modern-day Israel, Christianity has spread worldwide and actively seeks converts. Followers in Switzerland (above) participate in an Easter season procession with lanterns and crosses.

BUDDHISM

Founded about 2,400 years ago in northern India by the Hindu prince Gautama Buddha, Buddhism spread throughout East and Southeast Asia. Buddhist temples have statues, such as the Mihintale Buddha (above) in Sri Lanka.

HINDUISM

Dating back more than 4,000 years, Hinduism is practiced mainly in India. Hindus follow sacred texts known as the Vedas and believe in reincarnation. During the festival of Navratri, which honors the goddess Durga, the Garba dance is performed (above).

CLOSE-UP

Now that's a BIG crowd!

It has been 1,200 years since the bishop of Rome became known as the pope. Today, the pope is still the head of the Roman Catholic Church. Every Easter Sunday about 100,000 people gather in St. Peter's Square in Vatican City to receive his blessing.

ISLAM

Muslims believe that the Koran, Islam's sacred book, records the words of Allah (God) as revealed to the Prophet Muhammad beginning around A.D. 610. Believers (above) circle the Kaaba in the Haram Mosque in Mecca, Saudi Arabia, the spiritual center of the faith.

JUDAISM

The traditions, laws, and beliefs of Judaism date back to Abraham (the Patriarch) and the Torah (the first five books of the Old Testament). Followers pray before the Western Wall (above), which stands below Islam's Dome of the Rock in Jerusalem.

197

STUMP YOUR PARENTS

CULTURE CONNECTION QUIZ

Give your 'rents a crash course in culture by testing their knowledge of happenings around the world. ANSWERS BELOW

1 During the holiday of Sukkot, where do people eat and sleep?
a. their cars
b. restaurants
c. outdoor huts
d. their bedroom

2 **True or false?** Hinduism dates back more than 100,000 years.

ZEUS

3 Aside from being Zeus's son, Ares is also the Greek god of _____?

4 How many languages are spoken on Earth?
a. too many to count
b. 20
c. 50,000
d. more than 7,000

5 According to the Chinese Horoscope, 2015 is the year of the _____?

Not **STUMPED** yet?
Check out the *National Geographic Kids Quiz Whiz* collection for more crazy **CULTURE** questions!

Explore a New Culture

INDIAN STAMP

5-RUPEE COIN

INDIAN FLAG

You're a student, but you're also a citizen of the world. Writing a report on a foreign nation or your own country is a great way to better understand and appreciate how people in other parts of the world live. Pick the country of your ancestors, one that's been in the news, or one that you'd like to visit someday.

Passport to Success
A country report follows the format of an expository essay because you're "exposing" information about the country you choose.

Simple Steps

1. RESEARCH Gathering information is the most important step in writing a good country report. Look to Internet sources, encyclopedias, books, magazine and newspaper articles, and other sources to find important and interesting details about your subject.

2. ORGANIZE YOUR NOTES Put the information you gathered into a rough outline. For example, sort everything you found about the country's system of government, climate, etc.

3. WRITE IT UP Follow the basic structure of good writing: introduction, body, and conclusion. Remember that each paragraph should have a topic sentence that is then supported by facts and details. Incorporate the information from your notes, but make sure it's in your own words. And make your writing flow with good transitions and descriptive language.

4. ADD VISUALS Include maps, diagrams, photos, and other visual aids.

5. PROOFREAD AND REVISE Correct any mistakes, and polish your language. Do your best!

6. CITE YOUR SOURCES Be sure to keep a record of your sources.

Wonders of
Nature

Arenal Volcano erupts in Costa Rica's
Arenal Volcano National Park.

Weather and Climate

Weather is the condition of the atmosphere—temperature, precipitation, humidity, and wind—at a given place at a given time. Climate, however, is the average weather for a particular place over a long period of time. Different places on Earth have different climates, but climate is not a random occurrence. It is a pattern that is controlled by factors such as latitude, elevation, prevailing winds, the temperature of ocean currents, and location on land relative to water. Climate is generally constant, but evidence indicates that human activity is causing a change in the patterns of climate.

WEATHER EXTREMES

MOST SNOW RECORDED IN ONE SEASON: 1,140 inches (29 m) in Mount Baker, Washington, U.S.A.

FASTEST TEMPERATURE RISE: 49°F (27.2°C) **in 15 minutes, in Rapid City, South Dakota, U.S.A.**

MOST DAYS IN A ROW ABOVE 100°F (37.8°C): 160 days in Marble Bar, Western Australia

GLOBAL CLIMATE ZONES

Climatologists, people who study climate, have created different systems for classifying climates. One often-used system is called the Köppen system, which classifies climate zones according to precipitation, temperature, and vegetation. It has five major categories—Tropical, Dry, Temperate, Cold, and Polar—with a sixth category for locations where high elevations override other factors.

ARCTIC OCEAN

ARCTIC CIRCLE

ATLANTIC OCEAN

TROPIC OF CANCER

PACIFIC OCEAN

EQUATOR

PACIFIC OCEAN

INDIAN OCEAN

TROPIC OF CAPRICORN

ANTARCTIC CIRCLE

Climate

Tropical   Dry   Temperate   Cold   Polar

WEATHER COMPARISONS

Weather events can be so big and widespread that it's sometimes hard to comprehend them. For example, a single hurricane can cover hundreds of miles; its eye alone can be up to 200 miles (320 km) wide. That's about as far as Paris, France, is from London, England, U.K. But weather is also a part of daily life. Let's think about weather in terms of some everyday objects and events.

Is It Hot Enough to Fry an Egg on a Sidewalk?

It's possible for sidewalks to get hot enough (158°F/70°C), but once an egg hits the surface, the sidewalk cools. The sun alone can't cook the egg thoroughly.

How Fast Is a Hurricane?

A powerful hurricane can reach wind speeds of more than 155 miles an hour (249 kph). That's about as fast as some Indy cars speed around the track.

How Much Rain Is in a Snowfall?

Snowflakes come in many different shapes and sizes, so each snowfall contains a different amount of moisture. Rule of thumb: 10 inches (25 cm) of snow is equal to an inch (2.5 cm) of rain.

1 The largest hurricanes can measure ten miles (16 km) from top to bottom.

2 RAINDROPS are shaped more like hamburger buns than like teardrops!

3 A RAINDROP'S top speed is 18 mph (29 kph).

4 TORNADOES SPIN COUNTERCLOCKWISE IN THE NORTHERN HEMISPHERE AND CLOCKWISE IN THE SOUTHERN HEMISPHERE.

15 COOL THINGS ABOUT

5 The world's largest snowball fight had 5,387 participants.

6 THE HIGHEST WEATHER STATION ON EARTH IS LOCATED AT 26,000 FEET (7,925 M) ON MOUNT EVEREST.

7 In a double rainbow, the inner rainbow has the red on top. The outer one has the red on the bottom!

8 The lifetime of a typical fluffy cotton-ball-looking cumulus cloud is 5 to 40 minutes.

9 A LIGHTNING FLASH IS NO MORE THAN ONE INCH (2.5 CM) WIDE.

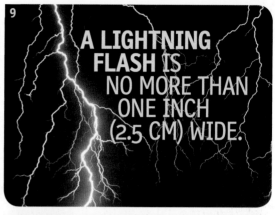

10 SOME PEOPLE THINK IT WILL BE A SEVERE WINTER IF SQUIRRELS HAVE BUSHY TAILS IN FALL, BUT SCIENTISTS HAVE NOT FOUND EVIDENCE TO SUPPORT THIS THEORY.

11 PINECONES can predict the weather! In dry weather, the scales open, and when rain is on the way, they close.

WEATHER

12 Satellites up to 1,000 miles (1,609 km) above Earth keep track of the weather below.

13 The world's **tallest snowman** was a girl! She measured 122 feet, 1 inch (37.21 m).

14 All snowflakes have six sides.

15 THERE IS FOG ON MARS.

Natural Disasters

Every world region has its share of natural disasters—the mix just varies from place to place. The Ring of Fire—grinding tectonic plate boundaries that follow the coasts of the Pacific Ocean—shakes with volcanic eruptions and earthquakes. Lives and livelihoods here and along other oceans can be swept away by tsunamis. North America's heartland endures blizzards in winter and tornadoes that can strike in spring, summer, or fall. Tropical cyclones batter many coastal areas in Asia and Australia with ripping winds, torrents of rain, and huge storm surges along their deadly paths.

HURRICANE!

HURRICANES IN 2015

HELLO, MY NAME IS . . .

Hurricane names come from six official international lists. The names alternate between male and female. When a storm becomes a hurricane, a name from the list is used, in alphabetical order. Each list is reused every six years. A name "retires" if that hurricane caused a lot of damage or many deaths.

Ana
Bill
Claudette
Danny
Erika
Fred
Grace
Henri
Ida
Joaquin
Kate
Larry
Mindy
Nicholas
Odette
Peter
Rose
Sam
Teresa
Victor
Wanda

A monster storm with 150-mile-an-hour (241-kph) winds churns west across the Atlantic Ocean. Scientists at the National Hurricane Center in Miami have tracked it for days using satellite images. Now they're worried it may threaten the United States.

It's time for the "hurricane hunters" to go to work! All ships and airplanes have been warned away from this monster. But two four-engine airplanes head toward the storm. Their mission? To collect data inside the hurricane that will tell meteorologists where the storm is going, when it will get there, and how violent it will be.

The word "hurricane" comes from Huracan, the god of big winds and evil spirits once worshipped by the Maya people of Central America. These superstrong storms—which usually last about nine days—are the most destructive during their first 12 hours onshore, when high winds can topple homes and cause major flooding.

To help people prepare for a hurricane that's hustling to shore, the U.S. National Oceanic and Atmospheric Administration (NOAA) sends out the hurricane hunters, who fly straight into the storm to determine characteristics such as temperature, air pressure, wind speed, and wind direction. It's a dangerous job, but by mission's end, the hunters' work will help to keep everyone in the hurricane's path safe.

Scale of Hurricane Intensity

CATEGORY	ONE	TWO	THREE	FOUR	FIVE
DAMAGE	Minimal	Moderate	Extensive	Extreme	Catastrophic
WINDS	74–95 mph (119–153 kph)	96–110 mph (154–177 kph)	111–129 mph (178–208 kph)	130–156 mph (209–251 kph)	157 mph or higher (252+ kph)
	(DAMAGE refers to wind and water damage combined.)				

Wildfire!

During the summer of 2013, a fire erupted in Stanislaus National Forest in northern California, U.S.A., eventually spreading into nearby Yosemite National Park. Within days, over 250,000 acres (101,100 ha) had been charred, making it one of the worst wildfires in California's history. In some spots, the fire burned so intensely that it wiped out trees and other vegetation, leaving an eerie, barren moonscape.

How do wildfires start? Often, they're sparked by a careless act by a human, such as leaving a campfire unattended or irresponsibly disposing of a cigarette. Some are deliberately set, or are ignited by lightning strikes or fallen power lines. However they begin, wildfires can quickly rage out of control.

Highly trained forest firefighters are equipped and experienced to fight huge forest fires. Some even parachute into a remote area to battle the blaze. In addition to the work of skilled firefighters, a break in the weather can also help in beating a wildfire. Rain assisted in containing the Yosemite fire.

Flood!

The Danube River, which usually peacefully flows through cities and towns in Austria, Hungary, Germany, and other parts of central Europe, swelled to epic levels the spring of 2013. In Budapest, the river hit a record high of 29 feet (8.9 m) before finally receding a few days later.

Although flash floods can occur quickly and be quite dangerous, most floods develop slowly, giving residents time to prepare. In Europe, crews of volunteers placed millions of sandbags along the Danube's banks in an attempt to prevent the water from spilling into the streets, and thousands of people in the affected areas were evacuated. Still, the flood caused serious problems. The Danube's flooding stalled road and subway traffic, submerged small towns and farmland, and racked up several billion dollars in damages.

How to Survive Lightning

Caught off guard by a sudden thunderstorm? Avoid becoming a human glow stick with these easy tips.

SEEK SHELTER
If you see lightning and can't count to 30 before you hear thunder, get into an enclosed structure or vehicle as soon as you can. Remain there for 30 minutes after the last thunderclap.

DON'T BE A TREE HUGGER
Lightning often strikes the tallest thing around, so don't look for shelter under tall trees. That goes double for telephone or electrical poles.

GO SWIMMING LATER
Water is conductive, meaning it can transfer the lightning's electricity to you. Stay away from bodies of water, even puddles. If you're in the pool, get out!

LIGHTEN THE LOAD
Metal is also conductive. If you're wearing anything with metal in it—a backpack, a belt, jewelry—now's the time to get rid of it.

SHORTEN IT UP
If you're out in the open, make yourself as small as possible. Crouch with your head between your knees. Not being the tallest object around may protect you from a direct strike.

BECOME A LONER
If you're with a bunch of people, space yourselves more than 15 feet (4.6 m) apart so that lightning won't jump from person to person.

Tsunami Heroes

RESCUED OR REUNITED, ANIMALS AND PEOPLE PULL TOGETHER AFTER A HUGE NATURAL DISASTER.

When a 9.0-magnitude earthquake struck off the coast of Honshu, Japan, in 2011, it knocked people off their feet and made tall buildings sway. Then things got even worse. Miles offshore, the massive movement created a series of huge waves called a tsunami, which rushed toward the island nation. Walls of water as tall as 30 feet (9 m) crashed into the coast and wiped out everything in the way—and separated humans from their pets. Many animal lovers went out of their way to help animals in need after the tsunami. Here are two stories of survival and hope.

DOG AT SEA

SAFE ON LAND

PUP RESCUED FROM ROOF

Three weeks after the disaster, a helicopter crew spots a dog pacing across the roof of a wrecked house floating more than a mile (1.6 km) offshore. A rescue team reaches the canine by canoe, carrying her aboard a larger boat on a stretcher. A woman from a nearby town sees the rescue on the local news and instantly recognizes her missing pet, a two-year-old mixed breed named Ban. Dog and owner are happily reunited—safe and on dry land.

PORPOISE SURVIVES STRANDING

A tiny porpoise is spotted in a flooded rice field, more than a mile (1.6 km) away from the shore. Pet shop owner Ryo Taira wades into the water, grabs the three-foot (1-m)-long animal and cradles it in his arms. He then wraps the exhausted porpoise in wet towels and drives it to a nearby beach. As soon as it's placed into the sea, the porpoise springs back to life and energetically swims away.

RESCUED

THE WATER CYCLE

RISING UP

Some of the water and spray from the waterfall in this picture will **evaporate** into the air. In other bodies of water, heat from the sun causes some water to evaporate, or turn into water vapor, or gas. This water vapor rises from the stream, river, or lake and goes into the air.

HANGING OUT

Water covers more than 70 percent of Earth's surface in the form of oceans, lakes, and rivers. When water ends up on land from rain, snow, or hail, it may soak into the earth, becoming part of the ground-water and leaving the water cycle for a while.

Scientists think that the water we drink, bathe in, and use to grow crops today has been here on Earth since long before the time of the dinosaurs. It has just been moving around and around in the atmosphere in a nearly endless cycle. But there's not much water in the air. In fact, if all of the atmosphere's water rained down at once, it would cover the globe only to a depth of one inch (2.5 cm). It's a good thing, then, that we have the water cycle—Earth's original recycling project. Here's how it works:

CHILLING OUT

As water vapor cools in the air, it **condenses.** This means that it changes back into liquid form. You will notice the same kind of thing happening if you pour a cold glass of water on a hot day. Water forms on the outside of the glass. The water vapor in the warm air touches the cold glass and turns to liquid.

FALLING DOWN

After so much water has condensed that the air can't hold it anymore, it falls as **precipitation**—rain, hail, sleet, or snow—into Earth's oceans, lakes, and rivers.

RUNNING OFF

Melted snow and rain that run downhill eventually end up in large bodies of water. The transfer of land water to the ocean is called **runoff.**

LOCATED AT THE BORDER OF CHINA AND VIETNAM, THE DETIAN WATERFALL IS ONE OF THE LARGEST WATERFALLS IN ASIA. ITS NAME MEANS "VIRTUOUS HEAVEN."

THE OC

PACIFIC OCEAN

STATS

Surface area
65,436,200 sq mi (169,479,000 sq km)

Portion of Earth's water area
47 percent

Greatest depth
Challenger Deep
(in the Mariana Trench)
-36,070 ft (-10,994 m)

Surface temperatures
Summer high: 90°F (32°C)
Winter low: 28°F (-2°C)

Tides
Highest: 30 ft (9 m) near Korean peninsula
Lowest: 1 ft (0.3 m) near Midway Islands

Cool creatures: giant Pacific octopus,
bottlenose whale, clownfish, great
white shark

ATLANTIC OCEAN

STATS

Surface area
35,338,500 sq mi (91,526,300 sq km)

Portion of Earth's water area
25 percent

Greatest depth
Puerto Rico Trench
-28,232 ft (-8,605 m)

Surface temperatures
Summer high: 90°F (32°C)
Winter low: 28°F (-2°C)

Tides
Highest: 52 ft (16 m)
Bay of Fundy, Canada
Lowest: 1.5 ft (0.5 m)
Gulf of Mexico and Mediterranean Sea

Cool creatures: blue whale, Atlantic spotted
dolphin, sea turtle

GREAT WHITE SHARK

GREEN SEA TURTLE

EANS

INDIAN OCEAN

STATS

Surface area
28,839,800 sq mi (74,694,800 sq km)

Portion of Earth's water area
21 percent

Greatest depth
Java Trench
-23,376 ft (-7,125 m)

Surface temperatures
Summer high: 93°F (34°C)
Winter low: 28°F (-2°C)

Tides
Highest: 36 ft (11 m)
Lowest: 2 ft (0.6 m)
Both along Australia's west coast

Cool creatures: humpback whale, Portuguese man-of-war, dugong (sea cow)

DUGONG

ARCTIC OCEAN

STATS

Surface area
5,390,000 sq mi (13,960,100 sq km)

Portion of Earth's water area
4 percent

Greatest depth
Molloy Deep
-18,599 ft (-5,669 m)

Surface temperatures
Summer high: 41°F (5°C)
Winter low: 28°F (-2°C)

Tides
Less than 1 ft (0.3 m) variation throughout the ocean

Cool creatures: beluga whale, orca, harp seal, narwhal

ORCA

To see the major oceans and bays in relation to landmasses, look at the map on pages 260 and 261.

Coral Reefs

Just below the surface of the Caribbean Sea's crystal-clear water, miles (km) of vivid corals grow in fantastic shapes that shelter tropical fish of every color. Coral reefs account for a quarter of all life in the ocean and are often called the rain forests of the sea. Like big apartment complexes for sea creatures, coral reefs provide a tough limestone skeleton for fish, clams, and other organisms to live in— and plenty of food for them to eat, too.

And how does the coral get its color? It's all about the algae that cling to its limestone polyps. Algae and coral live together in a mutually helpful relationship. The coral provides a home to the algae and helps the algae convert sunlight to food that the corals consume. But as beautiful as coral reefs are, they are also highly sensitive. A jump of even 2°F (1.1°C) in water temperature makes the reef rid itself of the algae, leaving the coral with a sickly, bleached look. Pollution is another threat; it can poison the sensitive corals. Humans pose a threat, too: One clumsy kick from a swimmer can destroy decades of coral growth.

QUEEN ANGELFISH

MANTA RAY

Try This!

FOOD FOR YOUR GARDEN!

Grow a healthy garden and reduce waste by using leftovers to make your own compost, which is organic material that adds nutrients to the soil.

GROW VEGGIES AND FLOWERS

RECYCLE THE NATURAL WAY

By composting you reduce the need for chemical fertilizers in your yard, and you send less waste to landfills. Yard trimmings and food scraps make up about 25 percent of the trash from cities and towns in the United States. So put that banana peel to good use. Turn it—and a lot of other things in your trash can—into environmentally helpful compost. By making natural fertilizer you will help the environment *and* have a great excuse to play with your food!

HOW TO MAKE COMPOST

1. Choose a dry, shady spot to create your compost pile.

2. Use a bin with a tight-fitting lid and plenty of airholes to hold your compost ingredients. In the bin, start with a 6-inch (15-cm) layer of dry "brown" material (see examples in the list below right). Break down large pieces before you place them in the bin.

3. Add a 3-inch (8-cm) layer of "green" materials (see list). Add a little bit of soil to this layer.

4. Mix the brown and green layers.

5. Finish with another 3-inch (8-cm) layer of brown materials.

6. Add water until the contents are moist. If you accidentally add too much water, just add more brown materials to the bin. Mix your compost pile every week or two.

7. After one to four months, the compost will be almost ready. When it is dark brown and moist, and you can't identify the original ingredients, wait two more weeks. Then add your finished compost to your garden.

COMPOST THESE

"BROWN" MATERIALS
Dead leaves
Eggshells
Twigs
Shredded newspaper
Nutshells

"GREEN" MATERIALS
Grass clippings
Fruit and vegetable scraps
Coffee grounds
Tea bags

217

Biomes

A BIOME, OFTEN CALLED A MAJOR LIFE ZONE, is one of the natural world's major communities where plants and animals adapt to their specific surroundings. Biomes are classified depending on the predominant vegetation, climate, and geography of a region. They can be divided into six major types: forest, fresh water, marine, desert, grassland, and tundra. Each biome consists of many ecosystems.

Biomes are extremely important. Balanced ecological relationships among biomes help to maintain the environment and life on Earth as we know it. For example, an increase in one species of plant, such as an invasive one, can cause a ripple effect throughout the whole biome.

Because biomes can be fragile in this way, it is important to protect them from negative human activity, such as deforestation and pollution. We must work to conserve these biomes and the unique organisms that live within them.

FOREST

The forest biomes have been evolving for about 420 million years. Today, forests occupy about one-third of Earth's land area. There are three major types of forests: tropical, temperate, and boreal (taiga). Forests are home to a diversity of plants, some of which may hold medicinal qualities for humans, as well as thousands of animal species, some still undiscovered. Forests can also absorb carbon dioxide, a greenhouse gas, and give off oxygen.

FRESH WATER

Most water on Earth is salty, but freshwater ecosystems—including lakes, ponds, wetlands, rivers, and streams—usually contain water with less than one percent salt concentration. The countless animal and plant species that live in a freshwater biome vary from continent to continent, but include algae, frogs, turtles, fish, and the larvae of many insects. Throughout the world, people use food, medicine, and other resources from this biome.

MARINE

The marine biome covers almost three-fourths of Earth's surface, making it the largest habitat on our planet. The four oceans make up the majority of the saltwater marine biome. Coral reefs are considered to be the most biodiverse of any of the biome habitats. The marine biome is home to more than one million plant and animal species. Some of the largest animals on Earth, such as the blue whale, live in the marine biome.

DESERT

Covering about one-fifth of Earth's surface, deserts are places where precipitation is less than 10 inches (25 cm) per year. Although most deserts are hot, there are other kinds as well. The four major kinds of deserts in the world are hot, semiarid, coastal, and cold. Far from being barren wastelands, deserts are biologically rich habitats with a vast array of animals and plants that have adapted to the harsh conditions there.

GRASSLAND

Biomes called grasslands are characterized by having grasses instead of large shrubs or trees. Grasslands generally have precipitation for only about half to three-fourths of the year. If it were more, they would become forests. Widespread around the world, grasslands can be divided into two types: tropical (savannas) and temperate. Grasslands are home to some of the largest land animals on Earth, such as elephants, hippopotamuses, rhinoceroses, and lions.

TUNDRA

The coldest of all biomes, a tundra is characterized by an extremely cold climate, simple vegetation, little precipitation, poor nutrients, and a short growing season. There are two types of tundra: arctic and alpine. A very fragile environment, a tundra is home to few kinds of vegetation. Surprisingly, though, there are quite a few animal species that can survive the tundra's extremes, such as wolves, caribou, and even mosquitoes.

STUMP YOUR PARENTS

WONDERS OF NATURE QUIZ

Are your folks one with nature? Test them to see how much they know about the great outdoors. ANSWERS BELOW

① **True or false?** You can fry an egg on a sidewalk.

② **Which is not a hurricane name in 2015?**
a. Wanda
b. George
c. Rose
d. Joaquin

③ **What's the best way to protect yourself from a lightning strike?**
a. get out of the pool
b. remove your belt
c. seek shelter
d. all of the above

④ **In which ocean would you find a Portuguese man-of-war?**
a. Atlantic Ocean
b. Arctic Ocean
c. Indian Ocean
d. Pacific Ocean

⑤ **How much of the Earth's surface is covered by deserts?**
a. One-fifth
b. Half
c. One-tenth
d. Two-thirds

Not **STUMPED** yet?
Check out the *National Geographic Kids Quiz Whiz* collection for more crazy **NATURE** questions!

ANSWERS:
1. False. While it can get hot enough, the sidewalk would cool too quickly to actually fry the egg; 2. b; 3. d; 4. c; 5. a

SPEAK NATURALLY

Oral Reports Made Easy

Does the thought of public speaking start your stomach churning like a tornado? Would you rather get caught in an avalanche than give a speech?

Giving an oral report does not have to be a natural disaster. The basic format is very similar to a written essay. There are two main elements that make up a good oral report—the writing and the presentation. As you write your oral report, remember that your audience will be hearing the information as opposed to reading it. Follow the guidelines below, and there will be clear skies ahead.

Writing Your Material

Follow the steps in the "How to Write a Perfect Essay" section on p. 116, but prepare your report to be spoken rather than written. Try to keep your sentences short and simple. Long, complex sentences are harder to follow. Limit yourself to just a few key points. You don't want to overwhelm your audience with too much information. To be most effective, hit your key points in the introduction, elaborate on them in the body, and then repeat them once again in your conclusion.

An oral report has three basic parts:

- **Introduction**—This is your chance to engage your audience and really capture their interest in the subject you are presenting. Use a funny personal experience or a dramatic story, or start with an intriguing question.

- **Body**—This is the longest part of your report. Here you elaborate on the facts and ideas you want to convey. Give information that supports your main idea, and expand on it with specific examples or details. In other words, structure your oral report in the same way you would a written essay so that your thoughts are presented in a clear and organized manner.

- **Conclusion**—This is the time to summarize the information and emphasize your most important points to the audience one last time.

Preparing Your Delivery

1 Practice makes perfect.
Practice! Practice! Practice! Confidence, enthusiasm, and energy are key to delivering an effective oral report, and they can best be achieved through rehearsal. Ask family and friends to be your practice audience and give you feedback when you're done. Were they able to follow your ideas? Did you seem knowledgeable and confident? Did you speak too slowly or too fast, too softly or too loudly? The more times you practice giving your report, the more you'll master the material. Then you won't have to rely so heavily on your notes or papers, and you will be able to give your report in a relaxed and confident manner.

2 Present with everything you've got.
Be as creative as you can. Incorporate videos, sound clips, slide presentations, charts, diagrams, and photos. Visual aids help stimulate your audience's senses and keep them intrigued and engaged. They can also help to reinforce your key points. And remember that when you're giving an oral report, you're a performer. Take charge of the spotlight and be as animated and entertaining as you can. Have fun with it.

3 Keep your nerves under control.
Everyone gets a little nervous when speaking in front of a group. That's normal. But the more preparation you've done—meaning plenty of researching, organizing, and rehearsing—the more confident you'll be. Preparation is the key. And if you make a mistake or stumble over your words, just regroup and keep going. Nobody's perfect, and nobody expects you to be.

History Happens

Completed in 1894, Tower Bridge spans
the Thames River in London, England, U.K.

PACKING FOR THE AFTERLIFE

BOATS

Egyptians believed the sun god traveled to the afterlife each night by boat. Entombed model boats—and even full-size versions—helped the dead make that same voyage.

IMAGINE HOW YOU'D

FEEL IF YOU BOARDED A PLANE FOR A LONG TRIP

and realized you forgot to pack. To the ancient Egyptians, who viewed death as the start of a great journey, passing into the afterlife unprepared was equally unsettling. That's why family and friends filled the tombs of their dearly departed with everything they would need in the hereafter.

Graves of poor Egyptians were packed with just the essentials: food, cosmetics, and clothes. The ornate burial chambers of pharaohs overflowed with treasures and art. Browse these grave goodies recovered from ancient Egyptian tombs.

FOOD

Family members left food offerings outside a tomb to nourish their loved one's spirit. Paintings of feasts on tomb walls or sculptures of food trays were thought to provide magical bottomless buffets.

GAMES

Board games like Senet provided eternal entertainment.

CLOTHES

Most tombs were stocked with chests of clothes, fine linens, sandals, and other attire. It would be unseemly to spend eternity naked, after all.

COFFINS

Coffins were carved in the likeness of the deceased so that spirits could recognize their own bodies.

SERVANTS

Summoned to life by a spell, carved figures known as shabtis served as laborers in the afterlife. One pharaoh's tomb contained nearly a thousand of these ancient action figures.

JEWELRY

The adage "You can't take it with you" would have horrified wealthy Egyptians, who packed their tombs with their favorite jewelry.

225

Ancient World ADVENTURE

ANGKOR WAT

WHERE: Cambodia
BUILT: A.D. 1113 to A.D.1150

COOL FACT: Created to honor the Hindu god Vishnu, Angkor Wat remains the largest religious complex in the world. It's still protected by a 4-mile (6.4-km)-long moat!

BOROBUDUR

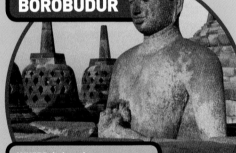

WHERE: Indonesia
BUILT: About A.D. 778 to A.D. 850

COOL FACT: The world's largest Buddhist monument, this temple is made from two million rocks and took about 75 years to build.

FORBIDDEN CITY

WHERE: China
BUILT: Between A.D. 1406 and A.D. 1420

COOL FACT: The 180-acre (73-ha) imperial compound in Beijing is rumored to have more than 9,999 rooms and was home to 24 Chinese emperors over a nearly 500-year span.

Ever wonder what it was like on Earth thousands of years ago? Check out these amazing ancient sites. Visiting them is like taking a time machine into the past!

PYRAMIDS AT GIZA

WHERE: Egypt
BUILT: About 2500 B.C.

COOL FACT: These massive pyramids—built as tombs for Egypt's pharaohs—are part of a complex that included a palace, temples, and boat pits. The largest pyramid is 481 feet (147 m) tall and is made from 2.3 million stone blocks.

TIMBUKTU

PALENQUE

WHERE: Mexico
BUILT: About A.D. 500

COOL FACT: This ancient Maya city-state's buildings, including temples and tombs, were built without the use of metal tools, pack animals, or even the wheel.

WHERE: Mali
BUILT: About A.D. 1100

COOL FACT: Once known as the fabled "City of Gold," Africa's Timbuktu was a center of learning and culture in the 15th and 16th centuries and is home to a still standing university.

The ancient Olmec gave the cocoa tree, used to make chocolate, its earliest known name: KAKAWA.

2

ACCORDING TO A CHINESE LEGEND, **TEA DRINKING** ORIGINATED WHEN DRIED TEA LEAVES FELL INTO A CUP OF WATER SERVED TO AN EMPEROR.

3

People have lived in **the world's oldest neighborhood**—Iraq's the Citadel—for at least 7,000 years.

15 COOL THINGS ABOUT

4

ANCIENT EGYPTIAN KIDS PLAYED HOCKEY WITH STICKS MADE FROM PALM BRANCHES.

5

Roads built by the ancient Romans are still intact and in use today, from Europe to the Middle East.

6

People in ancient India **stitched up wounds** with hair and plants such as flax and hemp.

7

An Inca burial site was found 20,702 feet (6,310 m) high in the Andes Mountains.

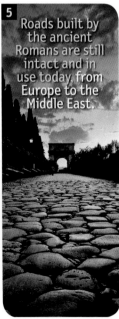

8 Ancient Celts regarded WILD PIGS AS SACRED.

9 IN ANCIENT GREECE, COINS WERE DECORATED WITH IMAGES OF BEES.

10 IN CHINA, the earliest writing— about 1200 B.C.— was inscribed on the BONES OF ANIMALS.

11 Bright red skeletal remains of the ancient Maya reveal they coated their dead in the red mineral CINNABAR.

ANCIENT CULTURES

12 Horse riding began about 6,000 years ago in Central Asia.

13 CITIZENS OF THE ANCIENT GREEK CITY-STATE OF SPARTA—SPARTANS— VOTED BY POUNDING ON THEIR SHIELDS.

14 Australian Aborigines, the world's oldest living culture, have existed for at least 50,000 years.

15 The Romans believed cinnamon was sacred. Wreaths made from the plant's leaves often decorated Roman temples.

Knight Life

Protector of the Castle

It started with a childhood full of boring chores and ended at age 21 with a ceremonial smack to the head that knocked some men on their tails. The road to knighthood was long and rough, but the journey was often worth the trouble. Successful knights found fortune and glory.

In times of war and peace, knights led a dangerous life. These professional warriors were charged with protecting the lord's land from invaders, leading the castle's men-at-arms during sieges, and fighting on behalf of the church. Between battles, they competed in deadly games called tournaments to sharpen their skills.

In exchange for military service, knights were granted their own lands—along with peasants to farm it—and noble titles. The mightiest knights rose to rival lords in power and property. Sir Ulrich von Liechtenstein, one of the 13th century's most famous knights, owned three castles.

Not just anyone could become a knight. Armor, weapons, and warhorses cost more than a typical peasant might earn in a lifetime, so knights often hailed from noble families. They started their training early in life—at the age most kids today begin first grade.

Lord Lore

England's royal family still grants knighthood to actors, scientists, and other accomplished citizens.

How to Become a Knight

1. Serve as a Page

A boy destined for knighthood left home at age 7 to become a servant in a great lord's castle. The page learned courtly manners, received a basic education, and played rough with other pages.

2. Squire for a Knight

Once he turned 14, a page became a squire for a knight. He learned about armor by cleaning his master's suit and helping him dress for battle. He practiced fighting with swords, shields, and other weaponry. Most important of all, he learned to attack from the saddle of a huge warhorse—the type of mounted combat knights were famous for.

3. Get Dubbed

By age 21, a squire was ready for his dubbing ceremony. He knelt before his lord or lady and received a hard slap to help him remember his oath. (This brutal blow later evolved into a friendlier sword tap on the shoulders.) The newly dubbed knight was given the title "sir" and could seek service at a lord's castle.

Knightly Numbers

55 pounds (25 kg) of armor weighed down a knight on the battlefield.

45 years was the life expectancy of most knights.

45 days per year was the typical term of service a knight owed his lord.

Good knights acted chivalrously, which meant they protected the weak, treated women with respect, served the church, and were generous and humble.

MYSTERY of the BURIED TREASURE

TRUE STORY

AN ANCIENT STASH OF GOLD AND SILVER WORTH MILLIONS OF DOLLARS IS UNCOVERED IN A FARMER'S FIELD.

Beep! The man stops suddenly as his metal detector sounds off. Something is buried under the English field he's been exploring. Is it a worthless piece of junk—or something far more valuable?

The man's discovery turns out to be more than 3,500 pieces of gold and silver treasure buried by ancient warriors at least 1,300 years ago. Archaeologists uncovered sword handles, helmet pieces, and shield decorations. Some were studded with jewels or engraved with animals.

The treasure is worth about $5.5 million. But archaeologists are more excited about what it could tell us about these ancient warriors.

MYSTERIOUS PEOPLE

The treasure was buried by people called the Anglo-Saxons, who settled in England after arriving from Germany starting around A.D. 410. Archaeologists think it may have belonged to the Anglo-Saxon ruler, King Penda of Mercia.

The Anglo-Saxons lived in the Dark Ages, once believed to be a time when little was happening in art or culture. But the treasure helps confirm that the Anglo-Saxon period was a time of great change and amazing artistry.

SECRETS OF THE TREASURE

Anglo-Saxons were considered fierce warriors, and they cared about their weapons. But the quality of the metalwork shows they were also artists. Craftsmen created tiny, detailed engravings without magnifying lenses.

The treasure may also shed new light on where Anglo-Saxons lived. Because it was found in western England, rather than in the south or east, where archaeologists believed early Anglo-Saxons settled, this may mean the people had traveled farther than once thought.

Still, archaeologists may have more questions than answers. Why weren't there any items belonging to women? Was the treasure buried for safekeeping, or to mark a victory?

The answers to these mysteries may come with further study, but more than anything, this discovery has brought the people of the Anglo-Saxon era to life.

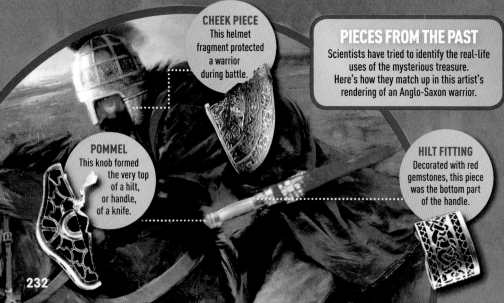

CHEEK PIECE
This helmet fragment protected a warrior during battle.

PIECES FROM THE PAST
Scientists have tried to identify the real-life uses of the mysterious treasure. Here's how they match up in this artist's rendering of an Anglo-Saxon warrior.

POMMEL
This knob formed the very top of a hilt, or handle, of a knife.

HILT FITTING
Decorated with red gemstones, this piece was the bottom part of the handle.

THE AMAZING HOUDINI!
Death-Defying Magic Tricks
REVEALED

Throughout history, many magicians have wowed audiences with their amazing illusions. But there has only been one Harry Houdini. Known for his death-defying magic tricks, Houdini, who died in 1926, was one of the most fearless illusionists of all time. Here is the scoop about two of his most legendary stunts.

VANISHING ELEPHANT

The Trick: Houdini promises to make Jenny, a 4,000-pound (1,814-kg) elephant, disappear.

What You See: Houdini coaxes Jenny into an enormous wooden box and closes its front curtain. A moment later, he reopens it and she's gone.

What You Don't See: The box has a secret back door. Houdini closes the curtain and Jenny is lured out the back exit by the smell of her favorite food.

SUSPENDED STRAITJACKET

The Trick: Hanging by his feet from a building while wearing a straitjacket, Houdini vows to free himself—without falling!

What You See: Houdini wriggles against the straps of his straitjacket, freeing one arm at a time. Pulling the jacket over his head, he drops to the ground below.

What You Don't See: Legend has it that Houdini took a deep breath to expand his chest and keep the straitjacket loose. Then he used his flexibility to help him wriggle free.

Secrets of the

SCIENTISTS USE CUTTING-EDGE TECHNOLOGY TO UNCOVER NEW EVIDENCE ABOUT HOW THE SHIP SANK.

Sunday, April 14, 1912: The R.M.S. *Titanic* steams across the North Atlantic Ocean. The 882-foot (269-m)-long passenger ship carries 2,208 people on its maiden voyage from Southampton, England, to New York City, in the United States of America.

Suddenly, a dark shape appears. An iceberg scrapes the ship, and within three hours, the *Titanic* sinks. Almost 1,500 people lose their lives.

Scientists have closely studied the *Titanic*'s wreck on the ocean floor since it was discovered in 1985. Recently, National Geographic Explorer-in-Residence James Cameron—the director of the movie *Titanic*—assembled a team of experts to examine the shipwreck anew. Using 3-D modeling and state-of-the-art technology, the experts reveal new clues about how the *Titanic* sank.

FLOODING

It might have been possible for the ship to sink more slowly, allowing more people to survive. Many of the ship's portholes were found open—most likely because passengers were airing out their rooms and never closed them. This caused the ship to take on water faster.

Something similar also may have happened in one of the grand lobbies, where a large door was found open. "The size of the door is twice the size of the original iceberg damage," Cameron says. "This would have sped up the sinking of the ship."

BREAKING

As the *Titanic* took on water, the front of the ship, called the bow, sank below the surface, causing the back, or stern, to lift into the air. The great stress broke the ship in half. "When the *Titanic* broke in half and the bow pulled away, the bottom likely remained attached to the back of the ship until it, too, was pulled apart," Cameron says.

EXPLORER JAMES CAMERON PILOTS AN UNDERWATER VEHICLE CALLED A SUBMERSIBLE.

SINKING

In its final resting place, the bow looks remarkably intact. But the stern looks like a bomb destroyed it. Why? The bow was filled with water when it sank, so the pressure was the same on the inside as the outside. The stern, however, sank with lots of air inside and imploded from the pressure.

FINAL IMPACT

The sinking ship created a massive trail of water that followed it downward at 20 to 25 miles an hour (32 to 40 kph). Experts think that this water trail pummeled the *Titanic* after it hit bottom. "Millions of gallons of water came pushing down on it," Cameron says. With all this new information, is our understanding of the *Titanic* tragedy complete? "I think we have a very good picture of what happened," Cameron says. "But there will always be mysteries."

Titanic

TITANIC
·19· ·12·
LONDON

SUPERSIZE SHIP
The *Titanic* was almost as long as three football fields. With its smokestacks, the ship was as tall as a 17-story building.

NATIONAL GEOGRAPHIC KiDS
SCANNER

SCAN THIS PAGE!
GET BONUS MOBILE CONTENT! Download the free NG Kids scanner app. Directions on inside front cover.

TITANIC

WHAT IF...
Scientists know a lot about how the *Titanic* sank, but other factors contributed as well.

SAILING SCHEDULE
The *Titanic* set sail more than three weeks behind schedule. If the ship had left on time, an iceberg probably wouldn't have been in its path.

FROM CALM TO CHAOS
The sea was unusually calm on April 14, 1912. Waves would have made the iceberg easier to spot.

MISSED MESSAGES
Two messages were telegraphed from other ships to warn the *Titanic* of icebergs, but they never reached the captain.

We asked oceanographer and National Geographic Explorer-in-Residence Robert Ballard, who led the team that discovered the *Titanic* in 1985, what it felt like to make the discovery of the century.

"**My first reaction** was one of excitement and celebration. But we were at the **very spot** on the **cold North Atlantic Ocean** where it all happened. So then we had **a quiet moment of remembrance.**"

235

WAR!

Since the beginning of time, different countries, territories, and cultures have feuded with each other over land, power, and politics. Major military conflicts include the following wars:

1095–1291 THE CRUSADES
Starting late in the 11th century, these wars over religion were fought in the Middle East for nearly 200 years.

1337–1453 HUNDRED YEARS' WAR
France and England battled over rights to land for more than a century before the French eventually drove the English out in 1453.

1754–1763 FRENCH AND INDIAN WAR (part of Europe's Seven Years' War)
A nine-year war between the British and French for control of North America.

1775–1783 AMERICAN REVOLUTION
Thirteen British colonies in America united to reject the rule of the British government and to form the United States of America.

1861–1865 AMERICAN CIVIL WAR
Occurred when the northern states (the Union) went to war with the southern states, which had seceded, or withdrawn, to form the Confederate States of America. Slavery was one of the key issues in the Civil War.

1910–1920 MEXICAN REVOLUTION
The people of Mexico revolted against the rule of dictator President Porfirio Díaz, leading to his eventual defeat and to a democratic government.

1914–1918 WORLD WAR I
The assassination of Austria's Archduke Ferdinand by a Serbian nationalist sparked this wide-spreading war. The U.S. entered after Germany sunk the British ship *Lusitania,* killing more than 120 Americans.

1918–1920 RUSSIAN CIVIL WAR
Following the 1917 Russian Revolution, this conflict pitted the Communist Red Army against the foreign-backed White Army. The Red Army won, leading to the establishment of the Union of Soviet Socialist Republics (U.S.S.R.) in 1922.

1936–1939 SPANISH CIVIL WAR
Aid from Italy and Germany helped the Nationalists gain victory over the Communist-supported Republicans. The war resulted in the loss of more than 300,000 lives and increased tension in Europe leading up to World War II.

1939–1945 WORLD WAR II
This massive conflict in Europe, Asia, and North Africa involved many countries that aligned with the two sides: the Allies and the Axis. After the bombing of Pearl Harbor in Hawaii in 1941, the U.S. entered the war on the side of the Allies. More than 50 million people died during the war.

1946–1949 CHINESE CIVIL WAR
Also known as the "War of Liberation," this pitted the Communist and Nationalist parties in China against each other. The Communists won.

1950–1953 KOREAN WAR
Kicked off when the Communist forces of North Korea, with backing from the Soviet Union, invaded their democratic neighbor to the south. A coalition of 16 countries from the United Nations stepped in to support South Korea.

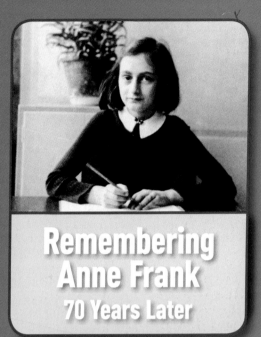

Remembering Anne Frank
70 Years Later

1950s–1975 VIETNAM WAR
Fought between the Communist North, supported by allies including China, and the government of South Vietnam, supported by the United States and other anticommunist nations.

1967 SIX-DAY WAR
A battle for land between Israel and the states of Egypt, Jordan, and Syria. The outcome resulted in Israel's gaining control of coveted territory, including the Gaza Strip and the West Bank.

1991–PRESENT SOMALI CIVIL WAR
Began when Somalia's last president, a dictator named Mohamed Siad Barre, was overthrown. The war has led to years of fighting and anarchy.

2001–2014 WAR IN AFGHANISTAN
After attacks in the United States by the terrorist group al Qaeda, a coalition that eventually included more than 40 countries invaded Afghanistan to find Osama bin Laden and other al Qaeda members and to dismantle the Taliban. Bin Laden was killed in a U.S. covert operation in 2011. The North Atlantic Treaty Organization (NATO) took control of the coalition's combat mission in 2003. That combat mission ended in 2014.

2003–2011 WAR IN IRAQ
A coalition led by the U.S., and including Britain, Australia, and Spain, invaded Iraq over suspicions that Iraq had weapons of mass destruction.

Imagine one day you're just a regular, happy kid living in a normal home with your normal family. And the next, you're in hiding from German Nazi soldiers in a secret attic apartment where you'll stay for two years before you're found and sent to a concentration camp. This is the story of Anne Frank, one of the many tragic tales to emerge from World War II. For two years, while Anne and her family hid in an attic in Amsterdam, Netherlands, she documented her everyday thoughts as well as her frustration about the war. In diaries that were later shared by her father—the only family member to survive their horrific ordeal—Anne offered insight into what it was like to be persecuted for being Jewish and to endure the constant fear of being discovered. Her work, *The Diary of a Young Girl,* has since been read by millions.

Now, 70 years since Anne's untimely death in 1945 at age 15, we remember this amazing girl and the other victims of the Holocaust, which claimed the lives of nearly six million people. Even today, it is difficult to comprehend the magnitude of this tragedy. That's why, no matter how much time passes, it is important that we never, ever forget.

The Constitution & the Bill of Rights

The United States Constitution was written in 1787 by a group of political leaders from the 13 states that made up the U.S. at the time. Thirty-nine men, including Benjamin Franklin and James Madison, signed the document to create a national government. While some feared the creation of a strong federal government, all 13 states eventually ratified, or approved, the Constitution, making it the law of the land. The Constitution has three major parts: the preamble, the articles, and the amendments.

THE PREAMBLE outlines the basic purposes of the government: *We the People of the United States, in order to form a more perfect Union, establish justice, insure domestic tranquility, provide for the common defense, promote the general welfare, and secure the blessings of liberty to ourselves and our posterity, do ordain and establish this Constitution for the United States of America.*

SEVEN ARTICLES outline the powers of Congress, the President, and the court system:

Article I outlines the legislative branch—the Senate and the House of Representatives—and its powers and responsibilities.

Article II outlines the executive branch—the Presidency—and its powers and responsibilities.

Article III outlines the judicial branch—the court system—and its powers and responsibilities.

Article IV describes the individual states' rights and powers.

Article V outlines the amendment process.

Article VI establishes the Constitution as the law of the land.

Article VII gives the requirements for the Constitution to be approved.

THE AMENDMENTS, or additions to the Constitution, were put in later as needed. In 1791, the first ten amendments, known as the **Bill of Rights**, were added. Since then another seventeen amendments have been added. This is the Bill of Rights:

1st Amendment: guarantees freedom of religion, speech, and the press, and the right to assemble and petition

2nd Amendment: discusses the militia and the right of people to bear arms

3rd Amendment: prohibits the military or troops from using private homes without consent

4th Amendment: protects people and their homes from search, arrest, or seizure without probable cause or a warrant

5th Amendment: grants people the right to have a trial and prevents punishment before prosecution; protects private property from being taken without compensation

6th Amendment: guarantees the right to a speedy and public trial

7th Amendment: guarantees a trial by jury in certain cases

8th Amendment: forbids "cruel and unusual punishments"

9th Amendment: states that the Constitution is not all-encompassing and does not deny people other, unspecified rights

10th Amendment: grants the powers not covered by the Constitution to the states and the people

Bet you didn't know

At just 4,543 words, the **U.S. CONSTITUTION** is the **OLDEST** and **SHORTEST NATIONAL CONSTITUTION.**

12 of the original 14 handwritten copies of the **BILL OF RIGHTS still survive today.**

Branches of Government

The **UNITED STATES GOVERNMENT** is divided into three branches: **executive, legislative**, and **judicial**. The system of checks and balances is a way to control power and to make sure one branch can't take the reins of government. For example, most of the President's actions require the approval of Congress. Likewise, the laws passed in Congress must be signed by the President before they can take effect.

White House

Executive Branch

The Constitution lists the central powers of the President: to serve as Commander in Chief of the armed forces; make treaties with other nations; grant pardons; inform Congress on the state of the union; and appoint ambassadors, officials, and judges. The executive branch includes the President and the 15 governmental departments.

Legislative Branch

This branch is made up of Congress—the Senate and the House of Representatives. The Constitution grants Congress the power to make laws. Congress is made up of elected representatives from each state. Each state has two representatives in the Senate, while the number of representatives in the House is determined by the size of the state's population. Washington, D.C., and the territories elect nonvoting representatives to the House of Representatives. The Founding Fathers set up this system as a compromise between big states—which wanted representation based on population—and small states—which wanted all states to have equal representation rights.

The U.S. Capitol in Washington, D.C.

Judicial Branch

The judicial branch is composed of the federal court system—the U.S. Supreme Court, the courts of appeals, and the district courts. The Supreme Court is the most powerful court. Its motto is "Equal Justice Under Law." This influential court is responsible for interpreting the Constitution and applying it to the cases that it hears. The decisions of the Supreme Court are absolute—they are the final word on any legal question.

There are nine justices on the Supreme Court. They are appointed by the President of the United States and confirmed by the Senate.

The U.S. Supreme Court Building in Washington, D.C.

239

The Indian Experience

Some American Indians of the Great Plains kept their drums in special buildings called "drum houses."

In winter, Lakota children traditionally played with sleds made from buffalo rib bones.

American Indians are indigenous to North and South America—they are the people who were here before Columbus and other European explorers came to these lands. They lived in nations, tribes, and bands across both continents. For decades following the arrival of Europeans in 1492, American Indians clashed with the newcomers who had ruptured the Indians' way of living.

Tribal Land

During the 19th century, both United States legislation and military action restricted the movement of American Indians, forcing them to live on reservations and attempting to dismantle tribal structures. For centuries Indians were often displaced or killed, or became assimilated into the general U.S. population. In 1924 the Indian Citizenship Act granted citizenship to all American Indians. Unfortunately, this was not enough to end the social discrimination and mistreatment that many Indians have faced. Today, American Indians living in the U.S. still face many challenges.

Healing the Past

Many members of the 560-plus recognized tribes in the United States live primarily on reservations. Some tribes have more than one reservation, while others have none. Together these reservations make up less than 3 percent of the nation's land area. The tribal governments on reservations have the right to form their own governments and to enforce laws, similar to individual states. Many feel that this sovereignty is still not enough to right the wrongs of the past: They hope for a change in the U.S. government's relationship with American Indians.

A Lakota woman in traditional costume. Black Hills, South Dakota, U.S.A.

GEORGE WASHINGTON'S REAL LOOK

WITH HELP FROM SCIENCE, THESE WAX FIGURES SOLVE THE MYSTERY OF WHAT THE FIRST U.S. PRESIDENT LOOKED LIKE.

Did George Washington really look like the portrait on the dollar bill, which appears above? Without photos, no one knew for sure. So officials at Mount Vernon, Washington's Virginia estate, called the experts. Using scientific methods, they accurately re-created Washington at the ages of 19, 45 (big picture), and 57. Here's how they gave Washington a makeover.

FACE In 1785, artist Jean-Antoine Houdon created a mask of Washington after laying plaster-soaked gauze over his face. The mask was a near-perfect match of Washington's face, so scientists scanned it into a computer to create a 3-D image (right) that accurately showed Washington's facial features.

HAIR Because Washington often powdered his hair, not many people knew what his real hair color was. That's why experts examined Washington's hair samples (left, in center) and written descriptions by people who knew him. That confirmed once and for all that the President had reddish brown hair.

Washington, age 19

JAW Washington started losing his teeth around age 24, which meant that his jaw changed shape over time. To determine what Washington's jawline would have looked like at 19, anthropologist Jeffrey Schwartz examined two sets of Washington's false teeth, which were scanned into a computer.

The result? Turns out the real George Washington was thinner than many artists portrayed him. And his face was actually broader and longer than how it looks on the dollar bill. "Basically," Schwartz says, "no one portrait represents him faithfully from head to toe."

Washington, age 57

241

The President of the United States is the chief of the executive branch, the Commander in Chief of the U.S. armed forces, and head of the federal government. Elected every four years, the President is the highest policy-maker in the nation. The 22nd Amendment (1951) says that no person may be elected to the office of President more than twice. There have been 44 Presidencies and 43 Presidents.

JAMES MONROE

5th President of the United States ★ *1817–1825*

BORN April 28, 1758, in
Westmoreland County, VA
POLITICAL PARTY Democratic-Republican
NO. OF TERMS two
VICE PRESIDENT Daniel D. Tompkins
DIED July 4, 1831, in New York, NY

GEORGE WASHINGTON

1st President of the United States ★ *1789–1797*

BORN Feb. 22, 1732, in
Pope's Creek, Westmoreland
County, VA
POLITICAL PARTY Federalist
NO. OF TERMS two
VICE PRESIDENT John Adams
DIED Dec. 14, 1799, at Mount Vernon, VA

JOHN QUINCY ADAMS

6th President of the United States ★ *1825–1829*

BORN July 11, 1767, in Braintree
(now Quincy), MA
POLITICAL PARTY Democratic-Republican
NO. OF TERMS one
VICE PRESIDENT John Caldwell Calhoun
DIED Feb. 23, 1848, at the U.S. Capitol,
Washington, DC

JOHN ADAMS

2nd President of the United States ★ *1797–1801*

BORN Oct. 30, 1735, in Braintree
(now Quincy), MA
POLITICAL PARTY Federalist
NO. OF TERMS one
VICE PRESIDENT Thomas Jefferson
DIED July 4, 1826, in Quincy, MA

A 2008 study named
JOHN QUINCY ADAMS
the fittest U.S. President
because of his
exercise routines.

HE SWAM IN THE POTOMAC RIVER.

THOMAS JEFFERSON

3rd President of the United States ★ *1801–1809*

BORN April 13, 1743, at Shadwell,
Goochland (now Albemarle)
County, VA
POLITICAL PARTY Democratic-Republican
NO. OF TERMS two
VICE PRESIDENTS 1st term: Aaron Burr
2nd term: George Clinton
DIED July 4, 1826, at Monticello,
Charlottesville, VA

ANDREW JACKSON

7th President of the United States ★ *1829–1837*

BORN March 15, 1767, in the Waxhaw
region, NC and SC
POLITICAL PARTY Democrat
NO. OF TERMS two
VICE PRESIDENTS 1st term:
John Caldwell Calhoun
2nd term: Martin Van Buren
DIED June 8, 1845, in Nashville, TN

JAMES MADISON

4th President of the United States ★ *1809–1817*

BORN March 16, 1751, at Belle Grove,
Port Conway, VA
POLITICAL PARTY Democratic-Republican
NO. OF TERMS two
VICE PRESIDENTS 1st term: George Clinton
2nd term: Elbridge Gerry
DIED June 28, 1836, at Montpelier,
Orange County, VA

MARTIN VAN BUREN

8th President of the United States ★ *1837–1841*

BORN Dec. 5, 1782,
in Kinderhook, NY
POLITICAL PARTY Democrat
NO. OF TERMS one
VICE PRESIDENT Richard M. Johnson
DIED July 24, 1862, in Kinderhook, NY

WILLIAM HENRY HARRISON

9th President of the United States ★ *1841*

BORN Feb. 9, 1773, in Charles City County, VA

POLITICAL PARTY Whig

NO. OF TERMS one (cut short by death)

VICE PRESIDENT John Tyler

DIED April 4, 1841, in the White House, Washington, DC

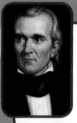

JOHN TYLER

10th President of the United States ★ *1841–1845*

BORN March 29, 1790, in Charles City County, VA

POLITICAL PARTY Whig

NO. OF TERMS one (partial)

VICE PRESIDENT none

DIED Jan. 18, 1862, in Richmond, VA

JAMES K. POLK

11th President of the United States ★ *1845–1849*

BORN Nov. 2, 1795, near Pineville, Mecklenburg County, NC

POLITICAL PARTY Democrat

NO. OF TERMS one

VICE PRESIDENT George Mifflin Dallas

DIED June 15, 1849, in Nashville, TN

ZACHARY TAYLOR

12th President of the United States ★ *1849–1850*

BORN Nov. 24, 1784, in Orange County, VA

POLITICAL PARTY Whig

NO. OF TERMS one (cut short by death)

VICE PRESIDENT Millard Fillmore

DIED July 9, 1850, in the White House, Washington, DC

MILLARD FILLMORE

13th President of the United States ★ *1850–1853*

BORN Jan. 7, 1800, in Cayuga County, NY

POLITICAL PARTY Whig

NO. OF TERMS one (partial)

VICE PRESIDENT none

DIED March 8, 1874, in Buffalo, NY

FRANKLIN PIERCE

14th President of the United States ★ *1853–1857*

BORN Nov. 23, 1804, in Hillsborough (now Hillsboro), NH

POLITICAL PARTY Democrat

NO. OF TERMS one

VICE PRESIDENT William Rufus De Vane King

DIED Oct. 8, 1869, in Concord, NH

JAMES BUCHANAN

15th President of the United States ★ *1857–1861*

BORN April 23, 1791, in Cove Gap, PA

POLITICAL PARTY Democrat

NO. OF TERMS one

VICE PRESIDENT John Cabell Breckinridge

DIED June 1, 1868, in Lancaster, PA

ABRAHAM LINCOLN

16th President of the United States ★ *1861–1865*

BORN Feb. 12, 1809, near Hodgenville, KY

POLITICAL PARTY Republican (formerly Whig)

NO. OF TERMS two (assassinated)

VICE PRESIDENTS 1st term: Hannibal Hamlin
2nd term: Andrew Johnson

DIED April 15, 1865, in Washington, DC

ANDREW JOHNSON

17th President of the United States ★ *1865–1869*

BORN Dec. 29, 1808, in Raleigh, NC

POLITICAL PARTY Democrat

NO. OF TERMS one (partial)

VICE PRESIDENT none

DIED July 31, 1875, in Carter's Station, TN

BEFORE BECOMING A POLITICIAN, ANDREW JOHNSON WAS A TAILOR.

ULYSSES S. GRANT

18th President of the United States ★ *1869–1877*

BORN April 27, 1822, in Point Pleasant, OH

POLITICAL PARTY Republican

NO. OF TERMS two

VICE PRESIDENTS 1st term: Schuyler Colfax
2nd term: Henry Wilson

DIED July 23, 1885, in Mount McGregor, NY

RUTHERFORD B. HAYES

19th President of the United States ★ *1877–1881*

BORN Oct. 4, 1822, in Delaware, OH

POLITICAL PARTY Republican

NO. OF TERMS one

VICE PRESIDENT William Almon Wheeler

DIED Jan. 17, 1893, in Fremont, OH

JAMES A. GARFIELD

20th President of the United States ★ *1881*

BORN Nov. 19, 1831, near Orange, OH

POLITICAL PARTY Republican

NO. OF TERMS one (assassinated)

VICE PRESIDENT Chester A. Arthur

DIED Sept. 19, 1881, in Elberon, NJ

CHESTER A. ARTHUR

21st President of the United States ★ *1881–1885*

BORN Oct. 5, 1829, in Fairfield, VT

POLITICAL PARTY Republican

NO. OF TERMS one (partial)

VICE PRESIDENT none

DIED Nov. 18, 1886, in New York, NY

GROVER CLEVELAND

22nd and 24th President of the United States
1885–1889 ★ *1893–1897*

BORN March 18, 1837, in Caldwell, NJ

POLITICAL PARTY Democrat

NO. OF TERMS two (nonconsecutive)

VICE PRESIDENTS 1st administration:
Thomas Andrews Hendricks
2nd administration:
Adlai Ewing Stevenson

DIED June 24, 1908, in Princeton, NJ

BENJAMIN HARRISON

23rd President of the United States ★ *1889–1893*

BORN Aug. 20, 1833, in North Bend, OH

POLITICAL PARTY Republican

NO. OF TERMS one

VICE PRESIDENT Levi Parsons Morton

DIED March 13, 1901, in Indianapolis, IN

WILLIAM MCKINLEY

25th President of the United States ★ *1897–1901*

BORN Jan. 29, 1843, in Niles, OH

POLITICAL PARTY Republican

NO. OF TERMS two (assassinated)

VICE PRESIDENTS 1st term:
Garret Augustus Hobart
2nd term:
Theodore Roosevelt

DIED Sept. 14, 1901, in Buffalo, NY

THEODORE ROOSEVELT

26th President of the United States ★ *1901–1909*

BORN Oct. 27, 1858, in New York, NY

POLITICAL PARTY Republican

NO. OF TERMS one, plus balance of McKinley's term

VICE PRESIDENTS 1st term: none
2nd term: Charles Warren Fairbanks

DIED Jan. 6, 1919, in Oyster Bay, NY

WILLIAM HOWARD TAFT

27th President of the United States ★ *1909–1913*

BORN Sept. 15, 1857, in Cincinnati, OH

POLITICAL PARTY Republican

NO. OF TERMS one

VICE PRESIDENT James Schoolcraft Sherman

DIED March 8, 1930, in Washington, DC

WOODROW WILSON

28th President of the United States ★ *1913–1921*

BORN Dec. 29, 1856, in Staunton, VA

POLITICAL PARTY Democrat

NO. OF TERMS two

VICE PRESIDENT Thomas Riley Marshall

DIED Feb. 3, 1924, in Washington, DC

WARREN G. HARDING

29th President of the United States ★ 1921–1923

BORN Nov. 2, 1865, in Caledonia
(now Blooming Grove), OH
POLITICAL PARTY Republican
NO. OF TERMS one (died while in office)
VICE PRESIDENT Calvin Coolidge
DIED Aug. 2, 1923, in San Francisco, CA

CALVIN COOLIDGE

30th President of the United States ★ 1923–1929

BORN July 4, 1872, in Plymouth, VT
POLITICAL PARTY Republican
NO. OF TERMS one, plus balance of
Harding's term
VICE PRESIDENTS 1st term: none
2nd term:
Charles Gates Dawes
DIED Jan. 5, 1933, in Northampton, MA

HERBERT HOOVER

31st President of the United States ★ 1929–1933

BORN Aug. 10, 1874,
in West Branch, IA
POLITICAL PARTY Republican
NO. OF TERMS one
VICE PRESIDENT Charles Curtis
DIED Oct. 20, 1964, in New York, NY

FRANKLIN D. ROOSEVELT

32nd President of the United States ★ 1933–1945

BORN Jan. 30, 1882, in Hyde Park, NY
POLITICAL PARTY Democrat
NO. OF TERMS four (died while in office)
VICE PRESIDENTS 1st & 2nd terms: John
Nance Garner; 3rd term:
Henry Agard Wallace;
4th term: Harry S. Truman
DIED April 12, 1945,
in Warm Springs, GA

HARRY S. TRUMAN

33rd President of the United States ★ 1945–1953

BORN May 8, 1884, in Lamar, MO
POLITICAL PARTY Democrat
NO. OF TERMS one, plus balance of
Franklin D. Roosevelt's term
VICE PRESIDENTS 1st term: none
2nd term:
Alben William Barkley
DIED Dec. 26, 1972, in Independence, MO

DWIGHT D. EISENHOWER

34th President of the United States ★ 1953–1961

BORN Oct. 14, 1890, in Denison, TX
POLITICAL PARTY Republican
NO. OF TERMS two
VICE PRESIDENT Richard M. Nixon
DIED March 28, 1969,
in Washington, DC

JOHN F. KENNEDY

35th President of the United States ★ 1961–1963

BORN May 29, 1917, in Brookline, MA
POLITICAL PARTY Democrat
NO. OF TERMS one (assassinated)
VICE PRESIDENT Lyndon B. Johnson
DIED Nov. 22, 1963,
in Dallas, TX

LYNDON B. JOHNSON

36th President of the United States ★ 1963–1969

BORN Aug. 27, 1908,
near Stonewall, TX
POLITICAL PARTY Democrat
NO. OF TERMS one, plus balance of
Kennedy's term
VICE PRESIDENTS 1st term: none
2nd term: Hubert
Horatio Humphrey
DIED Jan. 22, 1973, near San Antonio, TX

LYNDON B. JOHNSON'S BEAGLES WERE NAMED HIM AND HER.

RICHARD NIXON

37th President of the United States ★ *1969–1974*

BORN Jan. 9, 1913, in Yorba Linda, CA
POLITICAL PARTY Republican
NO. OF TERMS two (resigned)
VICE PRESIDENTS 1st term & 2nd term (partial): Spiro Theodore Agnew; 2nd term (balance): Gerald R. Ford
DIED April 22, 1994, in New York, NY

GERALD R. FORD

38th President of the United States ★ *1974–1977*

BORN July 14, 1913, in Omaha, NE
POLITICAL PARTY Republican
NO. OF TERMS one (partial)
VICE PRESIDENT Nelson Aldrich Rockefeller
DIED Dec. 26, 2006, in Rancho Mirage, CA

JIMMY CARTER

39th President of the United States ★ *1977–1981*

BORN Oct. 1, 1924, in Plains, GA
POLITICAL PARTY Democrat
NO. OF TERMS one
VICE PRESIDENT Walter Frederick (Fritz) Mondale

RONALD REAGAN

40th President of the United States ★ *1981–1989*

BORN Feb. 6, 1911, in Tampico, IL
POLITICAL PARTY Republican
NO. OF TERMS two
VICE PRESIDENT George H. W. Bush
DIED June 5, 2004, in Los Angeles, CA

MORE THAN 6,000 POUNDS (2,722 KG) OF JELLY BEANS—RONALD REAGAN'S FAVORITE CANDY— WERE SHIPPED TO THE WHITE HOUSE FOR HIS INAUGURATION.

GEORGE H. W. BUSH

41st President of the United States ★ *1989–1993*

BORN June 12, 1924, in Milton, MA
POLITICAL PARTY Republican
NO. OF TERMS one
VICE PRESIDENT James Danforth (Dan) Quayle III

WILLIAM J. CLINTON

42nd President of the United States ★ *1993–2001*

BORN Aug. 19, 1946, in Hope, AR
POLITICAL PARTY Democrat
NO. OF TERMS two
VICE PRESIDENT Albert Gore, Jr.

WILLIAM J. CLINTON
has two Grammy awards—both in the spoken word category.

GEORGE W. BUSH

43rd President of the United States ★ *2001–2009*

BORN July 6, 1946, in New Haven, CT
POLITICAL PARTY Republican
NO. OF TERMS two
VICE PRESIDENT Richard Bruce Cheney

A BASEBALL LOVER, GEORGE W. BUSH HAS A COLLECTION OF MORE THAN 250 SIGNED BASEBALLS.

BARACK OBAMA

44th President of the United States ★ *2009–present*

BORN Aug. 4, 1961, in Honolulu, HI
POLITICAL PARTY Democrat
NO. OF TERMS two
VICE PRESIDENT Joseph Biden

On the Money Quiz!

In 1869, George Washington became the first President to be featured on U.S. currency, seven years after the first dollar bill was put into print. In 1909, Teddy Roosevelt commissioned the penny featuring Abraham Lincoln to celebrate the popular President's 100th birthday. Today, more than 30 Presidents and other prominent historical figures are featured on various bills and coins. So, do you know which President's face appears on each bill—or coin? See if you can match the President to the correct currency.

1. Franklin D. Roosevelt
2. John F. Kennedy
3. Ulysses S. Grant
4. Abraham Lincoln
5. Thomas Jefferson
6. Andrew Jackson

A. 50-cent piece
B. nickel
C. $20 bill
D. dime
E. $5 bill
F. $50 bill

ANSWERS: 1. D; 2. A; 3. F; 4. E; 5. B; 6. C

CIVIL RIGHTS

Although the Constitution protects the civil rights of American citizens, it has not always been able to protect all Americans from persecution or discrimination. During the first half of the 20th century, many Americans, particularly African Americans, were subjected to widespread discrimination and racism. By the mid-1950s, many people were eager to end the bonds of racism and bring freedom to all men and women.

The civil rights movement of the 1950s and 1960s sought to end the racial discrimination against African Americans, especially in the southern states. The movement wanted to restore the fundamentals of economic and social equality to those who had been oppressed.

The Little Rock Nine

The Little Rock Nine study during the weeks when they were blocked from school.

September 4, 1957, marked the first day of school at Little Rock Central High in Little Rock, Arkansas. But this was no ordinary back-to-school scene: Armed soldiers surrounded the entrance, awaiting the arrival of Central's first ever African-American students. The welcome was not warm, however, as the students—now known as the Little Rock Nine—were refused entry into the school by the soldiers and a group of protesters, angry about the potential integration. This did not deter the students, and they gained the support of President Dwight D. Eisenhower to eventually earn their right to go to an integrated school. Today, the Little Rock Nine are still considered civil rights icons for challenging a racist system—and winning!

Key Events in the Civil Rights Movement

1954	The Supreme Court case *Brown* v. *Board of Education* declares school segregation illegal.
1955	Rosa Parks refuses to give up her bus seat to a white passenger and spurs a bus boycott.
1957	The Little Rock Nine help to integrate schools.
1960	Four black college students begin sit-ins at a restaurant in Greensboro, North Carolina.
1961	Freedom Rides to southern states begin as a way to protest segregation in transportation.
1963	Martin Luther King, Jr., leads the famous March on Washington.
1964	The Civil Rights Act, signed by President Lyndon B. Johnson, prohibits discrimination based on race, color, religion, sex, and national origin.
1967	Thurgood Marshall becomes the first African American to be named to the Supreme Court.
1968	President Lyndon B. Johnson signs the Civil Rights Act of 1968, which prohibits discrimination in the sale, rental, and financing of housing.

STONE OF HOPE:
THE LEGACY OF MARTIN LUTHER KING, JR.

Dr. Martin Luther King, Jr., born in Atlanta, Georgia, in 1929, never backed down in his stand against racism. He dedicated his life to achieving equality and justice for Americans of all colors. King experienced racial prejudice early in life. As an adult fighting for civil rights, his speeches, marches, and mere presence motivated people to fight for justice for all. His March on Washington in 1963 was one of the largest activist gatherings in our nation's history.

Sadly, King was assassinated by James Earl Ray on April 4, 1968. But his spirit lives on through a memorial on the National Mall in Washington, D.C. Built in 2011, 48 years after Dr. King's famous "I Have a Dream" speech, the memorial features a 30-foot (9-m) statue of Dr. King carved into a granite boulder named the "Stone of Hope."

Each year, thousands of visitors pay tribute to this inspirational figure, who will forever be remembered as one of the most prominent leaders of the civil rights movement.

EQUAL in '63 RIGHTS

"The time is always right to do what is right."

Martin Luther King, Jr. Memorial in Washington, D.C.

In 1964, at the age of 35, Martin Luther King, Jr., became the youngest person ever to win the Nobel Peace Prize.

Dr. King's "I Have a Dream" speech drew 250,000 people to the National Mall in Washington, D.C., in 1963.

WOMEN
Fighting for Equality

Women march for equality in Washington, D.C.

Today, women make up about half of the country's workforce. But a little over a century ago, less than 20 percent worked outside the home. In fact, they didn't even have the right to vote!

That began to change in the mid-1800s when women, led by pioneers like Elizabeth Cady Stanton and Susan B. Anthony, started speaking up about inequality. They organized public demonstrations, gave speeches, published documents, and wrote newspaper articles to express their ideas. In 1848, about 300 people attended the Seneca Falls Convention in New York to address the need for equal rights. By the late 1800s, the National American Woman Suffrage Association had made great strides toward giving women the freedom to vote. One by one, states began allowing women to vote. By 1920, the U.S. Constitution was amended, giving women across the country the ability to cast a vote during any election.

But the fight for equality did not end there. In the 1960s and 1970s, the women's rights movement experienced a rebirth, as feminists protested against injustices in areas such as the workplace and in education.

While these efforts enabled women to make great strides in our society, the efforts to even the playing field among men and women continue today.

Women first took part in the Olympic Games in 1900, participating in tennis, golf, sailing, croquet, and equestrian events.

New Zealand granted national voting rights to women in 1893.

Girls at a suffrage meeting, ca 1920

Key Events in Women's History

1848: **Elizabeth Cady Stanton** and **Lucretia Mott** organize the Seneca Falls Convention in New York. Attendees rally for equitable laws, equal educational and job opportunities, and the right to vote.

1920: **The 19th Amendment,** guaranteeing women the right to vote, is ratified.

1964: **Title VII of the Civil Rights Act of 1964,** which prohibits employment discrimination on the basis of sex, is successfully amended.

1966: **The National Organization for Women** (NOW), the largest feminist organization in the United States, is founded by women, including writer Betty Friedan; Rev. Pauli Murray, the first African-American female Episcopal priest; and Shirley Chisholm, the first African-American woman to run for President of the United States.

1971: **Gloria Steinem** heads up the National Women's Political Caucus, which encourages women to be active in government. She also launches *Ms.,* a magazine about women's issues.

1972: Congress approves **the Equal Rights Amendment** (ERA), proposing that women and men have equal rights under the law. It is ratified by 35 of the necessary 38 states, and is still not part of the U.S. Constitution.

1981: President Ronald Reagan appoints **Sandra Day O'Connor** as the first female Supreme Court justice.

1984: Democrat **Geraldine Ferraro** is nominated as a major party's first female vice presidential candidate.

1996: **Madeleine Albright** is appointed the first female Secretary of State.

2005: **Condoleezza Rice** becomes the first African-American woman to be appointed Secretary of State.

The Sharpshooter: Annie Oakley

In the male-dominated era of the Wild West, Annie Oakley broke the mold by becoming one of the most famous figures around. Born Phoebe Ann Moses in 1860, Oakley adopted her stage name after taking a role in Buffalo Bill's Wild West Show, which toured throughout the country for more than 15 years. A sharpshooter with great aim and accuracy, Oakley wowed audiences by showing off tricks like shooting holes through cards thrown into the air and hitting targets while looking in a mirror. Her skills earned her fame and fortune, much of which she shared with her family or charities for orphans. She also supported the Red Cross during World War I.

Annie Oakley

The Glass-Ceiling Breaker: Barbara Walters

It's hard to imagine a world without female television hosts and news anchors, but that's just what Barbara Walters was up against when she began her career in 1961. At the time, no woman had ever co-hosted a news program on TV. That all changed when Walters was tapped as the co-host of the *Today* show in 1974. She continued to bust through glass ceilings after joining *ABC Evening News* in 1976, becoming the first co-anchor of a network evening newscast. During her career, Walters has interviewed every President and First Lady from the Nixons through the Obamas, and she went on to create and co-host the daytime show *The View.* Although Walters is now retired from her hosting duties, her passion for storytelling and perseverance remain an inspiration to women around the world.

Barbara Walters
The View, 1997

STUMP YOUR PARENTS

HISTORY HAPPENS QUIZ

Test your parents to see if they're well-read on the past— or if it's time to hit the books. ANSWERS BELOW

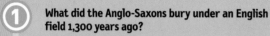

1 What did the Anglo-Saxons bury under an English field 1,300 years ago?

a. 3,500 pieces of gold and silver
b. diamond necklaces
c. dinosaur bones
d. a time capsule

2 **True or false?** Boys began training for knighthood when they were ten years old.

3 Where is Borobudur, the world's largest Buddhist monument?

a. Indonesia
b. Indiana
c. Malaysia
d. Cambodia

4 How tall was the *Titanic*?

a. 13 stories
b. 17 stories
c. 70 stories
d. as tall as 13 giraffes

5 Which of the following has not been recovered from an Egyptian tomb?

a. clothes
b. games
c. jewelry
d. popcorn

Not STUMPED yet?
Check out the *National Geographic Kids Quiz Whiz* collection for more crazy HISTORY questions!

ANSWERS:
1. a; 2. False. Boys began training at 7 years old.; 3. a; 4. b; 5. d

HOMEWORK HELP

Brilliant Biographies

A biography is the story of a person's life. It can be a brief summary or a long book. Biographers—those who write biographies—use many different sources to learn about their subjects. You can write your own biography of a famous person whom you find inspiring.

How to Get Started

Choose a subject you find interesting. If you think Cleopatra is cool, you have a good chance of getting your reader interested, too. If you're bored by ancient Egypt, your reader will be snoring after your first paragraph.

Your subject can be almost anyone: an author, an inventor, a celebrity, a politician, or a member of your family. To find someone to write about, ask yourself these simple questions:

1. Whom do I want to know more about?
2. What did this person do that was special?
3. How did this person change the world?

Do Your Research

- Find out as much about your subject as possible. Read books, news articles, and encyclopedia entries. Watch video clips and movies, and search the Internet. Conduct interviews, if possible.
- Take notes, writing down important facts and interesting stories about your subject.

Write the Biography

- Come up with a title. Include the person's name.
- Write an introduction. Consider asking a probing question about your subject.
- Include information about the person's childhood. When was this person born? Where did he or she grow up? Whom did he or she admire?
- Highlight the person's talents, accomplishments, and personal attributes.
- Describe the specific events that helped to shape this person's life. Did this person ever have a problem and overcome it?
- Write a conclusion. Include your thoughts about why it is important to learn about this person.
- Once you have finished your first draft, revise and then proofread your work.

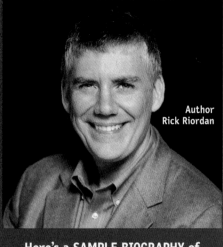

Author
Rick Riordan

Here's a SAMPLE BIOGRAPHY of Rick Riordan, best-selling author of the *Percy Jackson and the Olympians* and *The 39 Clues* series. Of course, there is so much more for you to discover, and write about on your own!

Rick Riordan—Author

Rick Riordan was born on June 5, 1964, in San Antonio, Texas, U.S.A. Born into a creative family—his mom was a musician and artist and his dad was a ceramicist—Riordan began writing in middle school, and he published his first short stories while attending college.

After graduating from University of Texas at Austin, Riordan went on to teach English to middle schoolers, spending his summers as a music director at a summer camp. Writing adult mysteries on the side, Riordan soon discovered his knack for writing for younger readers and published *The Lightning Thief*, the first book in the Percy Jackson series, in 2005. *The Sea of Monsters* soon followed. Before long, Riordan quit his teaching job to become a full-time writer.

Today Riordan has penned more than 35 books, firmly establishing himself as one of the most accomplished and well-known authors of our time. When he's not writing, Riordan—who lives with his wife, Becky, and their sons Haley and Patrick—likes to read, swim, play guitar, and travel with his family.

Geography
Rocks

KINDS OF MAPS

Maps are special tools that geographers use to tell a story about Earth. Maps can be used to show just about anything related to places. Some maps show physical features, such as mountains or vegetation. Maps can also show climates or natural hazards and other things we cannot easily see. Other maps illustrate different features on Earth—political boundaries, urban centers, and economic systems.

AN IMPERFECT TOOL

Maps are not perfect. A globe is a scale model of Earth with accurate relative sizes and locations. Because maps are flat, they involve distortions of size, shape, and direction. Also, cartographers—people who create maps— make choices about what information to include. Because of this, it is important to study many different types of maps to learn the complete story of Earth. Three commonly found kinds of maps are shown on this page.

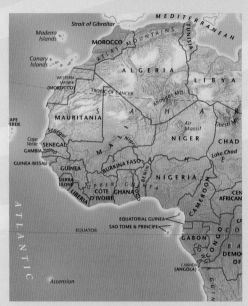

PHYSICAL MAPS. Earth's natural features—landforms, water bodies, and vegetation—are shown on physical maps. The map above uses color and shading to illustrate mountains, lakes, rivers, and deserts of western Africa. Country names and borders are added for reference, but they are not natural features.

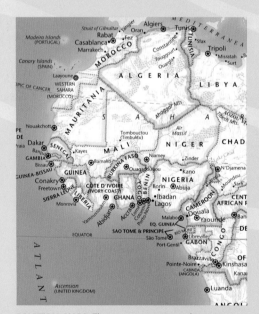

POLITICAL MAPS. These maps represent characteristics of the landscape created by humans, such as boundaries, cities, and place-names. Natural features are added only for reference. On the map above, capital cities are represented with a star inside a circle, while other cities are shown with black dots.

THEMATIC MAPS. Patterns related to a particular topic or theme, such as population distribution, appear on these maps. The map above displays the region's climate zones, which range from tropical wet (bright green) to tropical wet and dry (light green) to semiarid (dark yellow) to arid or desert (light yellow).

GEOGRAPHIC FEATURES

From roaring rivers to parched deserts, from underwater canyons to jagged mountains, Earth is covered with beautiful and diverse environments. Here are examples of the most common types of geographic features found around the world.

DESERT

Deserts are land features created by climate, specifically by a lack of water. Here, a camel caravan crosses the Sahara in North Africa.

VALLEY

Valleys, cut by running water or moving ice, may be broad and flat or narrow and steep, such as the Indus River Valley in Ladakh, India (above).

RIVER

As a river moves through flatlands, it twists and turns. Above, the Rio Los Amigos winds through a rain forest in Peru.

MOUNTAIN

Mountains are Earth's tallest landforms, and Mount Everest (above) rises highest of all, at 29,035 feet (8,850 m) above sea level.

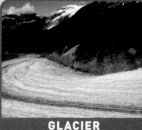

GLACIER

Glaciers—"rivers" of ice—such as Alaska's Hubbard Glacier (above) move slowly from mountains to the sea. Global warming is shrinking them.

CANYON

Steep-sided valleys called canyons are created mainly by running water. Buckskin Gulch in Utah (above) is the deepest slot canyon in the American Southwest.

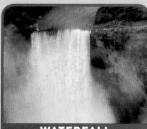

WATERFALL

Waterfalls form when a river reaches an abrupt change in elevation. Above, Kaieteur Falls, in Guyana, has a sheer drop of 741 feet (226 m).

THE POLITICAL WORLD

Earth's land area is made up of seven continents, but people have divided much of the land into smaller political units called countries. Australia is a continent made up of a single country, and Antarctica is set aside for scientific research. But the other five continents include almost 200 independent countries. The political map shown here depicts boundaries—imaginary lines created by treaties—that separate countries. Some boundaries, such as the one between the United States and Canada, are very stable and have been recognized for many years.

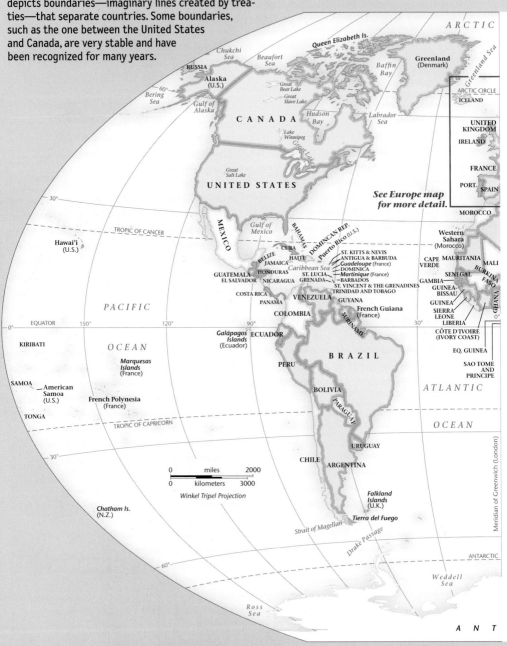

See Europe map for more detail.

Winkel Tripel Projection

Other boundaries, such as the one between Ethiopia and Eritrea in northeast Africa, are relatively new and still disputed. Countries come in all shapes and sizes. Russia and Canada are giants; others, such as Luxembourg, are small. Some countries are long and skinny—look at Chile in South America! Still other countries—such as Indonesia and Japan in Asia—are made up of groups of islands. The political map is a clue to the diversity that makes Earth so fascinating.

OCEAN

Severnaya Zemlya
New Siberian Islands
East Siberian Sea
Laptev Sea
Barents Sea
Kara Sea
Svalbard (Norway)
Novaya Zemlya

Bering Sea
Sea of Okhotsk

NORWAY SWEDEN FINLAND
DEN. GERMANY
EST. LATV. LITH. BELARUS
POLAND
UKRAINE MOLD.
ROMANIA GEORGIA
ITALY ALBANIA BULGARIA ARM.
GREECE TURKEY AZERB.
TUNISIA CYPRUS SYRIA
LEBANON IRAQ IRAN
ISRAEL JORDAN KUWAIT
ALGERIA LIBYA EGYPT
BAHRAIN QATAR U.A.E.
SAUDI ARABIA OMAN

RUSSIA
KAZAKHSTAN MONGOLIA
Lake Baikal
NORTH KOREA JAPAN
SOUTH KOREA
UZBEK. KYRGYZSTAN
TURKMEN. TAJIKISTAN
Caspian Sea
AFGHAN.
CHINA
PAKISTAN
NEPAL BHUTAN
BANGLADESH
INDIA MYANMAR (BURMA)
THAILAND LAOS VIETNAM
CAMBODIA

TAIWAN 30°
The People's Republic of China claims Taiwan as its 23rd province. Taiwan's government (Republic of China) maintains that there are two political entities.
Taiwan

NIGER CHAD SUDAN ERITREA YEMEN DJIBOUTI
NIGERIA CAMEROON C.A.R. SOUTH SUDAN ETHIOPIA SOMALIA
TOGO BENIN GABON CONGO DEM. REP. OF THE CONGO RWANDA BURUNDI UGANDA KENYA
Cabinda (Angola) TANZANIA SEYCHELLES
ANGOLA ZAMBIA COMOROS
ZIMBABWE MALAWI MOZAMBIQUE MADAGASCAR
NAMIBIA BOTSWANA Réunion (France)
SOUTH AFRICA LESOTHO SWAZILAND

Red Sea
Mediterranean Sea
Arabian Sea
Bay of Bengal
SRI LANKA
MALDIVES
60° 90°

South China Sea
Philippine Sea
PHILIPPINES
Northern Mariana Islands (U.S.)
Guam (U.S.)
PALAU
FEDERATED STATES OF MICRONESIA
BRUNEI MALAYSIA SINGAPORE
INDONESIA
TIMOR-LESTE (EAST TIMOR)
New Guinea PAPUA NEW GUINEA
SOLOMON ISLANDS
PACIFIC OCEAN
MARSHALL ISLANDS
KIRIBATI
NAURU EQUATOR 0°
TUVALU
150°

INDIAN OCEAN

Kerguelen Islands (France)

MAURITIUS

AUSTRALIA
Great Australian Bight
Tasman Sea
Tasmania
Coral Sea VANUATU FIJI
New Caledonia (France)
North Island
NEW ZEALAND
South Island
30°

CIRCLE 60°

Ross Sea

ARCTICA

THE PHYSICAL WORLD

Earth is dominated by large landmasses called continents—seven in all—and by an interconnected global ocean that is divided into four parts by the continents. More than 70 percent of Earth's surface is covered by oceans, and the remaining 30 percent is made up of land areas.

Different landforms give variety to the surface of the continents. The Rockies and the Andes mark the western edge of the Americas, and the Himalaya tower above southern Asia. The Plateau of Tibet forms the rugged core of Asia, while

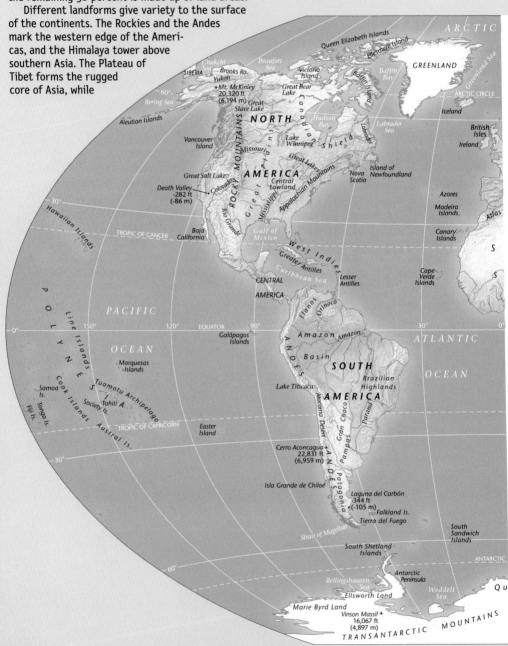

260

the Northern European Plain extends from the North Sea to the Ural Mountains. Much of Africa is a plateau, and dry plains cover large areas of Australia. Mountains rise more than 16,000 feet (4,877 m) above Antarctica's massive ice sheets. Mountains and trenches make the ocean floors as varied as any continent. A mountain chain called the Mid-Atlantic Ridge runs the length of the Atlantic Ocean. In the western Pacific, trenches drop deep into the ocean floor.

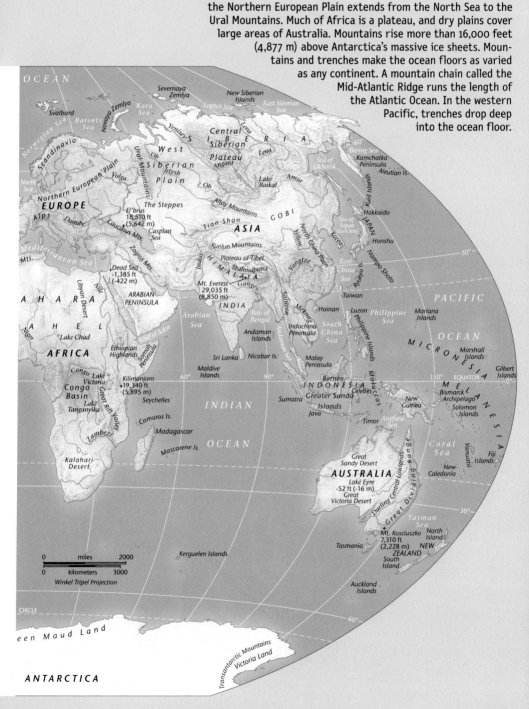

261

SPOTLIGHT ON
AFRICA

NATIONAL GEOGRAPHIC KIDS
SCANNER

SCAN THIS PAGE!
GET BONUS MOBILE
CONTENT! Download
the free NG Kids
scanner app. Directions
on inside front cover.

African lion
and cub

A
lion's roar
can be heard
up to 5 miles
(8 km) away.

In legends from
Tanzania, Africa,
witches ride on
hyenas, not
broomsticks.

The massive continent of Africa, where humankind began millions of years ago, is second to only Asia in size. Stretching nearly as far from west to east as it does from north to south, Africa is home to both the longest river in the world (the Nile) and the largest hot desert on Earth (Sahara).

Zulu woman in native costume

Beautiful Baskets

Young girls and women weave brightly colored baskets from grass and straw that have become a trademark of African cultures. The baskets are used for decoration and to store food.

Dry Land

One-third of Africa is covered in sand, bedrock, and stone. In the Sahara, there's only about 1 person per square mile (0.4 sq km), one of the lowest population densities on Earth.

Great Lakes

Three of the world's ten biggest lakes are in Africa. Lake Victoria, Lake Tanganyika, and Lake Malawi are found in the Great Rift Valley, which stretches from Ethiopia to Mozambique.

Unique Animals

Ninety percent of the animals found on the island of Madagascar evolved there and nowhere else. Many are endangered, including some of the numerous species of lemurs.

Top 5 Largest Animals

1. African elephant
   up to 14,000 pounds (6,350 kg)

2. Hippopotamus
   up to 8,000 pounds (3,630 kg)

3. White rhinoceros
   up to 7,920 pounds (3,600 kg)

4. Black rhinoceros
   up to 3,080 pounds (1,400 kg)

5. Giraffe
   up to 2,800 pounds (1,270 kg)

Downtown Johannesburg in South Africa

AFRICA

PHYSICAL

LAND AREA
11,608,000 sq mi
(30,065,000 sq km)

HIGHEST POINT
Kilimanjaro,
Tanzania
19,340 ft (5,895 m)

LOWEST POINT
Lake Assal, Djibouti
-512 ft (-156 m)

LONGEST RIVER
Nile
4,241 mi (6,825 km)

LARGEST LAKE
Victoria
26,800 sq mi
(69,500 sq km)

POLITICAL

POPULATION
1,099,579,000

LARGEST COUNTRY
Algeria
919,595 sq mi
(2,381,741 sq km)

LARGEST METROPOLITAN AREA
Lagos, Nigeria
Pop. 11,223,000

MOST DENSELY POPULATED COUNTRY
Mauritius 1,646 people
per sq mi (636 per sq km)

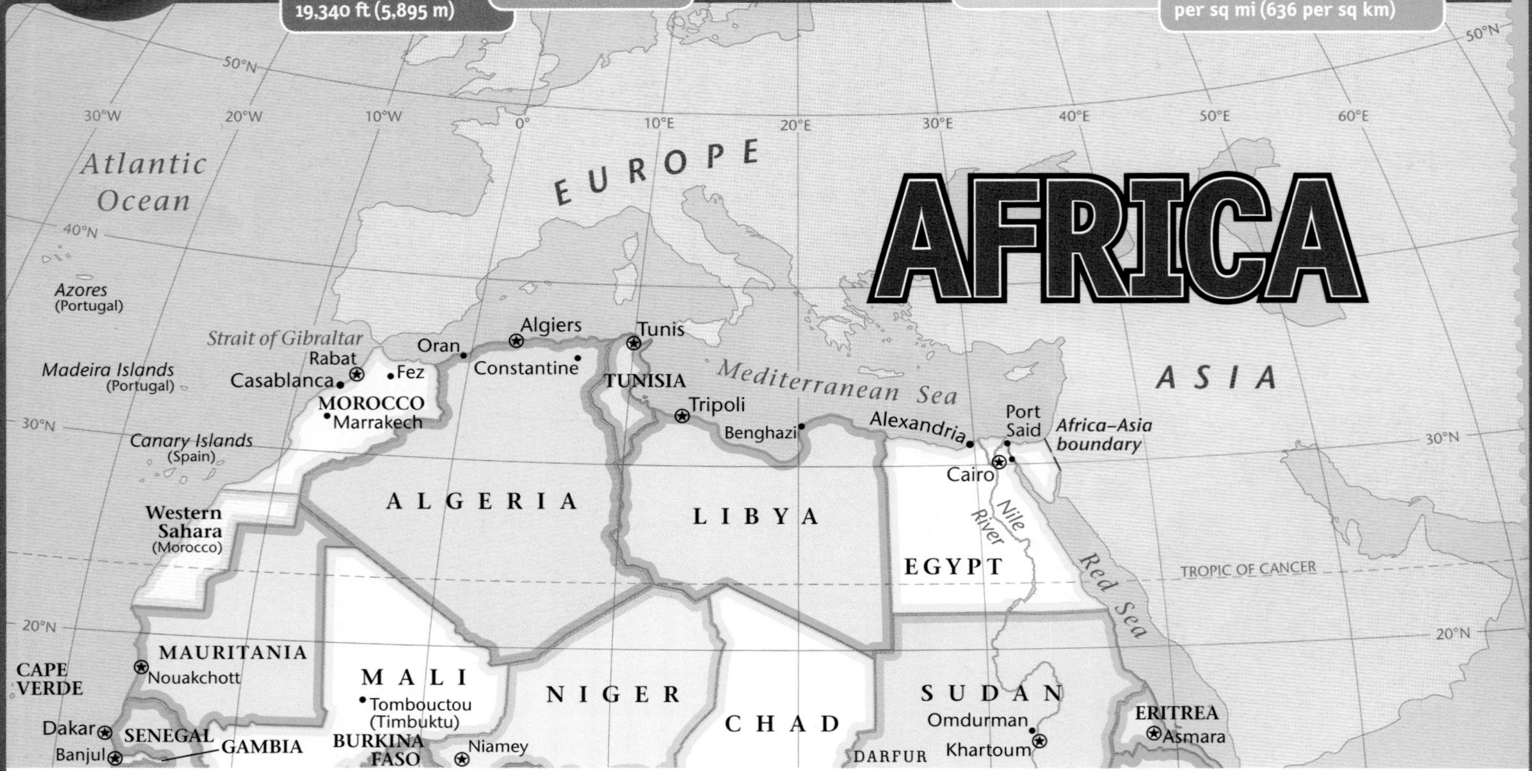

ASIA

EUROPE

Atlantic Ocean

Mediterranean Sea

Red Sea

TROPIC OF CANCER

Africa–Asia boundary

Nile River

Strait of Gibraltar

Azores (Portugal)

Madeira Islands (Portugal)

Canary Islands (Spain)

Algiers
Constantine
Oran
Tunis
TUNISIA
Tripoli
Benghazi
LIBYA

ALGERIA

Rabat
MOROCCO
Casablanca
Fez
Marrakech

Western Sahara (Morocco)

MAURITANIA
Nouakchott

CAPE VERDE
Dakar
SENEGAL
Banjul
GAMBIA

MALI
Tombouctou (Timbuktu)
BURKINA FASO

NIGER
Niamey

CHAD

SUDAN
Omdurman
Khartoum
DARFUR

EGYPT
Cairo
Alexandria
Port Said

ERITREA
Asmara

264

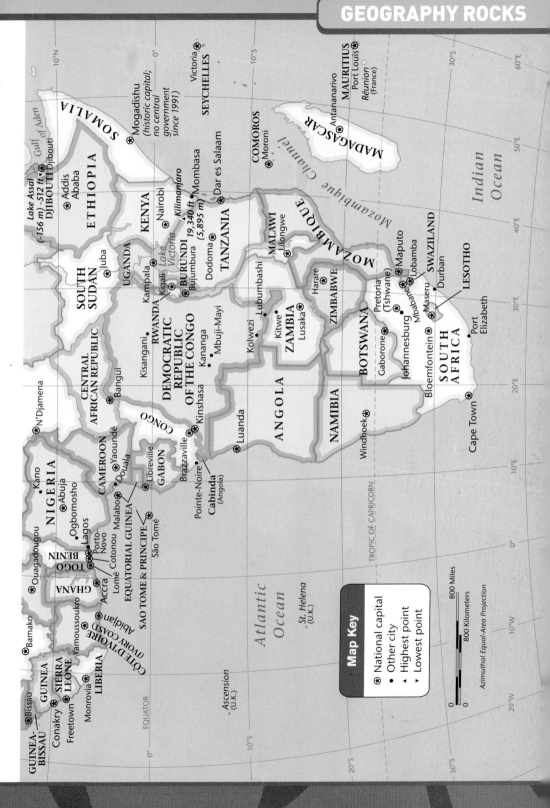

Map Key

⊛ National capital
• Other city
▲ Highest point
▼ Lowest point

800 Miles
800 Kilometers
Azimuthal Equal-Area Projection

MAURITIUS
Port Louis
Réunion (France)

Antananarivo
MADAGASCAR

Indian Ocean

Mozambique Channel

COMOROS
Moroni

SEYCHELLES
Victoria ⊛

SOMALIA
Mogadishu (historic capital; no central government since 1991)

Gulf of Aden
Djibouti
DJIBOUTI
Lake Assal (-156 m) -512 ft ▼

Addis Ababa
ETHIOPIA

Juba
SOUTH SUDAN

UGANDA
Kampala
Nairobi
KENYA
Kilimanjaro 19,340 ft ▲ (5,895 m)
Mombasa

RWANDA
Kigali
BURUNDI
Bujumbura
Lake Victoria

Dar es Salaam
TANZANIA
Dodoma

MALAWI
Lilongwe

Lubumbashi

MOZAMBIQUE

CENTRAL AFRICAN REPUBLIC
Bangui

DEMOCRATIC REPUBLIC OF THE CONGO
Kisangani
Mbuji-Mayi
Kananga
Kinshasa

Kolwezi
Kitwe •
ZAMBIA
Lusaka

Harare
ZIMBABWE

Pretoria (Tshwane)
Mbabane
SWAZILAND
Maputo
Lobamba
Maseru
LESOTHO
Durban

Johannesburg
Bloemfontein
SOUTH AFRICA
Port Elizabeth

BOTSWANA
Gaborone

NAMIBIA
Windhoek ⊛

Cape Town

ANGOLA
Luanda

CONGO
Brazzaville
Pointe-Noire
Cabinda (Angola)

GABON
Libreville

CAMEROON
Yaoundé
Douala
EQUATORIAL GUINEA
Malabo
São Tomé
SAO TOME & PRINCIPE

N'Djamena

NIGERIA
Kano
Abuja
Ogbomosho
Lagos
Porto-Novo
BENIN
TOGO
Cotonou
Lomé

Ouagadougou

GHANA
Accra
Yamoussoukro
CÔTE D'IVOIRE (IVORY COAST)
Abidjan

Bamako
GUINEA
Conakry
SIERRA LEONE
Freetown
Monrovia
LIBERIA
GUINEA-BISSAU
Bissau

Atlantic Ocean

St. Helena (U.K.)

Ascension (U.K.)

TROPIC OF CAPRICORN

EQUATOR

Gulf of Guinea

SPOTLIGHT ON
ANTARCTICA

Elephant seals living along the coast can stay underwater for up to two hours.

Winds in Antarctica can gust to more than 200 miles an hour (322 kph).

Elephant seal

This frozen continent may be a cool place to visit, but unless you're a penguin, you probably wouldn't want to hang out in Antarctica for long. The fact that it's the coldest, windiest, and driest continent helps explain why humans never colonized this ice-covered land surrounding the South Pole.

A seasonal Argentine scientific research station, Almirante Brown is also a popular stop for tourists.

Bare Ground

Just 2 percent of the continent is not covered by ice. In Dry Valleys, a 1,500-square-mile (3,885-sq-km) area of bare land, high winds blast away snow and prevent an ice buildup.

Warm Waters

Deception Island's geothermal pools are a popular spot for the 15,000 tourists who visit Antarctica each year. Activity from an underwater active volcano keeps the waters warm.

Stealth Seals

Native to Antarctica, Weddell seals are the world's southernmost animal. The rarely seen animals spend most of their time below ice, and they breathe through holes in the ice's surface.

Cool Blooms

Yes, flowers do grow on Antarctica! Two species of flowering plants, including the Antarctic pearlwort, grow along the Antarctic Peninsula and on some islands.

Extreme Antarctica

Highest recorded temperature
59°F (15°C), 1974

Lowest recorded temperature
-135.8°F (-93.2°C), 2010

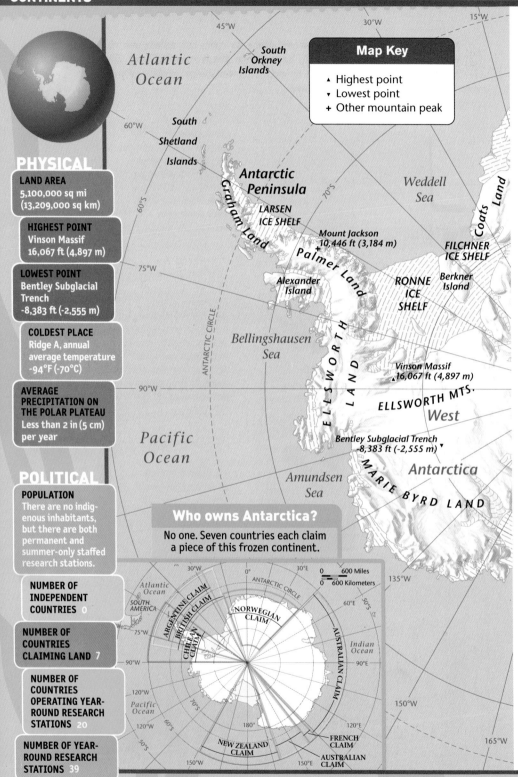

Atlantic
Ocean

South
Orkney
Islands

South
Shetland
Islands

Antarctic
Peninsula

Graham Land

LARSEN
ICE SHELF

Weddell
Sea

Coats Land

Mount Jackson
10,446 ft (3,184 m)

Palmer Land

FILCHNER
ICE SHELF

RONNE
ICE
SHELF

Berkner
Island

Alexander
Island

ANTARCTIC CIRCLE

Bellingshausen
Sea

ELLSWORTH LAND

Vinson Massif
16,067 ft (4,897 m)

ELLSWORTH MTS.

West

Pacific
Ocean

Bentley Subglacial Trench
-8,383 ft (-2,555 m)

Antarctica

Amundsen
Sea

MARIE BYRD LAND

Map Key

▲ Highest point
▼ Lowest point
+ Other mountain peak

PHYSICAL

LAND AREA
5,100,000 sq mi
(13,209,000 sq km)

HIGHEST POINT
Vinson Massif
16,067 ft (4,897 m)

LOWEST POINT
Bentley Subglacial
Trench
-8,383 ft (-2,555 m)

COLDEST PLACE
Ridge A, annual
average temperature
-94°F (-70°C)

**AVERAGE
PRECIPITATION ON
THE POLAR PLATEAU**
Less than 2 in (5 cm)
per year

POLITICAL

POPULATION
There are no indig-
enous inhabitants,
but there are both
permanent and
summer-only staffed
research stations.

**NUMBER OF
INDEPENDENT
COUNTRIES** 0

**NUMBER OF
COUNTRIES
CLAIMING LAND** 7

**NUMBER OF
COUNTRIES
OPERATING YEAR-
ROUND RESEARCH
STATIONS** 20

**NUMBER OF YEAR-
ROUND RESEARCH
STATIONS** 39

Who owns Antarctica?

No one. Seven countries each claim
a piece of this frozen continent.

Atlantic
Ocean

SOUTH
AMERICA

ARGENTINE CLAIM

BRITISH CLAIM

CHILEAN CLAIM

NORWEGIAN
CLAIM

ANTARCTIC CIRCLE

AUSTRALIAN CLAIM

Indian
Ocean

Pacific
Ocean

NEW ZEALAND
CLAIM

FRENCH
CLAIM

AUSTRALIAN
CLAIM

0   600 Miles
0   600 Kilometers

ANTARCTICA

FIMBUL
ICE SHELF

RIISER-LARSEN
ICE SHELF

Q U E E N   M A U D   L A N D

ENDERBY
LAND

Indian
Ocean

Valkyrie
Dome

MacKenzie Bay

Lambert
Glacier

AMERY ICE SHELF

AMERICAN

HIGHLAND

Ridge A

WEST
ICE SHELF

T R A N S A N T A R C T I C   M O U N T A I N S

POLAR PLATEAU

East

South Pole

Antarctica

SHACKLETON
ICE SHELF

80°S

ROSS
ICE
SHELF

Roosevelt
Island

Taylor
Glacier

Ross Island

Mount Erebus
12,448 ft
(3,794 m)

Ross
Sea

VICTORIA LAND

70°S

W I L K E S   L A N D

Talos
Dome

120°E

60°S

Indian
Ocean

South
Magnetic
Pole (2013)

180°

0   600 Miles

0   600 Kilometers

Azimuthal Equidistant Projection

150°E

135°E

0°   15°E   30°E   45°E   60°E   75°E   90°E   105°E

SPOTLIGHT ON
ASIA

Shwedagon Pagoda in Yangon (Rangoon), Myanmar (Burma)

The Shwedagon Pagoda (right) is topped with 5,448 diamonds and 2,317 rubies, sapphires, and other gems.

Archery is the national sport of Bhutan, a country in southern Asia.

270

Made up of 46 countries, Asia is the world's largest continent. And just how big is it? From western Turkey to the eastern tip of Russia, Asia spans nearly half the globe! Home to four billion citizens—that's three out of five people on the planet—Asia's population is bigger than that of all the other continents combined.

Kuala Lumpur, Malaysia

Rare Breed

Native to Indonesia, Southeast Asia, and Malaysia, the rare binturong—or bear cat—has a cat's face, a bear's body, and a tail that's as long as its body.

Popular Passage

Each year about 70,000 merchant ships cross the Strait of Malacca between Malaysia and Indonesia. The most direct route between India and China, this channel serves as an important shipping lane.

Go Bananas

Bananas have grown in Southeast Asia for over 7,000 years. Today, the Philippines is one of the world's largest exporters of the fruit.

On the Move

About a third of the population of Mongolia moves seasonally, living in portable huts called ger while traveling up to 70 miles (112 km) on foot to find food sources for their livestock.

Asia's Tallest Buildings

Burj Khalifa	Makkah Clock Royal Tower	Taipei 101	Shanghai World Financial Center	International Commerce Centre
Dubai, U.A.E. 2,717 feet (828 m)	Mecca, Saudi Arabia 1,972 feet (601 m)	Taiwan 1,667 feet (508 m)	Shanghai, China 1,614 feet (492 m)	Hong Kong, China 1,588 feet (484 m)

Komodo dragon in Indonesia

ASIA

PHYSICAL

LAND AREA
17,208,000 sq mi
(44,570,000 sq km)

HIGHEST POINT
Mount Everest,
China–Nepal
29,035 ft (8,850 m)

LOWEST POINT
Dead Sea,
Israel–Jordan
-1,385 ft (-422 m)

COLDEST PLACE
Yangtze, China
3,880 mi (6,244 km)

**LARGEST LAKE
ENTIRELY IN ASIA**
Lake Baikal, Russia
12,200 sq mi
(31,500 sq km)

POLITICAL

POPULATION
4,302,088,000

**LARGEST
METROPOLITAN AREA**
Tokyo, Japan
Pop. 37,217,000

**LARGEST COUNTRY
ENTIRELY IN ASIA**
China
3,705,405 sq mi
(9,596,960 sq km)

**MOST DENSELY
POPULATED COUNTRY**
Singapore
21,349 people
per sq mi
(8,248 per sq km)

Map labels

EUROPE

Europe
Asia

Yekaterinburg
Nizhniy Tagil
Magnitogorsk
Tyumen'
Chelyabinsk
Omsk

Dardanelles
Bosporus
İzmir
TURKEY
Ankara
ARMENIA
GEORGIA
Tbilisi
Yerevan
Baku
TURKMENISTAN
Astana
Qaraghandy
KAZAKHSTAN
Mediterranean Sea

LEBANON
Beirut
Jerusalem
Damascus
SYRIA
Amman
ISRAEL
Dead Sea
-1,385 ft
(-422 m)
JORDAN
AZERBAIJAN
Baghdad
Ashgabat
UZBEKISTAN
Tashkent
Bishkek
Almaty
KYRGYZSTAN
Samarqand
Dushanbe
TAJIKISTAN
IRAQ
Basra
Tehran
Mashhad
AFGHANISTAN
Hotan
Medina
KUWAIT
Kuwait City
IRAN
Kabul
Islamabad
Rawalpindi
Lahore
Jeddah
SAUDI ARABIA
Manama
Mecca
Riyadh
Doha
BAHRAIN
QATAR
Dubai
Abu Dhabi
Muscat
PAKISTAN
Faisalabad
Delhi
New Delhi
NEPAL
Jaipur
Sanaa
OMAN
Karachi
Kanpur
Indore
Bhopal
Aden
YEMEN
UNITED ARAB
EMIRATES
Surat
Mumbai
(Bombay)
INDIA
Pune

AFRICA

Arabian
Sea
Hyderabad

EQUATOR

Bangalore
(Bengaluru)
Chennai
(Madras)

SRI
LANKA
Colombo
Sri Jayewardenepura Kotte
Male
MALDIVES

0   800 Miles
0   800 Kilometers
Two-point Equidistant Projection

Indian Ocean

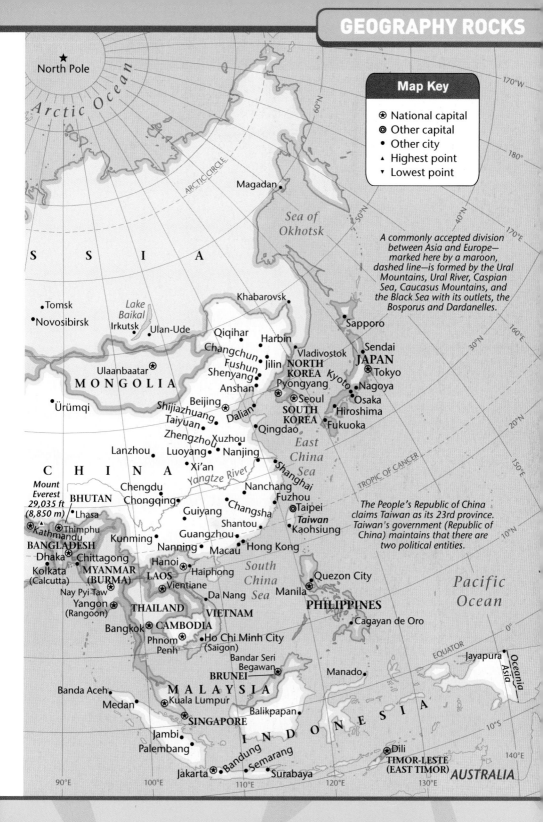

★ North Pole

Map Key

⊛ National capital
◎ Other capital
• Other city
▲ Highest point
▼ Lowest point

Arctic Ocean

ARCTIC CIRCLE

170°W

180°

R U S S I A

Magadan

Sea of Okhotsk

A commonly accepted division between Asia and Europe—marked here by a maroon, dashed line—is formed by the Ural Mountains, Ural River, Caspian Sea, Caucasus Mountains, and the Black Sea with its outlets, the Bosporus and Dardanelles.

170°E

•Tomsk
•Novosibirsk

Lake Baikal
Irkutsk•
•Ulan-Ude

Khabarovsk•

Sapporo•

Qiqihar• Harbin•
Changchun• •Vladivostok
Fushun• Jilin• **NORTH KOREA**
Shenyang• Pyongyang⊛
Anshan• •Seoul

Sendai•
JAPAN
Kyoto• •Tokyo
Nagoya•

Ulaanbaatar⊛

M O N G O L I A

•Ürümqi

Beijing⊛
Shijiazhuang• •Dalian
Taiyuan• **SOUTH KOREA**
Zhengzhou• Xuzhou• •Qingdao
Lanzhou• Luoyang• •Nanjing
•Xi'an
Yangtze River Shanghai•

Osaka•
Hiroshima•
•Fukuoka

160°E

50°N
40°N
30°N
20°N

East China Sea

C H I N A

Mount Everest 29,035 ft (8,850 m)
BHUTAN
•Lhasa
⊛Kathmandu ⊛Thimphu
BANGLADESH
•Dhaka •Chittagong
Kolkata (Calcutta)• **MYANMAR (BURMA)**
Nay Pyi Taw• **LAOS**
Yangon (Rangoon)• ⊛Vientiane
THAILAND
Bangkok⊛ **CAMBODIA**
Phnom Penh⊛ •Ho Chi Minh City (Saigon)

Chengdu•
Chongqing• •Changsha
Guiyang• Nanchang•
Kunming• Shantou•
Guangzhou•
Nanning• •Macau •Hong Kong
Hanoi⊛
•Haiphong
Da Nang•

Fuzhou•
◎Taipei
Taiwan
Kaohsiung•

TROPIC OF CANCER

150°E

The People's Republic of China claims Taiwan as its 23rd province. Taiwan's government (Republic of China) maintains that there are two political entities.

10°N

South China Sea

Manila⊛ ◎Quezon City

PHILIPPINES

Pacific Ocean

•Cagayan de Oro

VIETNAM

Bandar Seri Begawan⊛
BRUNEI
M A L A Y S I A
•Kuala Lumpur
⊛**SINGAPORE**

Manado•

EQUATOR

Oceania
Asia
Jayapura•

0°

Banda Aceh•
Medan•

Jambi•
Palembang•

Balikpapan•

I N D O N E S I A

10°S

Jakarta⊛ Bandung• •Semarang
•Surabaya

⊛Dili
TIMOR-LESTE (EAST TIMOR) *AUSTRALIA*

90°E 100°E 110°E 120°E 130°E 140°E

SPOTLIGHT ON
AUSTRALIA,
NEW ZEALAND, AND OCEANIA

More kangaroos than people live in Australia.

In Papua New Guinea, sunken ships from World War II are popular attractions for scuba divers.

Ifalik Island in Papua New Guinea

G'day, mate! This vast region, covering almost 3.3 million square miles (8.5 million sq km), includes Australia—the world's smallest and flattest continent—and New Zealand, as well as a fleet of mostly tiny islands scattered across the Pacific Ocean. Also known as "down under," all of the countries in this region are in the Southern Hemisphere, and below the Equator.

Aborigine children in ceremonial dress

Sporty Citizens

There's no doubt Australians are athletic: 70 percent of people over age 15 participate in sports more than once a week. Rugby, football, and cricket are fan favorites.

Don't Look Down!

Auckland, New Zealand's SkyJump offers daring visitors a wild ride. You can bungee jump off a 630-foot (192-m) -high platform on New Zealand's tallest man-made structure.

Cow Country

Australia, a top cattle producer, is home to about 29 million cows. Anna Creek Cattle Station in South Australia is the world's largest cattle ranch. It's slightly larger than Israel!

Giant Reef

The Great Barrier Reef, found off the east coast of Australia, is big enough to be seen from space. It's teeming with sea life, like whales, dolphins, sea turtles, snakes, coral, and fish.

Australia: Continent or Island?

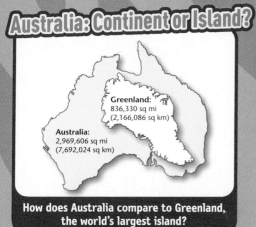

Greenland:
836,330 sq mi
(2,166,086 sq km)

Australia:
2,969,606 sq mi
(7,692,024 sq km)

How does Australia compare to Greenland, the world's largest island?

Numbat

275

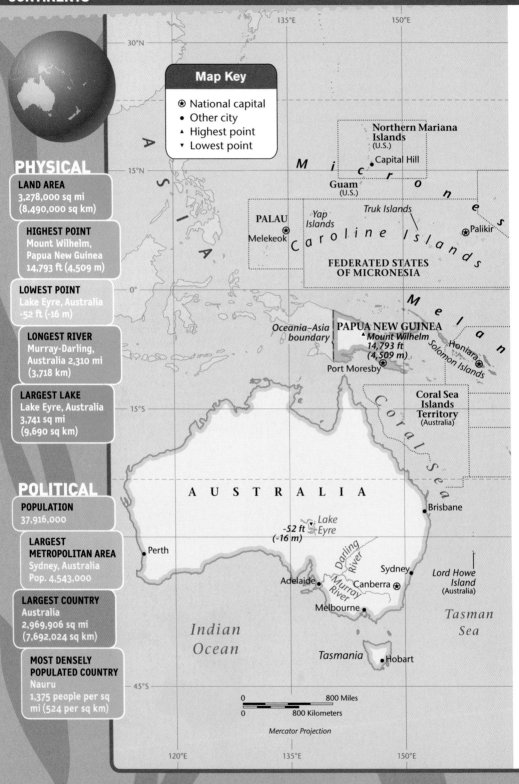

PHYSICAL

LAND AREA
3,278,000 sq mi
(8,490,000 sq km)

HIGHEST POINT
Mount Wilhelm,
Papua New Guinea
14,793 ft (4,509 m)

LOWEST POINT
Lake Eyre, Australia
-52 ft (-16 m)

LONGEST RIVER
Murray-Darling,
Australia 2,310 mi
(3,718 km)

LARGEST LAKE
Lake Eyre, Australia
3,741 sq mi
(9,690 sq km)

POLITICAL

POPULATION
37,916,000

**LARGEST
METROPOLITAN AREA**
Sydney, Australia
Pop. 4,543,000

LARGEST COUNTRY
Australia
2,969,906 sq mi
(7,692,024 sq km)

**MOST DENSELY
POPULATED COUNTRY**
Nauru
1,375 people per sq
mi (524 per sq km)

Map Key

⊛ National capital
• Other city
▲ Highest point
▼ Lowest point

Northern Mariana
Islands
(U.S.)
⊛ Capital Hill

Guam
(U.S.)

PALAU
Melekeok

Yap
Islands
Truk Islands

Caroline Islands
⊛ Palikir

FEDERATED STATES
OF MICRONESIA

Oceania–Asia
boundary

PAPUA NEW GUINEA
▲ Mount Wilhelm
14,793 ft
(4,509 m)
Port Moresby

Honiara ⊛
Solomon Islands

Coral Sea
Islands
Territory
(Australia)

Coral Sea

AUSTRALIA

Brisbane

▼ Lake
-52 ft   Eyre
(-16 m)

Darling River

Murray River

Perth

Adelaide
Canberra ⊛
Sydney

Lord Howe
Island
(Australia)

Melbourne

Indian
Ocean

Tasman
Sea

Tasmania
• Hobart

0   800 Miles
0   800 Kilometers

Mercator Projection

276

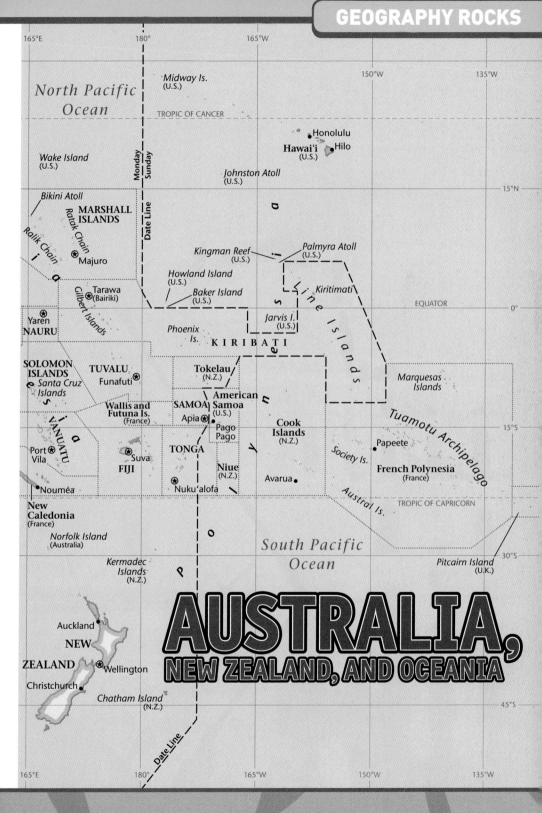

165°E   180°   165°W   150°W   135°W

North Pacific Ocean

Midway Is. (U.S.)

TROPIC OF CANCER

Honolulu
Hawai'i Hilo
(U.S.)

Wake Island (U.S.)

Monday / Sunday

Johnston Atoll (U.S.)

15°N

Bikini Atoll

MARSHALL ISLANDS

Ratak Chain

Date Line

Kingman Reef (U.S.)

Palmyra Atoll (U.S.)

Ralik Chain

Majuro

Gilbert Islands

Howland Island (U.S.)

Line Islands

Kiritimati

Tarawa (Bairiki)

Baker Island (U.S.)

EQUATOR   0°

Yaren
NAURU

Phoenix Is.

Jarvis I. (U.S.)

KIRIBATI

SOLOMON ISLANDS
Santa Cruz Islands

TUVALU
Funafuti

Tokelau (N.Z.)

Marquesas Islands

15°S

VANUATU

Wallis and Futuna Is. (France)

SAMOA
Apia

American Samoa (U.S.)
Pago Pago

Tuamotu Archipelago

Port Vila

Suva
FIJI

TONGA

Niue (N.Z.)

Cook Islands (N.Z.)

Society Is.

Papeete

French Polynesia (France)

Nouméa

Nuku'alofa

Avarua

Austral Is.

TROPIC OF CAPRICORN

New Caledonia (France)

Norfolk Island (Australia)

South Pacific Ocean

Pitcairn Island (U.K.)

30°S

Kermadec Islands (N.Z.)

AUSTRALIA, NEW ZEALAND, AND OCEANIA

Auckland

NEW ZEALAND

Wellington

Christchurch

Chatham Island (N.Z.)

45°S

Date Line

165°E   180°   165°W   150°W   135°W

SPOTLIGHT ON
EUROPE

The Louvre first opened as a museum during the French Revolution in 1793.

The Rubik's Cube was invented in Hungary, a country in Europe.

Louvre Museum in Paris, France

A cluster of islands and peninsulas jutting west from Asia, Europe is bordered by the Atlantic and Arctic Oceans and more than a dozen seas. Here you'll find a variety of scenery, from mountains to countryside to coastlines. Europe is also known for its rich culture and fascinating history, which make it one of the most-visited continents on the planet.

Bagpiper in Scotland, U.K.

Name Game

The origin of Europe's name is often attributed to Europa, a princess in Greek mythology. It may also be based on the Greek, Phoenician, or Semitic words describing the land to the west.

Europa on euro coin

Spot On

Dalmatians get their name from Dalmatia, a region of Croatia along the Adriatic Sea. The spotted canines have served as border guard dogs during conflicts in the region.

Rock Monkeys

Macaques are the only nonhuman primates found in Europe. They have been living on Gibraltar, a narrow peninsula at the southern edge of Spain, for centuries.

Great Big Sea

About the same size as Japan, the Caspian Sea is the world's biggest body of water that's surrounded by land. It's home to sturgeon, endangered fish whose eggs (roe) are used to make caviar.

Europe's 6 Most Visited Cities*

1. **London, England**
   15.96 million visitors

2. **Paris, France**
   13.92 million visitors

3. **Istanbul, Turkey**
   10.37 million visitors

4. **Barcelona, Spain**
   8.41 million visitors

5. **Milan, Italy**
   6.83 million visitors

6. **Rome, Italy**
   6.71 million visitors

*2013

Brandenburg Gate in Berlin, Germany

PHYSICAL

LAND AREA
3,841,000 sq mi
(9,947,000 sq km)

HIGHEST POINT
El'brus, Russia
18,510 ft (5,642 m)

LOWEST POINT
Caspian Sea
-92 ft (-28 m)

LONGEST RIVER
Volga, Russia
2,290 mi
(3,685 km)

**LARGEST LAKE
ENTIRELY IN EUROPE**
Ladoga, Russia
6,900 sq mi
(17,872 sq km)

POLITICAL

POPULATION
739,517,000

**LARGEST
METROPOLITAN AREA**
Moscow, Russia
Pop. 11,621,000

**LARGEST COUNTRY
ENTIRELY IN EUROPE**
Ukraine
233,090 sq mi
(603,700 sq km)

**MOST DENSELY
POPULATED COUNTRY**
Monaco
46,250 people per sq
mi (18,500 per sq km)

Map Key

⊛ National capital
• Other city
▫ Small country
▲ Highest point
▾ Lowest point

Jan Mayen
(Norway)

30°W 20°W 10°W 0°

Reykjavík
ICELAND

Norwegian Sea

ARCTIC CIRCLE

60°N

Faroe Islands
(Denmark)

Shetland
Islands

Orkney Islands

Oslo

SCOTLAND

Göteborg

N. IRELAND Glasgow
Edinburgh

North Sea

IRELAND Belfast

DENMARK

Dublin **UNITED KINGDOM**
Copenhagen

Liverpool Manchester
WALES Birmingham Kiel

50°N

Cardiff ENGLAND Hamburg

*Atlantic
Ocean* The **NETH.**
Hague Amsterdam Berlin

London

Brussels **GERMANY**

BELGIUM Frankfurt

Paris **LUX.** Prague

Nantes Munich
LIECH.

F R A N C E Zürich

*Bay of
Biscay* Bern **SWITZ.** **AUSTRIA**

Bordeaux Lyon Ljubljana
Milan **SLOV.**

40°N Turin Venice

Oporto Bilbao Toulouse Genoa
Valladolid **MONACO** **SAN
MARINO**

ANDORRA Nice
Madrid Zaragoza Marseille **ITALY**

Lisbon Corsica **VATICAN**
S P A I N Barcelona (France) **CITY** Rome

10°W Valencia *Sardinia*
(Italy) Naples

Seville Murcia *Balearic Is.*
(Spain)

Málaga *M e d i t e r r a*
Gibraltar (U.K.)

Messina
Palermo
Catania

0 400 Miles Sicily

0 400 Kilometers Valletta
A F R I C A **MALTA**

Azimuthal Equidistant Projection

0° 10°E

EUROPE

10°E 20°E 30°E 40°E 50°E 60°E 70°E

Barents Sea

•Murmansk

Asia
Europe

60°N

A S I A

•Arkhangel'sk

R U S S I A

N O R W A Y

S W E D E N

F I N L A N D

Lake Ladoga

⊕Helsinki

•St. Petersburg

•Stockholm
•Tallinn
ESTONIA

•Yaroslavl'

Volga River •Kazan'

•Ufa

•Tver'
⊕Moscow

•Nizhniy Novgorod

•Samara •Orenburg

Baltic Sea

Riga•
LATVIA

•Ryazan'

50°N

LITHUANIA
•Vitsyebsk
⊕Vilnius

•Smolensk

•Penza

•Saratov

KAZAKHSTAN

Kaliningrad
(Russia)

Gdańsk•
Kaunas•
⊕Minsk

•Bryansk

POLAND
⊕Warsaw
BELARUS
Homyel'•

•Kursk

Bydgoszcz•
•Łódź
•Wrocław •Kraków

⊕Kiev
Poltava•
L'viv• U K R A I N E
Vinnytsya

•Kharkiv

•Volgograd

•Astrakhan'

Donets'k•

CZECH REP.
(CZECHIA)

Vienna•
⊕ SLOVAKIA
⊕Bratislava
MOLDOVA
⊕Chişinău

•Dnipropetrovs'k
•Rostov

-92 ft
(-28 m)

⊕Budapest

Caspian Sea

HUNGARY
•Zagreb
CROATIA
ROMANIA
•Odesa
Simferopol'•

El'brus
(5,642 m) 18,510 ft •Groznyy

⊕Baku

BOSNIA &
HERZEGOVINA
•Belgrade Bucharest⊕
Sevastopol'•

•Sochi
GEORGIA

AZERBAIJAN

Sarajevo•
SERBIA
Black Sea

40°N

MONTENEGRO
KOSOVO
⊕Prishtina
•Varna

Podgorica•
⊕ BULGARIA
⊕Sofia

Tirana•⊕
⊕Skopje
MACED.
Bosporus

ALBANIA
•Thessaloníki
⊕Istanbul

T U R K E Y

Dardanelles

GREECE

⊕Athens

A commonly accepted division
between Asia and Europe—
marked here by a maroon,
dashed line—is formed by the
Ural Mountains, Ural River, Caspian
Sea, Caucasus Mountains, and
the Black Sea with its outlets, the
Bosporus and Dardanelles.

Sea

Crete
Nicosia⊕
CYPRUS

20°E 30°E 40°E

SPOTLIGHT ON
NORTH AMERICA

In the summer, the amount of water pouring over Niagara Falls each second could fill 13,000 bathtubs.

North America is home to only one marsupial, the opossum, which is active at night.

A nightly light show at Niagara Falls—on the border of Ontario, Canada, and New York, U.S.A.

From the Great Plains of the United States and Canada to the rain forests of Panama, North America stretches 5,500 miles (8,850 km) from north to south. The third largest continent, North America can be divided into five regions: the mountainous west (including parts of Mexico and Central America's western coast), the Great Plains, the Canadian Shield, the varied eastern region (including Central America's lowlands and coastal plains), and the Caribbean.

Mexican children perform mariachi music.

Coast to Coast

North America's 150,000-mile (241,402-km) coastline is the longest of any continent's. Canada alone claims 15 percent of the world's coastline—the most of any country.

Early Animals

Even though camels are associated with the Middle East, they actually originated in North America 45 million years ago. Dogs and horses also evolved on the continent.

Colossal Crystals

Mexico's Cave of Crystals contains some of the world's largest known natural crystals. They measure as long as 37.4 feet (11.4 m). That's almost as long as a school bus!

All Kinds of Climates

North America features all climate types, from the frozen tundra of Canada's Yukon Territory to the temperate rain forest of the Pacific Northwest coast to the Baja California desert.

5 Most Visited National Parks*

1. Great Smoky Mountains, U.S.A. 9,685,829
2. Grand Canyon, U.S.A. 4,421,352
3. Yosemite, U.S.A. 3,853,404
4. Yellowstone, U.S.A. 3,447,729
5. Banff, Canada 3,306,203**

Monarch butterfly

*2012 (National Park Service); **2012–2013 (Parks Canada)

EUROPE

ASIA

POLITICAL

POPULATION
556,558,000

LARGEST COUNTRY
Canada
3,855,103 sq mi
(9,984,670 sq km)

LARGEST METROPOLITAN AREA
Mexico City, Mexico
Pop. 20,446,000

MOST DENSELY POPULATED COUNTRY
Barbados / 1,524 people
per sq mi (588 per sq km)

PHYSICAL

LAND AREA
9,449,000 sq mi
(24,474,000 sq km)

HIGHEST POINT
Mount McKinley, Alaska
20,320 ft (6,194 m)

LOWEST POINT
Death Valley, California
-282 ft (-86 m)

LONGEST RIVER
Mississippi–Missouri,
United States
3,710 mi (5,970 km)

LARGEST LAKE
Lake Superior,
U.S.–Canada
31,700 sq mi
(82,100 sq km)

Map Key
⊛ National capital
• Other city
▲ Highest point
▼ Lowest point

Greenland
(Denmark)

CANADA

Montréal

Thunder Bay

Winnipeg

Edmonton

Calgary

Seattle

Vancouver

Victoria

Arctic Ocean

North Pole

ARCTIC CIRCLE

80°N

60°N

40°N

0°

20°W

40°W

40°N

180°

160°W

Alaska
(U.S.)

Anchorage

Mount McKinley
(6,194 m) 20,320 ft ▲

800 Miles
800 Kilometers

Azimuthal Equidistant Projection

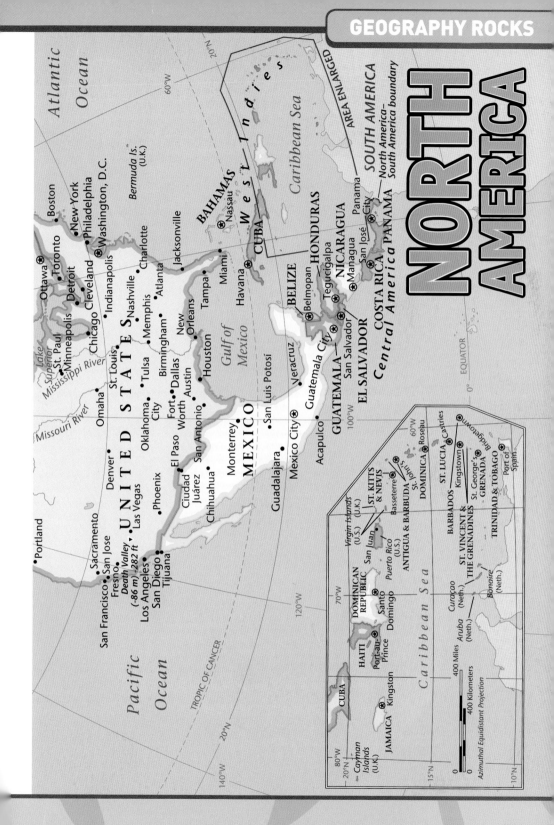

NORTH AMERICA

Atlantic Ocean

Pacific Ocean

Caribbean Sea

Gulf of Mexico

West Indies

SOUTH AMERICA

North America–
South America boundary

AREA ENLARGED

UNITED STATES

MEXICO

Central America

BAHAMAS

CUBA

BELIZE
GUATEMALA
EL SALVADOR
HONDURAS
NICARAGUA
COSTA RICA
PANAMA

Portland
San Francisco
San Jose
Fresno
Sacramento
Denver
Las Vegas
Phoenix
Los Angeles
San Diego
Tijuana
Death Valley (–86 m) –282 ft ▼
El Paso
Ciudad Juárez
Chihuahua
Monterrey
Guadalajara
Mexico City
Acapulco
San Luis Potosí
Omaha
Oklahoma City
Tulsa
Fort Worth
Dallas
Austin
San Antonio
Houston
New Orleans
Memphis
Birmingham
Nashville
St. Louis
Chicago
Minneapolis
St. Paul
Detroit
Cleveland
Indianapolis
Atlanta
Charlotte
Jacksonville
Tampa
Miami
Boston
New York
Philadelphia
Washington, D.C.
Ottawa
Toronto
Portland
Veracruz
Guatemala City
San Salvador
Belmopan
Tegucigalpa
Managua
San José
Panama City
Havana
Nassau
Lake Superior
Mississippi River
Missouri River

Bermuda Is. (U.K.)

Caribbean Sea

TROPIC OF CANCER

EQUATOR

CUBA
JAMAICA Kingston
Cayman Islands (U.K.)
HAITI
Port-au-Prince
DOMINICAN REPUBLIC
Santo Domingo
Puerto Rico (U.S.)
San Juan
Virgin Islands (U.S.)
ST. KITTS & NEVIS
Basseterre
ANTIGUA & BARBUDA
St. John's
DOMINICA
Roseau
ST. LUCIA Castries
BARBADOS
Bridgetown
ST. VINCENT & THE GRENADINES
Kingstown
GRENADA
St. George's
TRINIDAD & TOBAGO
Port of Spain
Curaçao (Neth.)
Aruba (Neth.)
Bonaire (Neth.)

400 Miles
400 Kilometers
0
0
Azimuthal Equidistant Projection

20°N
60°W
80°W
70°W
120°W
140°W
20°N
100°W
0°
60°W
15°N
10°N

285

SPOTLIGHT ON
SOUTH AMERICA

A sloth would take a month to travel a single mile (1.6 km).

About two-thirds of the world's emeralds come from Colombia, South America.

A southern two-toed sloth hangs from a branch in Brazil's Amazon rain forest.

South America is bordered by three major bodies of water—the Caribbean Sea, Atlantic Ocean, and Pacific Ocean. The world's fourth largest continent extends over a range of climates from tropical in the north to subarctic in the south. South America produces a rich diversity of natural resources, including nuts, fruits, sugar, grains, coffee, and chocolate.

A boy celebrates Carnival in Rio de Janeiro, Brazil

Up in the Air

Brazil, which makes up half of South America in area, is an airline industry leader. São Paulo–based company Embraer designs and builds commercial airplanes flown all around the world.

No Bones About It

In Peru, scientists discovered the remains of a megalodon, a 60-foot (18-m)-long whale-eating prehistoric shark. Another team unearthed 41-million-year-old rodent fossils.

Big Bird

The Andean condor, which lives exclusively in the mountains and valleys of the Andes, is the largest raptor in the world and the largest flying bird in South America.

Awesome Eruptions

There are several active volcanoes in South America. Tungurahua in Ecuador recently erupted with ash plumes as tall as 45,000 feet (13,716 m). They were spotted over 80 miles (129 km) away.

World's Tallest Waterfalls

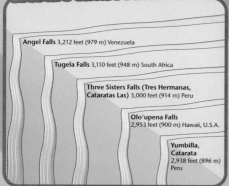

Angel Falls 3,212 feet (979 m) Venezuela

Tugela Falls 3,110 feet (948 m) South Africa

Three Sisters Falls (Tres Hermanas, Cataratas Las) 3,000 feet (914 m) Peru

Olo'upena Falls 2,953 feet (900 m) Hawaii, U.S.A.

Yumbilla, Catarata 2,938 feet (896 m) Peru

Casa Rosada in Buenos Aires, Argentina

PHYSICAL

LAND AREA
6,880,000 sq mi
(17,819,000 sq km)

HIGHEST POINT
Cerro Aconcagua,
Argentina
22,831 ft (6,959 m)

LOWEST POINT
Laguna del Carbón,
Argentina
-344 ft (-105 m)

LONGEST RIVER
Amazon
4,150 mi (6,679 km)

LARGEST LAKE
Lake Maracaibo,
Venezuela;
5,127 sq mi
(13,280 sq km)

POLITICAL

POPULATION
401,139,000

LARGEST COUNTRY
Brazil
3,287,612 sq mi
(8,514,877 sq km)

LARGEST METROPOLITAN AREA
São Paulo, Brazil
Pop. 19,924,000

MOST DENSELY POPULATED COUNTRY
Ecuador / 144 people per
sq mi (56 per sq km)

Map Key
⊛ National capital
• Other city
▲ Highest point
▼ Lowest point

Central
America

Caribbean
Sea

South America–
North America
boundary

Barranquilla

Maracaibo

Lake
Maracaibo

VENEZUELA

Caracas

Valencia

Barquisimeto

Medellín

⊛ Bogotá

COLOMBIA

Cali

⊛ Quito

ECUADOR

Guayaquil

Trujillo

Lima ⊛

P E R U

Cusco

B O L I V I A

Georgetown ⊛

GUYANA

Paramaribo ⊛

SURINAME

Cayenne
French Guiana
(France)

Manaus

Amazon River

B R A Z I L

Belém

Fortaleza

Natal

Recife

Salvador
(Bahia)

⊛ Brasília

EQUATOR

EQUATOR

10°N

0°

10°S

0°

10°S

40°W

50°W

60°W

70°W

80°W

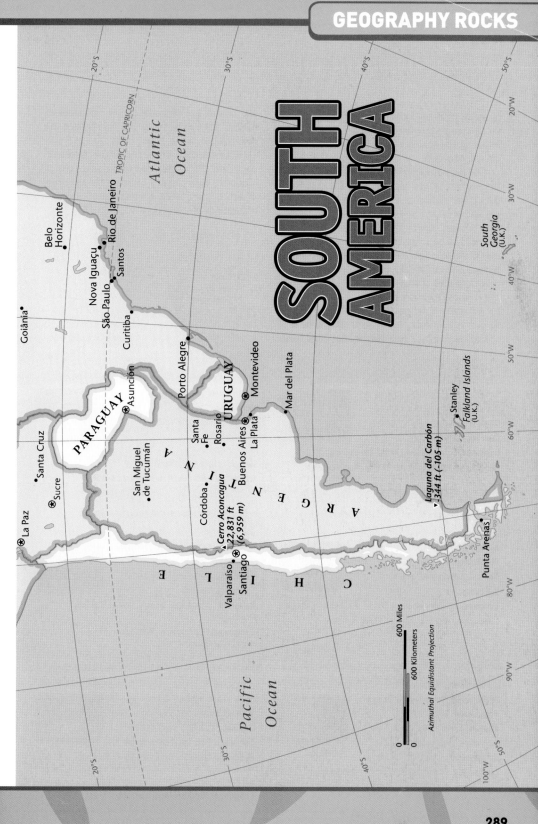

SOUTH AMERICA

Atlantic Ocean

Pacific Ocean

TROPIC OF CAPRICORN

20°S
30°S
40°S
50°S

20°W
30°W
40°W
50°W
60°W
70°W
80°W
90°W
100°W

Belo Horizonte
Rio de Janeiro
Nova Iguaçu
Santos
Goiânia
São Paulo
Curitiba
Porto Alegre

PARAGUAY
Asunción
Santa Cruz
Sucre
La Paz

URUGUAY
Montevideo
Mar del Plata
Santa Fe
Rosario
Buenos Aires
La Plata

San Miguel de Tucumán
Córdoba
Cerro Aconcagua
22,831 ft
(6,959 m)
Valparaíso
Santiago

A R G E N T I N A

C H I L E

Laguna del Carbón
-344 ft (-105 m)

Punta Arenas

Stanley
Falkland Islands
(U.K.)

South Georgia
(U.K.)

600 Miles
600 Kilometers
0
0
Azimuthal Equidistant Projection

COUNTRIES OF THE WORLD

The following pages present a general overview of all 195 independent countries recognized by the National Geographic Society, including the newest nation, South Sudan, which gained independence in 2011.

The flags of each independent country symbolize diverse cultures and histories. The statistical data cover highlights of geography and demography and provide a brief overview of each country. They present general characteristics and are not intended to be comprehensive. For example, not every language spoken in a specific country can be listed. Thus, languages shown are the most representative of that area. This is also true of the religions mentioned.

A country is defined as a political body with its own independent government, geographical space, and, in most cases, laws, military, and taxes.

Disputed areas such as Northern Cyprus and Taiwan, and dependencies of independent nations, such as Bermuda and Puerto Rico, are not included in this listing.

Note the color key at the bottom of the pages and the locator map below, which assign a color to each country based on the continent on which it is located. All information is accurate as of press time.

Color Key by Continent

Afghanistan

Area: 251,773 sq mi (652,090 sq km)
Population: 30,552,000
Capital: Kabul, pop. 3,097,000
Currency: afghani
Religions: Sunni Muslim, Shiite Muslim
Languages: Afghan Persian (Dari), Pashto, Turkic languages (primarily Uzbek and Turkmen), Baluchi, 30 minor languages (including Pashai)

Albania

Area: 11,100 sq mi (28,748 sq km)
Population: 2,774,000
Capital: Tirana, pop. 419,000
Currency: lek
Religions: Muslim, Albanian Orthodox, Roman Catholic
Languages: Albanian, Greek, Vlach, Romani, Slavic dialects

Algeria

Area: 919,595 sq mi (2,381,741 sq km)
Population: 38,290,000
Capital: Algiers, pop. 2,916,000
Currency: Algerian dinar
Religion: Sunni Muslim
Languages: Arabic, French, Berber dialects

Andorra

Area: 181 sq mi (469 sq km)
Population: 74,000
Capital: Andorra la Vella, pop. 23,000
Currency: euro
Religion: Roman Catholic
Languages: Catalan, French, Castilian, Portuguese

Angola

Area: 481,354 sq mi (1,246,700 sq km)
Population: 21,635,000
Capital: Luanda, pop. 5,068,000
Currency: kwanza
Religions: indigenous beliefs, Roman Catholic, Protestant
Languages: Portuguese, Bantu, and other African languages

Antigua and Barbuda

Area: 171 sq mi (442 sq km)
Population: 88,000
Capital: St. John's, pop. 27,000
Currency: East Caribbean dollar
Religions: Anglican, Seventh-day Adventist, Pentecostal, Moravian, Roman Catholic, Methodist, Baptist, Church of God, other Christian
Languages: English, local dialects

COLOR KEY ● Africa ● Australia, New Zealand, and Oceania

Argentina

Area: 1,073,518 sq mi
(2,780,400 sq km)
Population: 41,267,000
Capital: Buenos Aires,
pop. 13,528,000
Currency: Argentine peso
Religion: Roman Catholic
Languages: Spanish, English, Italian, German, French

Armenia

Area: 11,484 sq mi
(29,743 sq km)
Population: 3,048,000
Capital: Yerevan,
pop. 1,116,000
Currency: dram
Religions: Armenian Apostolic, other Christian
Language: Armenian

Australia

Area: 2,969,906 sq mi
(7,692,024 sq km)
Population: 23,106,000
Capital: Canberra,
pop. 399,000
Currency: Australian dollar
Religions: Roman Catholic, Anglican
Language: English

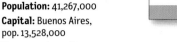

Austria

Area: 32,378 sq mi (83,858 sq km)
Population: 8,511,000
Capital: Vienna, pop. 1,720,000
Currency: euro
Religions: Roman Catholic, Protestant, Muslim
Language: German

Azerbaijan

Area: 33,436 sq mi
(86,600 sq km)
Population: 9,418,000
Capital: Baku, pop. 2,123,000
Currency: Azerbaijani manat
Religion: Muslim
Language: Azerbaijani (Azeri)

Bahamas

Area: 5,382 sq mi
(13,939 sq km)
Population: 350,000
Capital: Nassau, pop. 254,000
Currency: Bahamian dollar
Religions: Baptist, Anglican, Roman Catholic,
Pentecostal, Church of God
Languages: English, Creole

Bahrain

Area: 277 sq mi (717 sq km)
Population: 1,131,000
Capital: Manama, pop. 262,000
Currency: Bahraini dinar
Religions: Shiite Muslim, Sunni Muslim, Christian
Languages: Arabic, English, Farsi, Urdu

Bangladesh

Area: 55,598 sq mi
(143,998 sq km)
Population: 156,595,000
Capital: Dhaka, pop. 15,391,000
Currency: taka
Religions: Muslim, Hindu
Languages: Bangla (Bengali), English

Barbados

Area: 166 sq mi (430 sq km)
Population: 253,000
Capital: Bridgetown, pop. 122,000
Currency: Barbadian dollar
Religions: Anglican, Pentecostal, Methodist, other
Protestant, Roman Catholic
Language: English

Belarus

Area: 80,153 sq mi
(207,595 sq km)
Population: 9,463,000
Capital: Minsk, pop. 1,861,000
Currency: Belarusian ruble
Religions: Eastern Orthodox, other (includes Roman
Catholic, Protestant, Jewish, Muslim)
Languages: Belarusian, Russian

Belgium

Area: 11,787 sq mi (30,528 sq km)
Population: 11,164,000
Capital: Brussels, pop. 1,949,000
Currency: euro
Religions: Roman Catholic, other (includes Protestant)
Languages: Dutch, French

Belize

Area: 8,867 sq mi (22,965 sq km)
Population: 334,000
Capital: Belmopan, pop. 14,000
Currency: Belizean dollar
Religions: Roman Catholic, Protestant (includes Pentecostal, Seventh-day Adventist, Mennonite, Methodist)
Languages: Spanish, Creole, Mayan dialects, English, Garifuna (Carib), German

Benin

Area: 43,484 sq mi (112,622 sq km)
Population: 9,645,000
Capitals: Porto-Novo, pop. 314,000; Cotonou, pop. 924,000
Currency: Communauté Financière Africaine franc
Religions: Christian, Muslim, Vodoun
Languages: French, Fon, Yoruba, tribal languages

Bhutan

Area: 17,954 sq mi (46,500 sq km)
Population: 733,000
Capital: Thimphu, pop. 99,000
Currencies: ngultrum; Indian rupee
Religions: Lamaistic Buddhist, Indian- and Nepalese-influenced Hindu
Languages: Dzongkha, Tibetan dialects, Nepalese dialects

Bolivia

Area: 424,164 sq mi (1,098,581 sq km)
Population: 11,020,000
Capitals: La Paz, pop. 1,715,000; Sucre, pop. 307,000
Currency: boliviano
Religions: Roman Catholic, Protestant (includes Evangelical Methodist)
Languages: Spanish, Quechua, Aymara

Bosnia and Herzegovina

Area: 19,741 sq mi (51,129 sq km)
Population: 3,834,000
Capital: Sarajevo, pop. 389,000
Currency: konvertibilna marka (convertible mark)
Religions: Muslim, Orthodox, Roman Catholic
Languages: Bosnian, Croatian, Serbian

Botswana

Area: 224,607 sq mi (581,730 sq km)
Population: 1,866,000
Capital: Gaborone, pop. 202,000
Currency: pula
Religions: Christian, Badimo
Languages: Setswana, Kalanga

Brazil

Area: 3,287,612 sq mi (8,514,877 sq km)
Population: 195,527,000
Capital: Brasília, pop. 3,813,000
Currency: real
Religions: Roman Catholic, Protestant
Language: Portuguese

Brunei

Area: 2,226 sq mi (5,765 sq km)
Population: 407,000
Capital: Bandar Seri Begawan, pop. 16,000
Currency: Bruneian dollar
Religions: Muslim, Buddhist, Christian, other (includes indigenous beliefs)
Languages: Malay, English, Chinese

Bulgaria

Area: 42,855 sq mi (110,994 sq km)
Population: 7,260,000
Capital: Sofia, pop. 1,174,000
Currency: lev
Religions: Bulgarian Orthodox, Muslim
Languages: Bulgarian, Turkish, Roma

COLOR KEY ● Africa ● Australia, New Zealand, and Oceania

Burkina Faso

Area: 105,869 sq mi (274,200 sq km)
Population: 18,015,000
Capital: Ouagadougou, pop. 2,053,000
Currency: Communauté Financière Africaine franc
Religions: Muslim, indigenous beliefs, Christian
Languages: French, native African languages

Cambodia

Area: 69,898 sq mi (181,035 sq km)
Population: 14,406,000
Capital: Phnom Penh, pop. 1,550,000
Currency: riel
Religion: Theravada Buddhist
Language: Khmer

Burundi

Area: 10,747 sq mi (27,834 sq km)
Population: 10,892,000
Capital: Bujumbura, pop. 605,000
Currency: Burundi franc
Religions: Roman Catholic, indigenous beliefs, Muslim, Protestant
Languages: Kirundi, French, Swahili

Cameroon

Area: 183,569 sq mi (475,442 sq km)
Population: 21,491,000
Capital: Yaoundé, pop. 2,432,000
Currency: Communauté Financière Africaine franc
Religions: indigenous beliefs, Christian, Muslim
Languages: 24 major African language groups, English, French

You Are There!
Boromo, Burkina Faso

The beat of a tribal drum grows louder as you approach a clearing in a dusty field. There you join villagers crowding around a group of people wearing colorful costumes and giant wooden masks.

This is *Fête des Masques*, a mask festival celebrated by many tribes of Burkina Faso in western Africa during the dry season. In an ancient tradition, tribesmen ask their masks to protect their villages and to call for rain. Today's festivals—which can last for several days—feature elaborate dance-offs. It's considered a great honor to dance in the festival, but being able to watch it all unfold is just as cool.

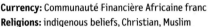

● Asia ● Europe ● North America ● South America

293

Canada

Area: 3,855,101 sq mi
(9,984,670 sq km)
Population: 35,250,000
Capital: Ottawa, pop. 1,208,000
Currency: Canadian dollar
Religions: Roman Catholic, Protestant (includes United Church, Anglican), other Christian
Languages: English, French

Cape Verde

Area: 1,558 sq mi (4,036 sq km)
Population: 515,000
Capital: Praia, pop. 132,000
Currency: Cape Verdean escudo
Religions: Roman Catholic (infused with indigenous beliefs), Protestant (mostly Church of the Nazarene)
Languages: Portuguese, Crioulo

Central African Republic

Area: 240,535 sq mi
(622,984 sq km)
Population: 4,676,000
Capital: Bangui, pop. 740,000
Currency: Communauté Financière Africaine franc
Religions: indigenous beliefs, Protestant, Roman Catholic, Muslim
Languages: French, Sangho, tribal languages

Chad

Area: 495,755 sq mi
(1,284,000 sq km)
Population: 12,209,000
Capital: N'Djamena, pop. 1,079,000
Currency: Communauté Financière Africaine franc
Religions: Muslim, Catholic, Protestant, animist
Languages: French, Arabic, Sara, more than 120 languages and dialects

Chile

Area: 291,930 sq mi
(756,096 sq km)
Population: 17,557,000
Capital: Santiago, pop. 6,034,000
Currency: Chilean peso
Religions: Roman Catholic, Evangelical
Language: Spanish

China

Area: 3,705,405 sq mi
(9,596,960 sq km)
Population: 1,357,372,000
Capital: Beijing, pop. 15,594,000
Currency: renminbi (yuan)
Religions: Taoist, Buddhist, Christian
Languages: Standard Chinese or Mandarin, Yue, Wu, Minbei, Minnan, Xiang, Gan, Hakka dialects

Colombia

Area: 440,831 sq mi
(1,141,748 sq km)
Population: 48,028,000
Capital: Bogotá, pop. 8,743,000
Currency: Colombian peso
Religion: Roman Catholic
Language: Spanish

ROASTED ANTS are a popular SNACK in Colombia.

Comoros

Area: 863 sq mi (2,235 sq km)
Population: 792,000
Capital: Moroni, pop. 54,000
Currency: Comoran franc
Religion: Sunni Muslim
Languages: Arabic, French, Shikomoro

Congo

Area: 132,047 sq mi (342,000 sq km)
Population: 4,355,000
Capital: Brazzaville, pop. 1,611,000
Currency: Communauté Financière Africaine franc
Religions: Christian, animist
Languages: French, Lingala, Monokutuba, local languages

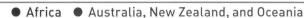

COLOR KEY ● Africa ● Australia, New Zealand, and Oceania

Costa Rica

Area: 19,730 sq mi
(51,100 sq km)
Population: 4,713,000
Capital: San José, pop. 1,515,000
Currency: Costa Rican colón
Religions: Roman Catholic, Evangelical
Languages: Spanish, English

Côte d'Ivoire (Ivory Coast)

Area: 124,503 sq mi
(322,462 sq km)
Population: 21,142,000
Capitals: Abidjan, pop. 4,288,000;
Yamoussoukro, pop. 966,000
Currency: Communauté Financière Africaine franc
Religions: Muslim, indigenous beliefs, Christian
Languages: French, Dioula, other native dialects

Croatia

Area: 21,831 sq mi
(56,542 sq km)
Population: 4,253,000
Capital: Zagreb, pop. 686,000
Currency: kuna
Religions: Roman Catholic, Orthodox
Language: Croatian

Cuba

Area: 42,803 sq mi
(110,860 sq km)
Population: 11,258,000
Capital: Havana, pop. 2,116,000
Currency: Cuban peso
Religions: Roman Catholic, Protestant, Jehovah's Witnesses, Jewish, Santería
Language: Spanish

Cyprus

Area: 3,572 sq mi (9,251 sq km)
Population: 1,135,000
Capital: Nicosia, pop. 253,000
Currencies: euro; new Turkish lira in Northern Cyprus
Religions: Greek Orthodox, Muslim, Maronite, Armenian Apostolic
Languages: Greek, Turkish, English

Czech Republic (Czechia)

Area: 30,450 sq mi (78,866 sq km)
Population: 10,521,000
Capital: Prague, pop. 1,276,000
Currency: koruny
Religion: Roman Catholic
Language: Czech

5 cool things about CZECH REPUBLIC

1. It took nearly 600 years to build St. Vitus Cathedral, the largest church in Prague, the nation's capital.

2. Czech chemist Otto Wichterle invented soft contact lenses.

3. The word "robot" comes from the Czech word *robota*, meaning "work."

4. The sugar cube was invented in the Czech town of Dačice in 1843.

5. Czech astronomers named a newly discovered asteroid after ice hockey star Dominik Hašek, who led the Czech team to gold in the 1998 Olympic Games.

Democratic Republic of the Congo

Area: 905,365 sq mi
(2,344,885 sq km)
Population: 71,128,000
Capital: Kinshasa, pop. 8,798,000
Currency: Congolese franc
Religions: Roman Catholic, Protestant, Kimbanguist, Muslim, syncretic sects, indigenous beliefs
Languages: French, Lingala, Kingwana, Kikongo, Tshiluba

Denmark

Area: 16,640 sq mi (43,098 sq km)
Population: 5,613,000
Capital: Copenhagen, pop. 1,206,000
Currency: Danish krone
Religions: Evangelical Lutheran, other Protestant, Roman Catholic
Languages: Danish, Faroese, Greenlandic, German, English as second language

Djibouti

Area: 8,958 sq mi
(23,200 sq km)
Population: 939,000
Capital: Djibouti, pop. 496,000
Currency: Djiboutian franc
Religions: Muslim, Christian
Languages: French, Arabic, Somali, Afar

Dominican Republic

Area: 18,704 sq mi
(48,442 sq km)
Population: 10,260,000
Capital: Santo Domingo,
pop. 2,191,000
Currency: Dominican peso
Religion: Roman Catholic
Language: Spanish

Dominica

Area: 290 sq mi (751 sq km)
Population: 71,000
Capital: Roseau, pop. 14,000
Currency: East Caribbean
dollar
Religions: Roman Catholic, Seventh-day Adventist,
Pentecostal, Baptist, Methodist, other Christian
Languages: English, French patois

Ecuador

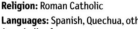

Area: 109,483 sq mi
(283,560 sq km)
Population: 15,789,000
Capital: Quito, pop. 1,622,000
Currency: U.S. dollar
Religion: Roman Catholic
Languages: Spanish, Quechua, other
Amerindian languages

You Are There!

The Galápagos Islands, Ecuador

Slip on a snorkel mask, fins, and a wet suit and dive under the waters surrounding the Galápagos Islands. Soon, you're face-to-face with a marine iguana, the only seagoing lizards on the planet. Watch as these scaly, spiky, dark gray reptiles dive down to feast on algae and seaweed before hopping back on land to warm up on the rocks. You may even see them sneeze out a noseful of salt water, which lands on their head. When the water dries, leaving the salt behind, these lizards get their trademark salty white "wigs."

But that's not all you see. The Galápagos Islands, located 600 miles (1,000 km) from mainland South America, are home to about 9,000 species of animals, including penguins, countless other birds, and the world's largest tortoise. So no matter where you roam, you're bound to spot something wild!

Egypt

Area: 386,874 sq mi
(1,002,000 sq km)
Population: 84,667,000
Capital: Cairo, pop. 11,169,000
Currency: Egyptian pound
Religions: Muslim (mostly Sunni), Coptic Christian
Languages: Arabic, English, French

El Salvador

Area: 8,124 sq mi
(21,041 sq km)
Population: 6,307,000
Capital: San Salvador,
pop. 1,605,000
Currency: U.S. dollar
Religions: Roman Catholic, Protestant
Languages: Spanish, Nahua

Equatorial Guinea

Area: 10,831 sq mi (28,051 sq km)
Population: 761,000
Capital: Malabo, pop. 137,000
Currency: Communauté
Financière Africaine franc
Religions: Christian (predominantly Roman Catholic),
pagan practices
Languages: Spanish, French, Fang, Bubi

Eritrea

Area: 45,406 sq mi
(117,600 sq km)
Population: 5,765,000
Capital: Asmara, pop. 712,000
Currency: nakfa
Religions: Muslim, Coptic Christian, Roman Catholic
Languages: Afar, Arabic, Tigre, Kunama, Tigrinya,
other Cushitic languages

Estonia

Area: 17,462 sq mi (45,227 sq km)
Population: 1,283,000
Capital: Tallinn, pop. 400,000
Currency: euro
Religions: Evangelical Lutheran, Orthodox
Languages: Estonian, Russian

Ethiopia

Area: 426,373 sq mi
(1,104,300 sq km)
Population: 89,209,000
Capital: Addis Ababa,
pop. 2,979,000
Currency: birr
Religions: Christian, Muslim, traditional
Languages: Amharic, Oromigna, Tigrinya, Guaragigna

Fiji

Area: 7,095 sq mi
(18,376 sq km)
Population: 860,000
Capital: Suva, pop. 177,000
Currency: Fijian dollar
Religions: Christian (Methodist, Roman Catholic,
Assembly of God), Hindu (Sanatan), Muslim (Sunni)
Languages: English, Fijian, Hindustani

Finland

Area: 130,558 sq mi
(338,145 sq km)
Population: 5,440,000
Capital: Helsinki, pop. 1,134,000
Currency: euro
Religion: Lutheran Church of Finland
Languages: Finnish, Swedish

France

Area: 210,026 sq mi
(543,965 sq km)
Population: 63,851,000
Capital: Paris, pop. 10,620,000
Currency: euro
Religions: Roman Catholic, Muslim
Language: French

Gabon

Area: 103,347 sq mi (267,667 sq km)
Population: 1,601,000
Capital: Libreville, pop. 686,000
Currency: Communauté Financière
Africaine franc
Religions: Christian, animist
Languages: French, Fang, Myene, Nzebi, Bapounou/
Eschira, Bandjabi

● Asia ● Europe ● North America ● South America

Gambia

Area: 4,361 sq mi (11,295 sq km)
Population: 1,884,000
Capital: Banjul, pop. 506,000
Currency: dalasi
Religions: Muslim, Christian
Languages: English, Mandinka, Wolof, Fula, other indigenous vernaculars

Greece

Area: 50,949 sq mi (131,957 sq km)
Population: 11,081,000
Capital: Athens, pop. 3,414,000
Currency: euro
Religion: Greek Orthodox
Languages: Greek, English, French

Georgia

Area: 26,911 sq mi (69,700 sq km)
Population: 4,541,000
Capital: Tbilisi, pop. 1,121,000
Currency: lari
Religions: Orthodox Christian, Muslim, Armenian-Gregorian
Languages: Georgian, Russian, Armenian, Azeri, Abkhaz

Grenada

Area: 133 sq mi (344 sq km)
Population: 112,000
Capital: St. George's, pop. 41,000
Currency: East Caribbean dollar
Religions: Roman Catholic, Anglican, other Protestant
Languages: English, French patois

ARCHAEOLOGISTS once unearthed a 1.8-million-year-old PREHUMAN SKULL IN GEORGIA.

Guatemala

Area: 42,042 sq mi (108,889 sq km)
Population: 15,428,000
Capital: Guatemala City, pop. 1,168,000
Currency: quetzal
Religions: Roman Catholic, Protestant, indigenous Maya beliefs
Languages: Spanish, 23 official Amerindian languages

Germany

Area: 137,847 sq mi (357,022 sq km)
Population: 80,572,000
Capital: Berlin, pop. 3,462,000
Currency: euro
Religions: Protestant, Roman Catholic, Muslim
Language: German

Guinea

Area: 94,926 sq mi (245,857 sq km)
Population: 11,793,000
Capital: Conakry, pop. 1,786,000
Currency: Guinean franc
Religions: Muslim, Christian, indigenous beliefs
Languages: French, ethnic languages

Ghana

Area: 92,100 sq mi (238,537 sq km)
Population: 26,088,000
Capital: Accra, pop. 2,573,000
Currency: Ghana cedi
Religions: Christian (Pentecostal/Charismatic, Protestant, Roman Catholic, other), Muslim, traditional beliefs
Languages: Asante, Ewe, Fante, Boron (Brong), Dagomba, Dangme, Dagarte (Dagaba), Akyem, Ga, English

Guinea-Bissau

Area: 13,948 sq mi (36,125 sq km)
Population: 1,677,000
Capital: Bissau, pop. 423,000
Currency: Communauté Financière Africaine franc
Religions: indigenous beliefs, Muslim, Christian
Languages: Portuguese, Crioulo, African languages

Guyana

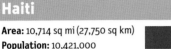

Area: 83,000 sq mi (214,969 sq km)
Population: 800,000
Capital: Georgetown, pop. 127,000
Currency: Guyanese dollar
Religions: Christian, Hindu, Muslim
Languages: English, Amerindian dialects, Creole, Hindustani, Urdu

Honduras

Area: 43,433 sq mi (112,492 sq km)
Population: 8,555,000
Capital: Tegucigalpa, pop. 1,088,000
Currency: lempira
Religions: Roman Catholic, Protestant
Languages: Spanish, Amerindian dialects

Haiti

Area: 10,714 sq mi (27,750 sq km)
Population: 10,421,000
Capital: Port-au-Prince, pop. 2,207,000
Currency: gourde
Religions: Roman Catholic, Protestant (Baptist, Pentecostal, other)
Languages: French, Creole

Hungary

Area: 35,919 sq mi (93,030 sq km)
Population: 9,892,000
Capital: Budapest, pop. 1,737,000
Currency: forint
Religions: Roman Catholic, Calvinist, Lutheran
Language: Hungarian

You Are There!
Copán, Honduras

Take a trip back in time with a visit to the ruins of Copán, the site of some of Central America's greatest Maya temples and tombs. Examine Maya artifacts and check out intricately carved sculptures and architectural highlights, such as the hieroglyphic stairway, which features 1,800 individual glyphs. Then imagine what life was like in this bustling and influential city thousands of years ago.

Iceland

Area: 39,769 sq mi
(103,000 sq km)
Population: 323,000
Capital: Reykjavík, pop. 206,000
Currency: Icelandic krona
Religion: Lutheran Church of Iceland
Languages: Icelandic, English, Nordic
languages, German

Indonesia

Area: 742,308 sq mi
(1,922,570 sq km)
Population: 248,527,000
Capital: Jakarta, pop. 9,769,000
Currency: Indonesian rupiah
Religions: Muslim, Protestant, Roman Catholic
Languages: Bahasa Indonesia (modified form of Malay),
English, Dutch, Javanese, local dialects

India

Area: 1,269,221 sq mi (3,287,270 sq km)
Population: 1,276,508,000
Capital: New Delhi, pop. 22,654,000
(part of Delhi metropolitan area)
Currency: Indian rupee
Religions: Hindu, Muslim
Languages: Hindi, 21 other official languages,
Hindustani (popular Hindi/Urdu variant in the north)

Iran

Area: 636,296 sq mi
(1,648,000 sq km)
Population: 76,521,000
Capital: Tehran, pop. 7,304,000
Currency: Iranian rial
Religions: Shiite Muslim, Sunni Muslim
Languages: Persian, Turkic, Kurdish, Luri,
Baluchi, Arabic

You Are There!
Cliffs of Moher, Ireland

Rising 702 feet (214 m) from the churning Atlantic Ocean, the Cliffs of Moher offer some of the most magical views in all of Ireland. Follow the winding path along the top of the cliffs for a gentle hike to cool spots like O'Brien's Tower, one of the highest points around. Climb to the top of the tower to take in the stunning surroundings of Galway Bay and the rocky landscape of the nearby Aran Islands.

Another can't-miss destination? The Hag's Head rock formation, which is said to resemble an old woman staring out to sea.

COLOR KEY ● Africa ● Australia, New Zealand, and Oceania

Iraq

Area: 168,754 sq mi
(437,072 sq km)
Population: 35,095,000
Capital: Baghdad, pop. 6,036,000
Currency: Iraqi dinar
Religions: Shiite Muslim, Sunni Muslim
Languages: Arabic, Kurdish, Assyrian, Armenian

Ireland

Area: 27,133 sq mi
(70,273 sq km)
Population: 4,598,000
Capital: Dublin, pop. 1,121,000
Currency: euro
Religions: Roman Catholic, Church of Ireland
Languages: Irish (Gaelic), English

Israel

Area: 8,550 sq mi (22,145 sq km)
Population: 8,054,000
Capital: Jerusalem, pop. 791,000
Currency: new Israeli sheqel
Religions: Jewish, Muslim
Languages: Hebrew, Arabic, English

Italy

Area: 116,345 sq mi
(301,333 sq km)
Population: 59,831,000
Capital: Rome, pop. 3,298,000
Currency: euro
Religions: Roman Catholic, Protestant, Jewish, Muslim
Languages: Italian, German, French, Slovene

Jamaica

Area: 4,244 sq mi
(10,991 sq km)
Population: 2,712,000
Capital: Kingston, pop. 571,000
Currency: Jamaican dollar
Religions: Protestant (Church of God, Seventh-day Adventist, Pentecostal, Baptist, Anglican, other)
Languages: English, English patois

Japan

Area: 145,902 sq mi (377,887 sq km)
Population: 127,301,000
Capital: Tokyo, pop. 37,217,000
Currency: yen
Religions: Shinto, Buddhist
Language: Japanese

Jordan

Area: 34,495 sq mi
(89,342 sq km)
Population: 7,309,000
Capital: Amman, pop. 1,179,000
Currency: Jordanian dinar
Religions: Sunni Muslim, Christian
Languages: Arabic, English

Kazakhstan

Area: 1,049,155 sq mi
(2,717,300 sq km)
Population: 17,031,000
Capital: Astana, pop. 664,000
Currency: tenge
Religions: Muslim, Russian Orthodox
Languages: Kazakh (Qazaq), Russian

Kenya

Area: 224,081 sq mi (580,367 sq km)
Population: 44,184,000
Capital: Nairobi, pop. 3,363,000
Currency: Kenyan shilling
Religions: Protestant, Roman Catholic, Muslim, indigenous beliefs
Languages: English, Kiswahili, many indigenous languages

Kiribati

Area: 313 sq mi (811 sq km)
Population: 106,000
Capital: Tarawa, pop. 44,000
Currency: Australian dollar
Religions: Roman Catholic, Protestant (Congregational)
Languages: I-Kiribati, English

Kosovo

Area: 4,203 sq mi (10,887 sq km)
Population: 1,824,000
Capital: Prishtina, pop. 600,000
Currency: euro
Religions: Muslim, Serbian Orthodox, Roman Catholic
Languages: Albanian, Serbian, Bosnian, Turkish, Roma

Kuwait

Area: 6,880 sq mi (17,818 sq km)
Population: 3,459,000
Capital: Kuwait City, pop. 2,406,000
Currency: Kuwaiti dinar
Religions: Sunni Muslim, Shiite Muslim
Languages: Arabic, English

Kyrgyzstan

Area: 77,182 sq mi (199,900 sq km)
Population: 5,665,000
Capital: Bishkek, pop. 839,000
Currency: som
Religions: Muslim, Russian Orthodox
Languages: Kyrgyz, Uzbek, Russian

Laos

Area: 91,429 sq mi (236,800 sq km)
Population: 6,736,000
Capital: Vientiane, pop. 810,000
Currency: kip
Religions: Buddhist, animist
Languages: Lao, French, English, various ethnic languages

Latvia

Area: 24,938 sq mi (64,589 sq km)
Population: 2,018,000
Capital: Riga, pop. 701,000
Currency: Latvian lat
Religions: Lutheran, Roman Catholic, Russian Orthodox
Languages: Latvian, Russian, Lithuanian

Lebanon

Area: 4,036 sq mi (10,452 sq km)
Population: 4,822,000
Capital: Beirut, pop. 2,022,000
Currency: Lebanese pound
Religions: Muslim, Christian
Languages: Arabic, French, English, Armenian

Lesotho

Area: 11,720 sq mi (30,355 sq km)
Population: 2,242,000
Capital: Maseru, pop. 239,000
Currencies: loti; South African rand
Religions: Christian, indigenous beliefs
Languages: Sesotho, English, Zulu, Xhosa

> **Workers discovered a 603-CARAT DIAMOND in a LESOTHO mine.**

Liberia

Area: 43,000 sq mi (111,370 sq km)
Population: 4,357,000
Capital: Monrovia, pop. 750,000
Currency: Liberian dollar
Religions: Christian, indigenous beliefs, Muslim
Languages: English, some 20 ethnic languages

Libya

Area: 679,362 sq mi (1,759,540 sq km)
Population: 6,518,000
Capital: Tripoli, pop. 1,127,000
Currency: Libyan dinar
Religion: Sunni Muslim
Languages: Arabic, Italian, English

COLOR KEY ● Africa ● Australia, New Zealand, and Oceania

Liechtenstein

Area: 62 sq mi (160 sq km)
Population: 37,000
Capital: Vaduz, pop. 5,000
Currency: Swiss franc
Religions: Roman Catholic, Protestant
Languages: German, Alemannic dialect

Lithuania

Area: 25,212 sq mi
(65,300 sq km)
Population: 2,956,000
Capital: Vilnius, pop. 546,000
Currency: litas
Religions: Roman Catholic, Russian Orthodox
Languages: Lithuanian, Russian, Polish

Luxembourg

Area: 998 sq mi (2,586 sq km)
Population: 543,000
Capital: Luxembourg,
pop. 94,000
Currency: euro
Religions: Roman Catholic, Protestant,
Jewish, Muslim
Languages: Luxembourgish, German, French

Macedonia

Area: 9,928 sq mi
(25,713 sq km)
Population: 2,066,000
Capital: Skopje, pop. 499,000
Currency: Macedonian denar
Religions: Macedonian Orthodox, Muslim
Languages: Macedonian, Albanian, Turkish

Madagascar

Area: 226,658 sq mi
(587,041 sq km)
Population: 22,550,000
Capital: Antananarivo,
pop. 1,987,000
Currency: Madagascar ariary
Religions: indigenous beliefs, Christian, Muslim
Languages: English, French, Malagasy

Malawi

Area: 45,747 sq mi
(118,484 sq km)
Population: 16,338,000
Capital: Lilongwe, pop. 772,000
Currency: Malawian kwacha
Religions: Christian, Muslim
Languages: Chichewa, Chinyanja, Chiyao, Chitumbuka

Malaysia

Area: 127,355 sq mi (329,847 sq km)
Population: 29,794,000
Capital: Kuala Lumpur,
pop. 1,556,000
Currency: ringgit
Religions: Muslim, Buddhist, Christian, Hindu
Languages: Bahasa Malaysia, English, Chinese, Tamil,
Telugu, Malayalam, Panjabi, Thai, indigenous languages

5 cool things about MALAYSIA

1. The Petronas Towers in Kuala Lumpur, Malaysia, have 32,000 windows.

2. Some Malaysian stick insects are 17 inches (45 cm) long—longer than a toaster!

3. Malaysia is home to about 150 snake species.

4. The giant *Rafflesia arnoldii*—known as the corpse flower for its stinky scent—is the state flower of Sabah, Malaysia.

5. There are over 135 different languages spoken in Malaysia.

Maldives

Area: 115 sq mi (298 sq km)
Population: 360,000
Capital: Male, pop. 132,000
Currency: rufiyaa
Religion: Sunni Muslim
Languages: Maldivian Dhivehi, English

Mali

Area: 478,841 sq mi (1,240,192 sq km)
Population: 15,461,000
Capital: Bamako, pop. 2,037,000
Currency: Communauté Financière Africaine franc
Religions: Muslim, indigenous beliefs
Languages: Bambara, French, numerous African languages

Marshall Islands

Area: 70 sq mi (181 sq km)
Population: 56,000
Capital: Majuro, pop. 31,000
Currency: U.S. dollar
Religions: Protestant, Assembly of God, Roman Catholic
Language: Marshallese

Malta

Area: 122 sq mi (316 sq km)
Population: 448,000
Capital: Valletta, pop. 198,000
Currency: euro
Religion: Roman Catholic
Languages: Maltese, English

Mauritania

Area: 397,955 sq mi (1,030,700 sq km)
Population: 3,712,000
Capital: Nouakchott, pop. 786,000
Currency: ouguiya
Religion: Muslim
Languages: Arabic, Pulaar, Soninke, French, Hassaniya, Wolof

You Are There!

Monte Carlo, Monaco

Monaco may be one of the smallest countries in the world, but that doesn't mean it lacks pizazz. Luxury cars, yachts, and hotels are commonplace in this three-mile (4.8-km)-long by half-mile (0.8-km)-wide principality. Adding to the glamour? The Monaco Grand Prix, which welcomes dozens of Formula One cars and their drivers from around the world each year.

COLOR KEY ● Africa ● Australia, New Zealand, and Oceania

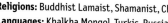

Mauritius

Area: 788 sq mi (2,040 sq km)
Population: 1,297,000
Capital: Port Louis, pop. 151,000
Currency: Mauritian rupee
Religions: Hindu, Roman Catholic, Muslim, other Christian
Languages: Creole, Bhojpuri, French

Mexico

Area: 758,449 sq mi (1,964,375 sq km)
Population: 117,574,000
Capital: Mexico City, pop. 20,446,000
Currency: Mexican peso
Religions: Roman Catholic, Protestant
Languages: Spanish, Mayan, other indigenous languages

Micronesia

Area: 271 sq mi (702 sq km)
Population: 107,000
Capital: Palikir, pop. 7,000
Currency: U.S. dollar
Religions: Roman Catholic, Protestant
Languages: English, Trukese, Pohnpeian, Yapese, other indigenous languages

Moldova

Area: 13,050 sq mi (33,800 sq km)
Population: 4,114,000
Capital: Chisinau, pop. 677,000
Currency: Moldovan leu
Religion: Eastern Orthodox
Languages: Moldovan, Russian, Gagauz

Monaco

Area: 0.8 sq mi (2.0 sq km)
Population: 37,000
Capital: Monaco, pop. 35,000
Currency: euro
Religion: Roman Catholic
Languages: French, English, Italian, Monegasque

Mongolia

Area: 603,909 sq mi (1,564,116 sq km)
Population: 2,792,000
Capital: Ulaanbaatar, pop. 1,184,000
Currency: togrog/tugrik
Religions: Buddhist Lamaist, Shamanist, Christian
Languages: Khalkha Mongol, Turkic, Russian

Montenegro

Area: 5,333 sq mi (13,812 sq km)
Population: 623,000
Capital: Podgorica, pop. 156,000
Currency: euro
Religions: Orthodox, Muslim, Roman Catholic
Languages: Serbian (Ijekavian dialect), Bosnian, Albanian, Croatian

Morocco

Area: 172,414 sq mi (446,550 sq km)
Population: 32,950,000
Capital: Rabat, pop. 1,843,000
Currency: Moroccan dirham
Religion: Muslim
Languages: Arabic, Berber dialects, French

Mozambique

Area: 308,642 sq mi (799,380 sq km)
Population: 24,336,000
Capital: Maputo, pop. 1,150,000
Currency: metical
Religions: Roman Catholic, Muslim, Zionist Christian
Languages: Emakhuwa, Xichangana, Portuguese, Elomwe, Cisena, Echuwabo, other local languages

Myanmar (Burma)

Area: 261,218 sq mi (676,552 sq km)
Population: 53,259,000
Capitals: Nay Pyi Taw, pop. 1,060,000; Yangon (Rangoon), pop. 4,457,000
Currency: kyat
Religions: Buddhist, Christian, Muslim
Languages: Burmese, minority ethnic languages

Namibia

Area: 318,261 sq mi
(824,292 sq km)
Population: 2,410,000
Capital: Windhoek, pop. 380,000
Currencies: Namibian dollar;
South African rand
Religions: Lutheran, other Christian, indigenous beliefs
Languages: Afrikaans, German, English

Nauru

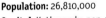

Area: 8 sq mi (21 sq km)
Population: 11,000
Capital: Yaren, pop. 11,000
Currency: Australian dollar
Religions: Protestant, Roman Catholic
Languages: Nauruan, English

Nepal

Area: 56,827 sq mi
(147,181 sq km)
Population: 26,810,000
Capital: Kathmandu, pop. 1,015,000
Currency: Nepalese rupee
Religions: Hindu, Buddhist, Muslim, Kirant
Languages: Nepali, Maithali, Bhojpuri, Tharu,
Tamang, Newar, Magar

Netherlands

Area: 16,034 sq mi
(41,528 sq km)
Population: 16,798,000
Capital: Amsterdam, pop. 1,056,000
Currency: euro
Religions: Roman Catholic, Dutch Reformed,
Calvinist, Muslim
Languages: Dutch, Frisian

New Zealand

Area: 104,454 sq mi
(270,534 sq km)
Population: 4,450,000
Capital: Wellington, pop. 410,000
Currency: New Zealand dollar
Religions: Anglican, Roman Catholic, Presbyterian,
other Christian
Languages: English, Maori

Nicaragua

Area: 50,193 sq mi
(130,000 sq km)
Population: 6,043,000
Capital: Managua, pop. 970,000
Currency: gold cordoba
Religions: Roman Catholic, Evangelical
Language: Spanish

Niger

Area: 489,191 sq mi (1,267,000 sq km)
Population: 16,916,000
Capital: Niamey, pop. 1,297,000
Currency: Communauté
Financière Africaine franc
Religions: Muslim, other (includes indigenous
beliefs and Christian)
Languages: French, Hausa, Djerma

Nigeria

Area: 356,669 sq mi
(923,768 sq km)
Population: 173,615,000
Capital: Abuja, pop. 2,153,000
Currency: naira
Religions: Muslim, Christian, indigenous beliefs
Languages: English, Hausa, Yoruba, Igbo (Ibo), Fulani

The National ANIMAL of Nigeria is the EAGLE.

North Korea

Area: 46,540 sq mi
(120,538 sq km)
Population: 24,720,000
Capital: Pyongyang,
pop. 2,843,000
Currency: North Korean won
Religions: Buddhist, Confucianist, some Christian
and syncretic Chondogyo
Language: Korean

Norway

Area: 125,004 sq mi
(323,758 sq km)
Population: 5,084,000
Capital: Oslo, pop. 915,000
Currency: Norwegian krone
Religion: Church of Norway (Lutheran)
Languages: Bokmal Norwegian, Nynorsk Norwegian, Sami

Pakistan

Area: 307,374 sq mi
(796,095 sq km)
Population: 190,709,000
Capital: Islamabad, pop. 919,000
Currency: Pakistani rupee
Religions: Sunni Muslim, Shiite Muslim
Languages: Punjabi, Sindhi, Siraiki, Pashto, Urdu, Baluchi, Hindko, English

Oman

Area: 119,500 sq mi
(309,500 sq km)
Population: 3,983,000
Capital: Muscat, pop. 743,000
Currency: Omani rial
Religions: Ibadhi Muslim, Sunni Muslim, Shiite Muslim, Hindu
Languages: Arabic, English, Baluchi, Urdu, Indian dialects

Palau

Area: 189 sq mi (489 sq km)
Population: 21,000
Capital: Melekeok, pop. 1,000
Currency: U.S. dollar
Religions: Roman Catholic, Protestant, Modekngei, Seventh-day Adventist
Languages: Palauan, Filipino, English, Chinese

You Are There!

Franz Josef Glacier, New Zealand

As your helicopter lifts into the cloudless sky, the landscape below rapidly changes from a lush green to an icy blue. You are flying high above New Zealand's Westland Tai Poutini National Park, home to the Franz Josef Glacier. Ranging from a height of 8,858 feet (2,700 m) above sea level down to just 787 feet (240 m), Franz Josef is one of the world's steepest glaciers. But it's also one of the most accessible, welcoming up to 2,700 visitors a day.

The best way to take in all of the glacier's glory? The chopper, of course, which gives you a brilliant bird's-eye view before landing. Then hike past funky formations, curving tunnels, and towering peaks—all formed by the majestic blue glacial ice.

● Asia   ● Europe   ● North America   ● South America

Panama

Area: 29,157 sq mi (75,517 sq km)
Population: 3,850,000
Capital: Panama City,
pop. 1,426,000
Currencies: balboa; U.S. dollar
Religions: Roman Catholic, Protestant
Languages: Spanish, English

Papua New Guinea

Area: 178,703 sq mi (462,840 sq km)
Population: 7,179,000
Capital: Port Moresby, pop. 343,000
Currency: kina
Religions: indigenous beliefs, Roman Catholic,
Lutheran, other Protestant
Languages: Melanesian Pidgin, 820 indigenous
languages

Paraguay

Area: 157,048 sq mi
(406,752 sq km)
Population: 6,798,000
Capital: Asunción, pop. 2,139,000
Currency: guarani
Religions: Roman Catholic, Protestant
Languages: Spanish, Guarani

5 cool things about PARAGUAY

1. Paraguay's flag features different designs on the front and back.

2. Located in the center of South America, Paraguay is sometimes called *Corazon de America* ("Heart of America").

3. Lace-making is a popular Paraguayan craft.

4. A musician in Paraguay makes instruments out of recycled trash from the country's largest landfill.

5. Paraguay completed the first railroad system in South America in 1889.

Peru

Area: 496,224 sq mi
(1,285,216 sq km)
Population: 30,475,000
Capital: Lima, pop. 9,130,000
Currency: nuevo sol
Religion: Roman Catholic
Languages: Spanish, Quechua, Aymara, minor
Amazonian languages

Philippines

Area: 115,831 sq mi
(300,000 sq km)
Population: 96,209,000
Capital: Manila,
pop. 11,862,000
Currency: Philippine peso
Religions: Roman Catholic, Muslim, other Christian
Languages: Filipino (based on Tagalog), English

Poland

Area: 120,728 sq mi
(312,685 sq km)
Population: 38,517,000
Capital: Warsaw, pop. 1,723,000
Currency: zloty
Religion: Roman Catholic
Language: Polish

Portugal

Area: 35,655 sq mi
(92,345 sq km)
Population: 10,460,000
Capital: Lisbon, pop. 2,843,000
Currency: euro
Religion: Roman Catholic
Languages: Portuguese, Mirandese

Qatar

Area: 4,448 sq mi
(11,521 sq km)
Population: 2,169,000
Capital: Doha, pop. 567,000
Currency: Qatari rial
Religions: Muslim, Christian
Languages: Arabic; English commonly
a second language

Romania

Area: 92,043 sq mi
(238,391 sq km)
Population: 21,269,000
Capital: Bucharest, pop. 1,937,000
Currency: new leu
Religions: Eastern Orthodox, Protestant,
Roman Catholic
Languages: Romanian, Hungarian

Russia

Area: 6,592,850 sq mi
(17,075,400 sq km)
Population: 143,493,000
Capital: Moscow, pop. 11,621,000
Currency: ruble
Religions: Russian Orthodox, Muslim
Languages: Russian, many minority languages
*Note: Russia is in both Europe and Asia, but its capital is in Europe,
so it is classified here as a European country.*

Rwanda

Area: 10,169 sq mi
(26,338 sq km)
Population: 11,116,000
Capital: Kigali, pop. 1,004,000
Currency: Rwandan franc
Religions: Roman Catholic, Protestant,
Adventist, Muslim
Languages: Kinyarwanda, French, English, Kiswahili

Samoa

Area: 1,093 sq mi (2,831 sq km)
Population: 190,000
Capital: Apia, pop. 37,000
Currency: tala
Religions: Congregationalist, Roman Catholic,
Methodist, Church of Jesus Christ of Latter-day
Saints, Assembly of God, Seventh-day Adventist
Languages: Samoan (Polynesian), English

San Marino

Area: 24 sq mi (61 sq km)
Population: 33,000
Capital: San Marino, pop. 4,000
Currency: euro
Religion: Roman Catholic
Language: Italian

Sao Tome and Principe

Area: 386 sq mi (1,001 sq km)
Population: 188,000
Capital: São Tomé,
pop. 64,000
Currency: dobra
Religions: Roman Catholic, Evangelical
Language: Portuguese

Saudi Arabia

Area: 756,985 sq mi
(1,960,582 sq km)
Population: 30,054,000
Capital: Riyadh, pop. 5,451,000
Currency: Saudi riyal
Religion: Muslim
Language: Arabic

Senegal

Area: 75,955 sq mi
(196,722 sq km)
Population: 13,497,000
Capital: Dakar, pop. 3,035,000
Currency: Communauté
Financière Africaine franc
Religions: Muslim, Christian (mostly Roman Catholic)
Languages: French, Wolof, Pulaar, Jola, Mandinka

Serbia

Area: 29,913 sq mi (77,474 sq km)
Population: 7,136,000
Capital: Belgrade, pop. 1,135,000
Currency: Serbian dinar
Religions: Serbian Orthodox, Roman Catholic, Muslim
Languages: Serbian, Hungarian

Seychelles

Area: 176 sq mi (455 sq km)
Population: 93,000
Capital: Victoria, pop. 27,000
Currency: Seychelles rupee
Religions: Roman Catholic, Anglican, other Christian
Languages: Creole, English

Sierra Leone

Area: 27,699 sq mi (71,740 sq km)
Population: 6,242,000
Capital: Freetown, pop. 941,000
Currency: leone
Religions: Muslim, indigenous beliefs, Christian
Languages: English, Mende, Temne, Krio

Slovakia

Area: 18,932 sq mi (49,035 sq km)
Population: 5,414,000
Capital: Bratislava, pop. 434,000
Currency: euro
Religions: Roman Catholic, Protestant, Greek Catholic
Languages: Slovak, Hungarian

Singapore

Area: 255 sq mi (660 sq km)
Population: 5,444,000
Capital: Singapore, pop. 5,188,000
Currency: Singapore dollar
Religions: Buddhist, Muslim, Taoist, Roman Catholic, Hindu, other Christian
Languages: Mandarin, English, Malay, Hokkien, Cantonese, Teochew, Tamil

Slovenia

Area: 7,827 sq mi (20,273 sq km)
Population: 2,060,000
Capital: Ljubljana, pop. 273,000
Currency: euro
Religions: Roman Catholic, Muslim, Orthodox
Languages: Slovene, Croatian, Serbian

You Are There!

Singapore Flyer, Singapore

Imagine strapping yourself into a Ferris wheel and being lifted so high in the sky, you can see nearly 30 miles (45 km) away. Well, in Singapore, you don't have to imagine: You can do just that in real life! Just take a spin on the Singapore Flyer—one of the world's highest observation wheels, which, at 541 feet (165 m), stands about 50 stories high. A standout on Singapore's iconic skyline along the Singapore River, the Flyer offers an unrivaled 360° view of famous sites and even neighboring countries.

COLOR KEY ● Africa ● Australia, New Zealand, and Oceania

Solomon Islands

Area: 10,954 sq mi
(28,370 sq km)
Population: 581,000
Capital: Honiara, pop. 68,000
Currency: Solomon Islands dollar
Religions: Church of Melanesia, Roman Catholic,
South Seas Evangelical, other Christian
Languages: Melanesian pidgin, 120 indigenous languages

Somalia

Area: 246,201 sq mi
(637,657 sq km)
Population: 10,383,000
Capital: Mogadishu, pop. 1,554,000
Currency: Somali shilling
Religion: Sunni Muslim
Languages: Somali, Arabic, Italian, English

South Africa

Area: 470,693 sq mi (1,219,090 sq km)
Population: 52,982,000
Capitals: Pretoria (Tshwane),
pop. 1,501,000; Bloemfontein,
pop. 468,000; Cape Town, pop. 3,562,000
Currency: rand
Religions: Zion Christian, Pentecostal, Catholic,
Methodist, Dutch Reformed, Anglican, other Christian
Languages: IsiZulu, IsiXhosa, Afrikaans, Sepedi, English

South Korea

Area: 38,321 sq mi
(99,250 sq km)
Population: 50,220,000
Capital: Seoul, pop. 9,736,000
Currency: South Korean won
Religions: Christian, Buddhist
Languages: Korean, English

South Sudan

Area: 248,777 sq mi
(644,329 sq km)
Population: 9,782,000
Capital: Juba, pop. 269,000
Currency: South Sudan pound
Religions: animist, Christian
Languages: English, Arabic, regional languages (Dinke,
Nuer, Bari, Zande, Shilluk)

Spain

Area: 195,363 sq mi (505,988 sq km)
Population: 46,647,000
Capital: Madrid, pop. 6,574,000
Currency: euro
Religion: Roman Catholic
Languages: Castilian Spanish, Catalan,
Galician, Basque

Sri Lanka

Area: 25,299 sq mi
(65,525 sq km)
Population: 20,501,000
Capitals: Colombo, pop. 693,000;
Sri Jayewardenepura Kotte, pop. 126,000
Currency: Sri Lankan rupee
Religions: Buddhist, Muslim, Hindu, Christian
Languages: Sinhala, Tamil

St. Kitts and Nevis

Area: 104 sq mi (269 sq km)
Population: 55,000
Capital: Basseterre, pop. 12,000
Currency: East Caribbean dollar
Religions: Anglican, other Protestant,
Roman Catholic
Language: English

St. Lucia

Area: 238 sq mi (616 sq km)
Population: 170,000
Capital: Castries, pop. 21,000
Currency: East Caribbean
dollar
Religions: Roman Catholic, Seventh-day Adventist,
Pentecostal
Languages: English, French patois

St. Vincent and the Grenadines

Area: 150 sq mi (389 sq km)
Population: 108,000
Capital: Kingstown, pop. 31,000
Currency: East Caribbean dollar
Religions: Anglican, Methodist, Roman Catholic
Languages: English, French patois

Sudan

Area: 718,722 sq mi
(1,861,484 sq km)
Population: 34,186,000
Capital: Khartoum, pop. 4,632,000
Currency: Sudanese pound
Religions: Sunni Muslim, indigenous beliefs, Christian
Languages: Arabic, Nubian, Ta Bedawie, many diverse dialects of Nilotic, Nilo-Hamitic, Sudanic languages

Suriname

Area: 63,037 sq mi (163,265 sq km)
Population: 558,000
Capital: Paramaribo, pop. 278,000
Currency: Suriname dollar
Religions: Hindu, Protestant (predominantly Moravian), Roman Catholic, Muslim, indigenous beliefs
Languages: Dutch, English, Sranang Tongo, Hindustani, Javanese

Swaziland

Area: 6,704 sq mi (17,363 sq km)
Population: 1,238,000
Capitals: Mbabane, pop. 66,000; Lobamba, pop. 4,557
Currency: lilangeni
Religions: Zionist, Roman Catholic, Muslim
Languages: English, siSwati

Sweden

Area: 173,732 sq mi
(449,964 sq km)
Population: 9,592,000
Capital: Stockholm, pop. 1,385,000
Currency: Swedish krona
Religion: Lutheran
Languages: Swedish, Sami, Finnish

Switzerland

Area: 15,940 sq mi
(41,284 sq km)
Population: 8,078,000
Capital: Bern, pop. 353,000
Currency: Swiss franc
Religions: Roman Catholic, Protestant, Muslim
Languages: German, French, Italian, Romansh

Syria

Area: 71,498 sq mi (185,180 sq km)
Population: 21,898,000
Capital: Damascus, pop. 2,650,000
Currency: Syrian pound
Religions: Sunni, other Muslim (includes Alawite, Druze), Christian
Languages: Arabic, Kurdish, Armenian, Aramaic, Circassian

Tajikistan

Area: 55,251 sq mi
(143,100 sq km)
Population: 8,085,000
Capital: Dushanbe, pop. 739,000
Currency: somoni
Religions: Sunni Muslim, Shiite Muslim
Languages: Tajik, Russian

Tanzania

Area: 364,900 sq mi (945,087 sq km)
Population: 49,122,000
Capitals: Dar es Salaam, pop. 2,930,000; Dodoma, pop. 226,000
Currency: Tanzanian shilling
Religions: Muslim, indigenous beliefs, Christian
Languages: Kiswahili, Kiunguja, English, Arabic, local languages

Thailand

Area: 198,115 sq mi
(513,115 sq km)
Population: 66,185,000
Capital: Bangkok, pop. 8,426,000
Currency: baht
Religions: Buddhist, Muslim
Languages: Thai, English, ethnic dialects

Timor-Leste (East Timor)

Area: 5,640 sq mi
(14,609 sq km)
Population: 1,108,000
Capital: Dili, pop. 180,000
Currency: U.S. dollar
Religion: Roman Catholic
Languages: Tetum, Portuguese, Indonesian, English, indigenous languages

COLOR KEY ● Africa ● Australia, New Zealand, and Oceania

Togo

Area: 21,925 sq mi (56,785 sq km)
Population: 6,168,000
Capital: Lomé, pop. 1,524,000
Currency: Communauté Financière Africaine franc
Religions: indigenous beliefs, Christian, Muslim
Languages: French, Ewe, Mina, Kabye, Dagomba

Trinidad and Tobago

Area: 1,980 sq mi (5,128 sq km)
Population: 1,341,000
Capital: Port of Spain, pop. 66,000
Currency: Trinidad and Tobago dollar
Religions: Roman Catholic, Hindu, Anglican, Baptist
Languages: English, Caribbean Hindustani, French, Spanish, Chinese

Tonga

Area: 289 sq mi (748 sq km)
Population: 103,000
Capital: Nuku'alofa, pop. 25,000
Currency: pa'anga
Religion: Christian
Languages: Tongan, English

Tunisia

Area: 63,170 sq mi (163,610 sq km)
Population: 10,882,000
Capital: Tunis, pop. 790,000
Currency: Tunisian dinar
Religion: Muslim
Languages: Arabic, French

You Are There!

The Matterhorn, Switzerland

One of the most iconic peaks on the planet, this pyramid-shaped mountain stands apart among the stunning Swiss Alps. While only the most expert mountaineers should even attempt to climb to the top of the Matterhorn, you can enjoy a swift ride that gets you pretty close. The Klein-Matterhorn cable car lifts you more than two miles (3,820 m) above sea level to the highest scenic overlook in Europe.

● Asia ● Europe ● North America ● South America

Turkey

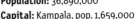

Area: 300,948 sq mi
(779,452 sq km)
Population: 76,083,000
Capital: Ankara, pop. 4,194,000
Currency: new Turkish lira
Religion: Muslim (mostly Sunni)
Languages: Turkish, Kurdish, Dimli (Zaza), Azeri, Kabardian, Gagauz

Turkmenistan

Area: 188,456 sq mi
(488,100 sq km)
Population: 5,240,000
Capital: Ashgabat, pop. 683,000
Currency: Turkmen manat
Religions: Muslim, Eastern Orthodox
Languages: Turkmen, Russian, Uzbek

5 cool things about TURKMENISTAN

1. There are more white marble buildings in the capital city of Ashgabat than in any other city in the world.

2. The massive Karakum Desert covers about 70 percent of Turkmenistan.

3. Turkmenistan is home to the world's largest indoor Ferris wheel.

4. Dinosaur footprints have been discovered in eastern Turkmenistan.

5. A crater in the Karakum Desert has been on fire for over 40 years.

Tuvalu

Area: 10 sq mi (26 sq km)
Population: 11,000
Capital: Funafuti, pop. 5,000
Currencies: Australian dollar; Tuvaluan dollar
Religion: Church of Tuvalu (Congregationalist)
Languages: Tuvaluan, English, Samoan, Kiribati

Uganda

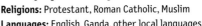

Area: 93,104 sq mi
(241,139 sq km)
Population: 36,890,000
Capital: Kampala, pop. 1,659,000
Currency: Ugandan shilling
Religions: Protestant, Roman Catholic, Muslim
Languages: English, Ganda, other local languages, Kiswahili, Arabic

Ukraine

Area: 233,090 sq mi
(603,700 sq km)
Population: 45,513,000
Capital: Kiev, pop. 2,829,000
Currency: hryvnia
Religions: Ukrainian Orthodox, Orthodox, Ukrainian Greek Catholic
Languages: Ukrainian, Russian

United Arab Emirates

Area: 30,000 sq mi
(77,700 sq km)
Population: 9,346,000
Capital: Abu Dhabi, pop. 942,000
Currency: Emirati dirham
Religion: Muslim
Languages: Arabic, Persian, English, Hindi, Urdu

United Kingdom

Area: 93,788 sq mi
(242,910 sq km)
Population: 64,092,000
Capital: London, pop. 9,005,000
Currency: British pound
Religions: Anglican, Roman Catholic, Presbyterian, Methodist
Languages: English, Welsh, Scottish form of Gaelic

United States

Area: 3,794,083 sq mi
(9,826,630 sq km)
Population: 316,158,000
Capital: Washington, D.C., pop. 617,996
Currency: U.S. dollar
Religions: Protestant, Roman Catholic
Languages: English, Spanish

COLOR KEY ● Africa ● Australia, New Zealand, and Oceania

Uruguay

Area: 68,037 sq mi
(176,215 sq km)
Population: 3,392,000
Capital: Montevideo, pop. 1,672,000
Currency: Uruguayan peso
Religion: Roman Catholic
Language: Spanish

Uzbekistan

Area: 172,742 sq mi
(447,400 sq km)
Population: 30,215,000
Capital: Tashkent,
pop. 2,227,000
Currency: Uzbekistani sum
Religions: Muslim (mostly Sunni), Eastern Orthodox
Languages: Uzbek, Russian, Tajik

Vanuatu

Area: 4,707 sq mi (12,190 sq km)
Population: 265,000
Capital: Port Vila, pop. 47,000
Currency: vatu
Religions: Presbyterian, Anglican, Roman Catholic,
other Christian, indigenous beliefs
Languages: more than 100 local languages, pidgin
(known as Bislama or Bichelama)

Vatican City

Area: 0.2 sq mi (0.4 sq km)
Population: 798
Capital: Vatican City, pop. 798
Currency: euro
Religion: Roman Catholic
Languages: Italian, Latin, French

Venezuela

Area: 352,144 sq mi
(912,050 sq km)
Population: 29,679,000
Capital: Caracas, pop. 3,242,000
Currency: bolivar
Religion: Roman Catholic
Languages: Spanish, numerous indigenous dialects

Vietnam

Area: 127,844 sq mi
(331,114 sq km)
Population: 89,721,000
Capital: Hanoi, pop. 2,955,000
Currency: dong
Religions: Buddhist, Roman Catholic
Languages: Vietnamese, English, French, Chinese, Khmer

Yemen

Area: 207,286 sq mi
(536,869 sq km)
Population: 25,235,000
Capital: Sanaa, pop. 2,419,000
Currency: Yemeni rial
Religions: Muslim, including Shaf'i (Sunni)
and Zaydi (Shiite)
Language: Arabic

Zambia

Area: 290,586 sq mi
(752,614 sq km)
Population: 14,187,000
Capital: Lusaka, pop. 1,802,000
Currency: Zambian kwacha
Religions: Christian, Muslim, Hindu
Languages: English, Bemba, Kaonda, Lozi, Lunda, Luvale,
Nyanja, Tonga, about 70 other indigenous languages

Zimbabwe

Area: 150,872 sq mi
(390,757 sq km)
Population: 13,038,000
Capital: Harare, pop. 1,542,000
Currency: Zimbabwean dollar
Religions: Syncretic (part Christian, part indigenous
beliefs), Christian, indigenous beliefs
Languages: English, Shona, Sindebele, tribal dialects

**THE SPRAY from
Victoria Falls—
a waterfall in
ZIMBABWE—can be
seen from more than
12 MILES (20 KM) away.**

THE POLITICAL
UNITED STATES

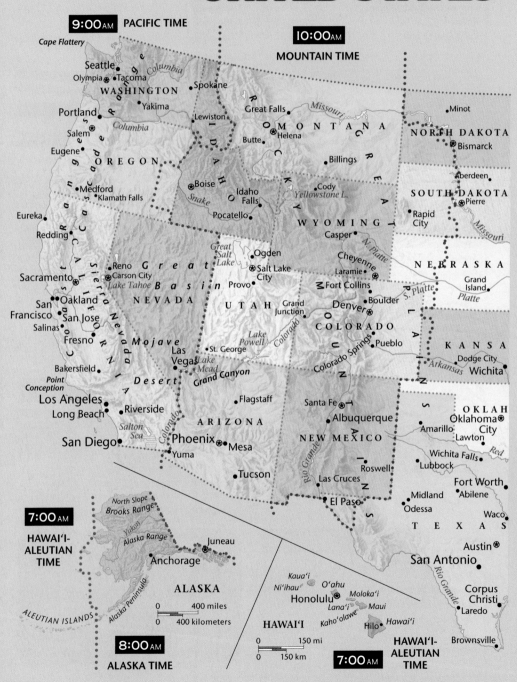

9:00AM **PACIFIC TIME**

10:00AM **MOUNTAIN TIME**

Cape Flattery

Seattle
Olympia⊛ Tacoma
WASHINGTON • Spokane
Portland • Yakima
Lewiston
Salem⊛ Columbia
Eugene•
OREGON
Great Falls • Missouri • Minot
M O N T A N A
Butte• Helena
Billings
NORTH DAKOTA
⊛ Bismarck
Aberdeen •
SOUTH DAKOTA
⊛ Pierre
Medford
Klamath Falls
•Boise
Idaho Falls
Snake
Cody
Yellowstone L.
Pocatello•
Eureka•
Redding•
Reno Great
Carson City
Lake Tahoe B a s i n
NEVADA
WYOMING
Casper•
Rapid City
Missouri
Great Salt Lake
•Ogden
⊛ Salt Lake City Provo• Cheyenne
Laramie•
Fort Collins
NEBRASKA
Grand Island•
Sacramento•
San Francisco• Oakland
San Jose
Salinas•
Fresno•
Bakersfield•
Point Conception
CALIFORNIA
Sierra Nevada
M o j a v e
Las Vegas
Lake Mead
D e s e r t
UTAH Grand Junction
Lake Powell
Colorado
Grand Canyon
St. George
Denver⊛ Boulder
COLORADO
Colorado Springs
Pueblo•
S. Platte
Platte
KANSA
Dodge City
Arkansas Wichita•
N. Platte
Los Angeles•
Long Beach•
Salton Sea
Riverside•
San Diego•
Colorado
Phoenix⊛• Mesa
Yuma•
ARIZONA
Flagstaff•
Santa Fe⊛
Albuquerque•
NEW MEXICO
Tucson•
Las Cruces•
El Paso•
Rio Grande
Amarillo•
Lawton•
OKLAH
Oklahoma⊛ City
Wichita Falls•
Lubbock•
Roswell•
Midland•
Odessa•
Fort Worth•
Abilene•
Waco•
T E X A S
Red
7:00AM **HAWAI'I-ALEUTIAN TIME**

North Slope
Brooks Range
Yukon
Alaska Range
Juneau⊛
Anchorage•
ALEUTIAN ISLANDS
Alaska Peninsula
ALASKA

0 ___ 400 miles
0 ___ 400 kilometers

8:00AM **ALASKA TIME**

Kaua'i
Ni'ihau O'ahu
Honolulu⊛ Moloka'i
Lana'i Maui
HAWAI'I Kaho'olawe
Hilo• Hawai'i

0 ___ 150 mi
0 ___ 150 km

Austin⊛
San Antonio•
Rio Grande
Corpus Christi•
Laredo•
Brownsville•

7:00AM **HAWAI'I-ALEUTIAN TIME**

Like a giant quilt, the United States is made up of 50 states. Each is unique, but together they make a national fabric held together by a constitution and a federal government. State boundaries, outlined in dotted lines on the map, set apart internal political units within the country. The national capital—Washington, D.C.—is marked by a star in a double circle. The capital of each state is marked by a star in a single circle.

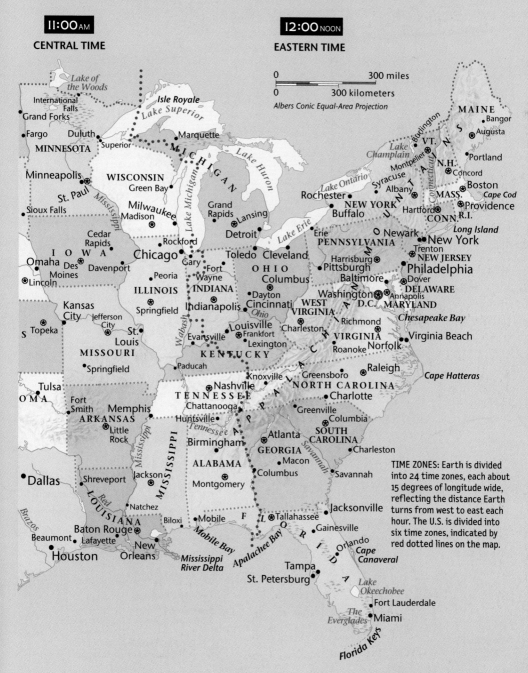

11:00 AM
CENTRAL TIME

12:00 NOON
EASTERN TIME

0 — 300 miles
0 — 300 kilometers
Albers Conic Equal-Area Projection

TIME ZONES: Earth is divided into 24 time zones, each about 15 degrees of longitude wide, reflecting the distance Earth turns from west to east each hour. The U.S. is divided into six time zones, indicated by red dotted lines on the map.

THE PHYSICAL UNITED STATES

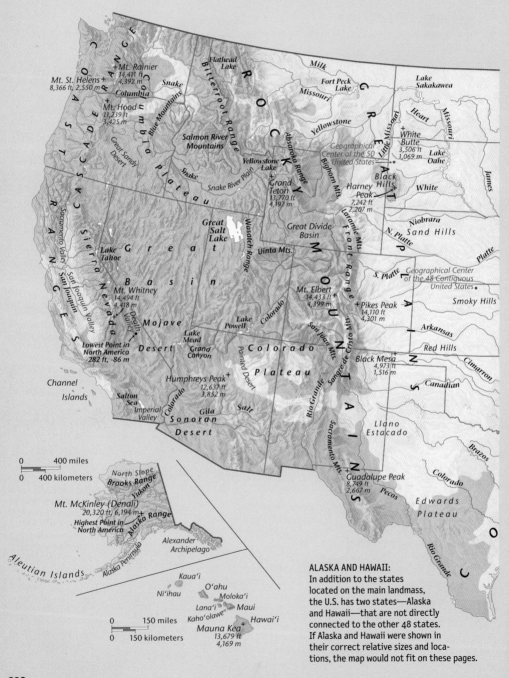

Mt. St. Helens +
8,366 ft, 2,550 m

Mt. Rainier
14,411 ft,
4,392 m

Snake

Columbia

Mt. Hood +
11,239 ft
3,425 m

Blue Mountains

C A S C A D E   R A N G E

CASCADE RANGE

Great Sandy
Desert

Columbia   Plateau

Flathead
Lake

Bitterroot Range

Salmon River
Mountains

Snake

Snake River Plain

R   O   C   K

Milk

Fort Peck
Lake

Missouri

Yellowstone

Absaroka Range

Yellowstone
Lake

Bighorn Mts.

+ Grand
Teton
13,770 ft
4,197 m

Geographical
Center of the 50
United States

Lake
Sakakawea

Heart

Missouri

+ White
Butte
3,506 ft
1,069 m

Little Missouri

Lake
Oahe

Black
Hills

Harney
Peak
7,242 ft
2,207 m

White

Niobrara

N. Platte

G   R   E   A   T

James

Sand Hills

Sacramento Valley

San Joaquin

Sierra   Nevada

Lake
Tahoe

G r e a t

B a s i n

Mt. Whitney
14,494 ft +
4,418 m

Death Valley

Lowest Point in
North America
-282 ft, -86 m

Mojave

Desert

Great
Salt
Lake

Wasatch Range

Uinta Mts.

Great Divide
Basin

Laramie Mts.

Front Range

M O U N T A I N S

Lake
Powell

Colorado

Mt. Elbert
14,433 ft +
4,399 m

San Juan Mts.

Geographical Center
of the 48 Contiguous
United States

S. Platte

+ Pikes Peak
14,110 ft
4,301 m

P   L   A   I   N   S

Platte

Smoky Hills

Arkansas

Red Hills

Lake
Mead

Grand
Canyon

Painted Desert

Colorado   Plateau

Sangre de Cristo Mts.

Black Mesa +
4,973 ft
1,516 m

Canadian

Channel
Islands

Salton
Sea

Imperial
Valley

Colorado

Humphreys Peak +
12,637 ft
3,852 m

Gila

Sonoran

Desert

Salt

Rio Grande

Sacramento Mts.

Llano
Estacado

Brazos

Colorado

ALASKA AND HAWAII:
In addition to the states
located on the main landmass,
the U.S. has two states—Alaska
and Hawaii—that are not directly
connected to the other 48 states.
If Alaska and Hawaii were shown in
their correct relative sizes and locations, the map would not fit on these pages.

Guadalupe Peak +
8,749 ft
2,667 m

Pecos

Edwards
Plateau

Rio Grande

0   400 miles

0   400 kilometers

North Slope

Brooks Range

Yukon

Mt. McKinley (Denali)
20,320 ft, 6,194 m +

Highest Point in
North America

Alaska Range

Aleutian Islands

Alaska Peninsula

Alexander
Archipelago

Kaua'i

Ni'ihau

O'ahu

Moloka'i

Lana'i   Maui

Kaho'olawe

Hawai'i

Mauna Kea +
13,679 ft
4,169 m

0   150 miles

0   150 kilometers

Stretching from the Atlantic Ocean in the east to the Pacific Ocean in the west, the United States is the third largest country (by area) in the world. Its physical diversity ranges from mountains to fertile plains and dry deserts. Shading on the map indicates changes in elevation, while colors show different vegetation patterns.

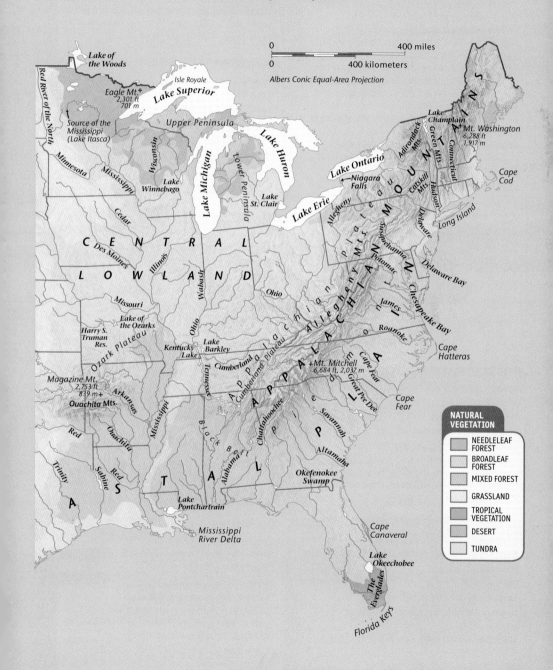

0 — 400 miles
0 — 400 kilometers
Albers Conic Equal-Area Projection

Lake of the Woods
Red River of the North
Isle Royale
Eagle Mt. 2,301 ft 701 m
Lake Superior
Source of the Mississippi (Lake Itasca)
Upper Peninsula
Minnesota
Wisconsin
Mississippi
Lake Winnebago
Cedar
Des Moines
C E N T R A L
L O W L A N D
Missouri
Illinois
Wabash
Lake Michigan
Lower Peninsula
Lake Huron
Lake St. Clair
Lake Erie
Ohio
Lake Ontario
Niagara Falls
Allegheny Plateau
Allegheny Mts.
Adirondack Mts.
Lake Champlain
Green Mts.
Connecticut
Catskill Mts.
Hudson
Delaware
Mt. Washington 6,288 ft 1,917 m
Cape Cod
Long Island
A P P A L A C H I A N   M O U N T A I N S
Susquehanna
Potomac
Delaware Bay
Chesapeake Bay
James
Roanoke
Cape Hatteras
Lake of the Ozarks
Harry S. Truman Res.
Ozark Plateau
Kentucky Lake
Lake Barkley
Cumberland
Cumberland Plateau
Tennessee
Mt. Mitchell 6,684 ft, 2,037 m
Cape Fear
Great Pee Dee
Magazine Mt. 2,753 ft 839 m
Arkansas
Ouachita Mts.
Ouachita
Mississippi
Red
Black Belt
Alabama
Chattahoochee
Savannah
Altamaha
C O A S T A L   P L A I N
Okefenokee Swamp
Cape Canaveral
Red
Sabine
Trinity
Lake Pontchartrain
Mississippi River Delta
Lake Okeechobee
The Everglades
Florida Keys

NATURAL VEGETATION

- NEEDLELEAF FOREST
- BROADLEAF FOREST
- MIXED FOREST
- GRASSLAND
- TROPICAL VEGETATION
- DESERT
- TUNDRA

THE STATES

From sea to shining sea, the United States of America is a nation of diversity. In the nearly 240 years since its creation, the nation has grown to become home to a wide range of peoples, industries, and cultures. The following pages present a general overview of all 50 states in the U.S.

The country is generally divided into five large regions: the Northeast, the Southeast, the Midwest, the Southwest, and the West. Though loosely defined, these zones tend to share important similarities, including climate, history, and geography. The color key below provides a guide to which states are in each region.

Flags of each state and highlights of demography and industry are also included. These details offer a brief overview of each state.

In addition, each state's official flower and bird are identified.

Color Key by Region

Alabama

Area: 52,419 sq mi (135,765 sq km)
Population: 4,822,023
Capital: Montgomery, pop. 205,293
Largest city: Birmingham, pop. 212,038
Industry: Retail and wholesale trade, services, government, finance, insurance, real estate, transportation, construction, communication
State flower/bird: Camellia/northern flicker

Alaska

Area: 663,267 sq mi (1,717,862 sq km)
Population: 731,449
Capital: Juneau, pop. 32,556
Largest city: Anchorage, pop. 298,610
Industry: Petroleum products, government, services, trade
State flower/bird: Forget-me-not/willow ptarmigan

Arizona

Area: 113,998 sq mi (295,256 sq km)
Population: 6,553,255
Capital: Phoenix, pop. 1,488,750
Largest city: Phoenix, pop. 1,488,750
Industry: Real estate, manufactured goods, retail, state and local government, transportation and public utilities, wholesale trade, health services
State flower/bird: Saguaro/cactus wren

Arkansas

Area: 53,179 sq mi (137,732 sq km)
Population: 2,949,131
Capital: Little Rock, pop. 196,537
Largest city: Little Rock, pop. 196,537
Industry: Services, food processing, paper products, transportation, metal products, machinery, electronics
State flower/bird: Apple blossom/mockingbird

California

Area: 163,696 sq mi (423,972 sq km)
Population: 38,041,430
Capital: Sacramento, pop. 475,516
Largest city: Los Angeles, pop. 3,857,799
Industry: Electronic components and equipment, computers and computer software, tourism, food processing, entertainment, clothing
State flower/bird: Golden poppy/California quail

San Francisco, California's **CABLE CARS** are considered mobile national monuments.

Colorado

Area: 104,094 sq mi (269,602 sq km)
Population: 5,187,582
Capital: Denver, pop. 634,265
Largest city: Denver, pop. 634,265
Industry: Real estate, government, durable goods, communications, health and other services, nondurable goods, transportation
State flower/bird: Columbine/lark bunting

Connecticut

Area: 5,543 sq mi (14,357 sq km)
Population: 3,590,347
Capital: Hartford, pop. 124,893
Largest city: Bridgeport, pop. 146,425
Industry: Transportation equipment, metal products, machinery, electrical equipment, printing and publishing, scientific instruments, insurance
State flower/bird: Mountain laurel/robin

> In 1895, a sandwich shop in **NEW HAVEN, CONNECTICUT,** served the first hamburger in U.S. history.

Delaware

Area: 2,489 sq mi (6,447 sq km)
Population: 917,092
Capital: Dover, pop. 37,089
Largest city: Wilmington, pop. 71,292
Industry: Food processing, chemicals, rubber and plastic products, scientific instruments, printing and publishing, financial services
State flower/bird: Peach blossom/blue hen chicken

Florida

Area: 65,755 sq mi (170,304 sq km)
Population: 19,317,568
Capital: Tallahassee, pop. 186,971
Largest city: Jacksonville, pop. 836,507
Industry: Tourism, health services, business services, communications, banking, electronic equipment, insurance
State flower/bird: Orange blossom/mockingbird

Georgia

Area: 59,425 sq mi (153,910 sq km)
Population: 9,919,945
Capital: Atlanta, pop. 443,775
Largest city: Atlanta, pop. 443,775
Industry: Textiles and clothing, transportation equipment, food processing, paper products, chemicals, electrical equipment, tourism
State flower/bird: Cherokee rose/brown thrasher

Hawaii

Area: 10,931 sq mi (28,311 sq km)
Population: 1,392,313
Capital: Honolulu, pop. 345,610
Largest city: Honolulu, pop. 345,610
Industry: Tourism, trade, finance, food processing, petroleum refining, stone, clay, glass products
State flower/bird: Hibiscus/Hawaiian goose (nene)

Idaho

Area: 83,570 sq mi (216,447 sq km)
Population: 1,595,728
Capital: Boise, pop. 212,303
Largest city: Boise, pop. 212,303
Industry: Electronics and computer equipment, tourism, food processing, forest products, mining
State flower/bird: Syringa (Lewis's mock orange)/ mountain bluebird

Illinois

Area: 57,914 sq mi (149,998 sq km)
Population: 12,875,255
Capital: Springfield, pop. 117,126
Largest city: Chicago, pop. 2,714,856
Industry: Industrial machinery, electronic equipment, food processing, chemicals, metals, printing and publishing, rubber and plastics, motor vehicles
State flower/bird: Violet/cardinal

Indiana

Area: 36,418 sq mi (94,322 sq km)
Population: 6,537,334
Capital: Indianapolis, pop. 834,852
Largest city: Indianapolis, pop. 834,852
Industry: Transportation equipment, steel, pharmaceutical and chemical products, machinery, petroleum, coal
State flower/bird: Peony/cardinal

Iowa

Area: 56,272 sq mi (145,743 sq km)
Population: 3,074,186
Capital: Des Moines, pop. 206,688
Largest city: Des Moines, pop. 206,688
Industry: Real estate, health services, industrial machinery, food processing, construction
State flower/bird: Wild rose/American goldfinch

Kansas

Area: 82,277 sq mi (213,097 sq km)
Population: 2,885,905
Capital: Topeka, pop. 127,939
Largest city: Wichita, pop. 385,577
Industry: Aircraft manufacturing, transportation equipment, construction, food processing, printing and publishing, health care
State flower/bird: Sunflower/western meadowlark

Kentucky

Area: 40,409 sq mi (104,659 sq km)
Population: 4,380,415
Capital: Frankfort, pop. 27,590
Largest city: Louisville, pop. 605,110
Industry: Manufacturing, services, government, finance, insurance, real estate, retail trade, transportation, wholesale trade, construction, mining
State flower/bird: Goldenrod/cardinal

Louisiana

Area: 51,840 sq mi (134,265 sq km)
Population: 4,601,893
Capital: Baton Rouge, pop. 230,058
Largest city: New Orleans, pop. 369,250
Industry: Chemicals, petroleum products, food processing, health services, tourism, oil and natural gas extraction, paper products
State flower/bird: Magnolia/brown pelican

Maine

Area: 35,385 sq mi (91,646 sq km)
Population: 1,329,192
Capital: Augusta, pop. 18,946
Largest city: Portland, pop. 66,214
Industry: Health services, tourism, forest products, leather products, electrical equipment
State flower/bird: White pine cone and tassel/chickadee

Maryland

Area: 12,407 sq mi (32,133 sq km)
Population: 5,884,563
Capital: Annapolis, pop. 38,620
Largest city: Baltimore, pop. 621,342
Industry: Real estate, federal government, health services, business services, engineering services
State flower/bird: Black-eyed Susan/northern (Baltimore) oriole

Massachusetts

Area: 10,555 sq mi (27,336 sq km)
Population: 6,646,144
Capital: Boston, pop. 636,479
Largest city: Boston, pop. 636,479
Industry: Electrical equipment, machinery, metal products, scientific instruments, printing and publishing, tourism
State flower/bird: Mayflower/chickadee

Michigan

Area: 96,716 sq mi (250,495 sq km)
Population: 9,883,360
Capital: Lansing, pop. 113,996
Largest city: Detroit, pop. 701,475
Industry: Motor vehicles and parts, machinery, metal products, office furniture, tourism, chemicals
State flower/bird: Apple blossom/robin

Minnesota

Area: 86,939 sq mi (225,172 sq km)
Population: 5,379,139
Capital: St. Paul, pop. 290,770
Largest city: Minneapolis, pop. 392,880
Industry: Real estate, banking and insurance, industrial machinery, printing and publishing, food processing, scientific equipment
State flower/bird: Showy lady's slipper/common loon

> Anoka, Minnesota, is known as the "Halloween Capital of the World."

Mississippi

Area: 48,430 sq mi (125,434 sq km)
Population: 2,984,926
Capital: Jackson, pop. 175,437
Largest city: Jackson, pop. 175,437
Industry: Petroleum products, health services, electronic equipment, transportation, banking, forest products, communications
State flower/bird: Magnolia/mockingbird

Missouri

Area: 69,704 sq mi (180,534 sq km)
Population: 6,021,988
Capital: Jefferson City, pop. 43,183
Largest city: Kansas City, pop. 464,310
Industry: Transportation equipment, food processing, chemicals, electrical equipment, metal products
State flower/bird: Hawthorn/eastern bluebird

Montana

Area: 147,042 sq mi (380,840 sq km)
Population: 1,005,141
Capital: Helena, pop. 29,134
Largest city: Billings, pop. 106,954
Industry: Forest products, food processing, mining, construction, tourism
State flower/bird: Bitterroot/western meadowlark

Nebraska

Area: 77,354 sq mi (200,346 sq km)
Population: 1,855,525
Capital: Lincoln, pop. 265,404
Largest city: Omaha, pop. 421,570
Industry: Food processing, machinery, electrical equipment, printing and publishing
State flower/bird: Goldenrod/western meadowlark

Nevada

Area: 110,561 sq mi (286,352 sq km)
Population: 2,758,931
Capital: Carson City, pop. 54,838
Largest city: Las Vegas, pop. 596,424
Industry: Tourism and gaming, mining, printing and publishing, food processing, electrical equipment
State flower/bird: Sagebrush/mountain bluebird

New Hampshire

Area: 9,350 sq mi (24,216 sq km)
Population: 1,320,718
Capital: Concord, pop. 42,630
Largest city: Manchester, pop. 110,209
Industry: Machinery, electronics, metal products
State flower/bird: Purple lilac/purple finch

New Jersey

Area: 8,721 sq mi (22,588 sq km)
Population: 8,864,590
Capital: Trenton, pop. 84,477
Largest city: Newark, pop. 277,727
Industry: Machinery, electronics, metal products, chemicals
State flower/bird: Violet/American goldfinch

5 cool things about NEW JERSEY

1. New Jersey is named after the island of Jersey in the English Channel.

2. New Jersey has more diner restaurants than any other state.

3. *Hadrosaurus foulkii* is New Jersey's official state dinosaur.

4. The world's largest statues of a tooth and an elephant are both found in New Jersey.

5. All of the streets in the game of Monopoly are actual streets in Atlantic City, New Jersey.

New Mexico

Area: 121,590 sq mi (314,917 sq km)
Population: 2,085,538
Capital: Santa Fe, pop. 69,204
Largest city: Albuquerque, pop. 555,417
Industry: Electronic equipment, state and local government, real estate, business services, federal government, oil and gas extraction, health services
State flower/bird: Yucca/roadrunner

New York

Area: 54,556 sq mi (141,300 sq km)
Population: 19,570,261
Capital: Albany, pop. 97,904
Largest city: New York City, pop. 8,336,697
Industry: Printing and publishing, machinery, computer products, finance, tourism
State flower/bird: Rose/eastern bluebird

North Carolina

Area: 53,819 sq mi (139,390 sq km)
Population: 9,752,073
Capital: Raleigh, pop. 423,179
Largest city: Charlotte, pop. 775,202
Industry: Real estate, health services, chemicals, tobacco products, finance, textiles
State flower/bird: Flowering dogwood/cardinal

NORTH CAROLINA is home to the FIRST MINIATURE GOLF COURSE.

North Dakota

Area: 70,700 sq mi (183,113 sq km)
Population: 699,628
Capital: Bismarck, pop. 64,751
Largest city: Fargo, pop. 109,779
Industry: Services, government, finance, construction, transportation, oil and gas
State flower/bird: Wild prairie rose/ western meadowlark

Ohio

Area: 44,825 sq mi (116,097 sq km)
Population: 11,544,225
Capital: Columbus, pop. 809,798
Largest city: Columbus, pop. 809,798
Industry: Transportation equipment, metal products, machinery, food processing, electrical equipment
State flower/bird: Scarlet carnation/cardinal

Oklahoma

Area: 69,898 sq mi (181,036 sq km)
Population: 3,814,820
Capital: Oklahoma City, pop. 599,199
Largest city: Oklahoma City, pop. 599,199
Industry: Manufacturing, services, government, finance, insurance, real estate
State flower/bird: Mistletoe/scissor-tailed flycatcher

Oregon

Area: 98,381 sq mi (254,806 sq km)
Population: 3,899,353
Capital: Salem, pop. 157,429
Largest city: Portland, pop. 603,106
Industry: Real estate, retail and wholesale trade, electronic equipment, health services, construction, forest products, business services
State flower/bird: Oregon grape/western meadowlark

Pennsylvania

Area: 46,055 sq mi (119,283 sq km)
Population: 12,763,536
Capital: Harrisburg, pop. 49,279
Largest city: Philadelphia, pop. 1,547,607
Industry: Machinery, printing and publishing, forest products, metal products
State flower/bird: Mountain laurel/ruffed grouse

Rhode Island

Area: 1,545 sq mi (4,002 sq km)
Population: 1,050,292
Capital: Providence, pop. 178,432
Largest city: Providence, pop. 178,432
Industry: Health services, business services, silver and jewelry products, metal products
State flower/bird: Violet/Rhode Island red

South Carolina

Area: 32,020 sq mi (82,932 sq km)
Population: 4,723,723
Capital: Columbia, pop. 131,686
Largest city: Columbia, pop. 131,686
Industry: Service industries, tourism, chemicals, textiles, machinery, forest products
State flower/bird: Yellow jessamine/Carolina wren

South Dakota

Area: 77,117 sq mi (199,732 sq km)
Population: 833,354
Capital: Pierre, pop. 13,914
Largest city: Sioux Falls, pop. 159,908
Industry: Finance, services, manufacturing, government, retail trade, transportation and utilities, wholesale trade, construction, mining
State flower/bird: Pasqueflower/ring-necked pheasant

COLOR KEY ● Northeast ● Southeast

Tennessee

Area: 42,143 sq mi (109,151 sq km)
Population: 6,456,243
Capital: Nashville, pop. 624,496
Largest city: Memphis, pop. 655,155
Industry: Service industries, chemicals, transportation equipment, processed foods, machinery
State flower/bird: Iris/mockingbird

Texas

Area: 268,581 sq mi (695,624 sq km)
Population: 26,059,203
Capital: Austin, pop. 842,592
Largest city: Houston, pop. 2,160,821
Industry: Chemicals, machinery, electronics and computers, food products, petroleum and natural gas, transportation equipment
State flower/bird: Bluebonnet/mockingbird

Utah

Area: 84,899 sq mi (219,888 sq km)
Population: 2,855,287
Capital: Salt Lake City, pop. 189,314
Largest city: Salt Lake City, pop. 189,314
Industry: Government, manufacturing, real estate, construction, health services, business services, banking
State flower/bird: Sego lily/California gull

Vermont

Area: 9,614 sq mi (24,901 sq km)
Population: 626,011
Capital: Montpelier, pop. 7,787
Largest city: Burlington, pop. 42,282
Industry: Health services, tourism, finance, real estate, computer components, electrical parts, printing and publishing, machine tools
State flower/bird: Red clover/hermit thrush

Virginia

Area: 42,774 sq mi (110,785 sq km)
Population: 8,185,867
Capital: Richmond, pop. 210,309
Largest city: Virginia Beach, pop. 447,021
Industry: Food processing, communication and electronic equipment, transportation equipment, printing, shipbuilding, textiles
State flower/bird: Flowering dogwood/cardinal

Washington

Area: 71,300 sq mi (184,666 sq km)
Population: 6,897,012
Capital: Olympia, pop. 47,698
Largest city: Seattle, pop. 634,535
Industry: Aerospace, tourism, food processing, forest products, paper products, industrial machinery, printing and publishing, metals, computer software
State flower/bird: Coast rhododendron/Amer. goldfinch

West Virginia

Area: 24,230 sq mi (62,755 sq km)
Population: 1,855,413
Capital: Charleston, pop. 51,018
Largest city: Charleston, pop. 51,018
Industry: Tourism, coal mining, chemicals, metal manufacturing, forest products, stone, clay, oil, glass products
State flower/bird: Rhododendron/cardinal

> West Virginia's **NEW RIVER** is one of the **OLDEST RIVERS IN THE WORLD.**

Wisconsin

Area: 65,498 sq mi (169,639 sq km)
Population: 5,726,398
Capital: Madison, pop. 240,323
Largest city: Milwaukee, pop. 598,916
Industry: Industrial machinery, paper products, food processing, metal products, electronic equipment, transportation
State flower/bird: Wood violet/robin

Wyoming

Area: 97,814 sq mi (253,337 sq km)
Population: 576,412
Capital: Cheyenne, pop. 61,537
Largest city: Cheyenne, pop. 61,537
Industry: Oil and natural gas, mining, generation of electricity, chemicals, tourism
State flower/bird: Indian paintbrush/western meadowlark

THE TERRITORIES

The United States has 14 territories—political divisions that are not states. Three of these are in the Caribbean Sea, and the other eleven are in the Pacific Ocean.

St. John, U.S. Virgin Islands

Convention Center, San Juan, Puerto Rico

Talofofo Falls, Guam

U.S. CARIBBEAN TERRITORIES

Puerto Rico
Area: 3,508 sq mi (9,086 sq km)
Population: 3,667,084
Capital: San Juan, pop. 2,475,000
Languages: Spanish, English

U.S. Virgin Islands
Area: 149 sq mi (386 sq km)
Population: 105,275
Capital: Charlotte Amalie, pop. 10,354
Languages: English, Spanish or Spanish Creole, French or French Creole

U.S. PACIFIC TERRITORIES

American Samoa
Area: 77 sq mi (199 sq km)
Population: 54,947
Capital: Pago Pago, pop. 3,656
Language: Samoan

Guam
Area: 217 sq mi (561 sq km)
Population: 159,914
Capital: Hagåtña (Agana), pop. 1,051
Languages: English, Chamorro, Philippine languages

Northern Mariana Islands
Area: 184 sq mi (477 sq km)
Population: 51,395
Capital: Saipan, pop. 48,220
Languages: Philippine languages, Chinese, Chamorro, English

Other U.S. Territories
Baker Island, Howland Island, Jarvis Island, Johnston Atoll, Kingman Reef, Midway Islands, Palmyra Atoll, Wake Island, Navassa Island (in the Caribbean)

THE U.S. CAPITAL

District of Columbia
Area: 68 sq mi (177 sq km)
Population: 632,323

Abraham Lincoln, who was President during the Civil War and a strong opponent of slavery, is remembered in the Lincoln Memorial, located at the opposite end of the National Mall from the U.S. Capitol Building.

COLOR KEY • Territories • Northeast

DESTINATION GUIDE

ALASKA

Though it's been a U.S. state for nearly 60 years, Alaska remains in a class of its own. Everything from its unique geography to its abundance of wildlife make Alaska a popular destination. Here are just a few of the many things you can do while visiting.

What to Do:

GREET GLACIERS. Get an up-close-and-personal peek at thousands of giant ice formations with a kayak trip on Glacier Bay. Paddle onto shore to spot wildlife, pick strawberries, or just sit back and watch ice break off glaciers and crash into the sea—a process called calving.

BEAR IT. Break out your binoculars and look for one of Alaska's most famous animals, the brown bear. At Katmai National Park in southern Alaska, you can safely watch bears feed on sockeye salmon from a viewing platform.

STAR GAZE. Clear skies over Alaska offer a dazzling display of the stars above. If you're lucky, you'll be treated to a stunning view of the colorful aurora borealis (also known as the Northern Lights), a natural light show.

GO FOR GOLD. Long after the Alaskan Gold Rush of the late 1880s, you can still seek out the shiny stuff. Try your luck by panning for gold in Alaska's hills and streams. (The beach east of Nome is a popular spot.)

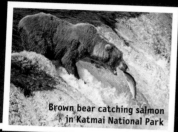

Brown bear catching salmon in Katmai National Park

Aurora borealis

Gold nugget

There are more bald eagles in Alaska than in all other states combined.

Migrating salmon can jump over waterfalls more than 12 feet (3.65 m) tall.

The 22 smallest U.S. states could all fit inside Alaska.

1

China's mountainous bamboo forests can rise sharply—but pandas can easily climb as much as **13,000 FEET** (3,962 m) up the slopes.

2

BEFORE THE 1400s IN EUROPE, **PORTUGAL'S SOUTHERN COAST WAS THOUGHT TO BE** THE EDGE OF THE KNOWN WORLD.

3

About **12,000 years ago,** the **Sahara** was covered with millions of trees.

15 COOL THINGS ABOUT

4

More people live in **TAMPA, FLORIDA, U.S.A.,** than in all of **ICELAND.**

Greetings from **TAMPA** FLORIDA

5

CANADA'S THOR PEAK IS THOUGHT TO HAVE THE WORLD'S LONGEST **UNINTERRUPTED CLIFF FACE.**

6

In Jordan's ancient city of Petra, buildings were carved directly into cliff walls.

7

BEIJING

BERLIN

BAKU

BERN

MORE CAPITAL CITIES START WITH THE LETTER *B* THAN WITH ANY OTHER LETTER.

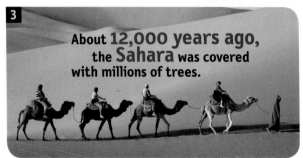

8

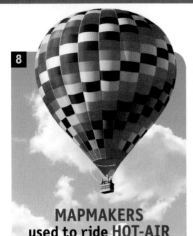

MAPMAKERS used to ride **HOT-AIR BALLOONS** to view and map land.

9

WHEN FORESTS FLOOD ALONG THE AMAZON RIVER, RIVER DOLPHINS SOMETIMES HAVE TO SWIM AROUND TREES.

11

THE SURFACE OF THE PACIFIC OCEAN COULD COVER ALL OF EARTH'S CONTINENTS COMBINED.

10

A MOTORCYCLE SWEPT TO SEA BY A 2011 TSUNAMI DRIFTED ALL THE WAY FROM JAPAN TO CANADA.

THE WORLD

12

INDONESIA'S REMOTE FOJA MOUNTAINS ARE HOME TO BIZARRE SPECIES SUCH AS THE PINOCCHIO-NOSED FROG.

13

HURRICANES NORTH OF THE EQUATOR SPIN IN THE OPPOSITE DIRECTION FROM ONES SOUTH OF THE EQUATOR.

15

The scorching deserts of North Africa don't hurt the sand cat—the animal's paw pads are covered in fur to protect its feet from heat.

14

THE CHOCOLATE HILLS IN THE PHILIPPINES ARE SHAPED LIKE **GIANT HERSHEY'S KISSES.**

Coolest Coasters

Check out the tallest, fastest, loopiest rides on the planet.

hurl -o- meter ★★★★★

THE LOOPIEST: COLOSSUS

WHERE Thorpe Park in Surrey, England

RIDE Riders on Colossus blast through ten upside-down loops, including two dizzying corkscrew turns and a loop shaped like a snake's head. One last loop awaits just when you think the ride is over.

COOL SCIENCE As riders enter a loop, the acceleration produces a force that pushes them away from the center of the circle. The force presses riders into their seats—even while upside down.

hurl -o- meter ★★★★

THE FASTEST: FORMULA ROSSA

WHERE Ferrari World in Abu Dhabi, United Arab Emirates

RIDE This coaster jumps from 0 to 149 miles an hour (0 to 240 kph) in less than five seconds. Because of its launch system, which is similar to those used in jet planes, riders must wear goggles to protect their eyes from sand and bugs.

COOL SCIENCE Formula Rossa's launch system is powered by hydraulics, which uses the pressure of fluids to build power. This power can be stored up and released with so much force that the ride hits incredible speeds.

hurl -o- meter ★★★★

THE TALLEST: KINGDA KA

WHERE Six Flags Great Adventure in Jackson, New Jersey, U.S.A.

RIDE Ka launches riders up a record-breaking 456-foot (139-m)-tall tower—higher than a 40-story building.

COOL SCIENCE When the ride reaches the top of the tower, it has built up potential energy for later. Once it begins to roll back down, potential energy becomes kinetic energy—the energy of motion, which helps the ride move without additional motors.

EXTREME WEIRDNESS

From AROUND the WORLD

WHAT'S HIS HAIR LOOK LIKE UNDER THE HAT?

BEARD VS. BEARD

WHAT European Beard and Mustache Championships

WHERE Leogang, Austria

DETAILS Talk about a manly competition. More than 150 well-groomed gentlemen participated in the contest, which included 17 categories—and a lot of hair spray. Contestants spruced up their facial art with curling irons, blow-dryers, and sculpting wax. Clippers were not welcome.

ROTTEN APPLE

WHAT Apple-shaped race car

WHERE Kiev, Ukraine

DETAILS This is one sour apple. The scowling fruit-shaped cart was part of a race against about 50 other wacky-looking vehicles. More than 30,000 people came to watch the event. The apple wasn't the fastest thing on wheels, but it did provide some juicy competition.

ORANGE YOU GLAD YOU KNOW ABOUT THIS APPLE?

SHARK GETS FRIENDLY

WHAT Polar Bear Swim

WHERE Vancouver, Canada

DETAILS One fake shark brings new meaning to the phrase "biting cold." Celebrating the new year, participants in this annual event wade into the chilly 44°F (6.7°C) waters of the English Bay wearing kooky costumes—or just their bathing suits. The plunge also raises money for charity. No coldhearted people here.

HE'S NOT FOOLING ANYONE.

HAUNTED HOTELS

Ghosts could be fellow guests in these creepy quarters.

Trips to historical sites can really make the past come to life. But at some popular spots, "living history" takes on a new meaning. Some people believe that these landmarks are home to ghosts, spirits, and downright spooky activity. Decide for yourself if these places are just creepy ... or actually haunted.

GREEN GHOST

WHAT: Tulloch Castle Hotel
WHERE: Dingwall, Scotland, U.K.
THE STORY: The daughter of a former owner of this 12th-century castle is said to wander the halls whispering "Why?" over and over. The ghost is nicknamed the Green Lady since she wears a long, elegant green dress.

CREEPY CASTLE

WHAT: Hampton Court Palace
WHERE: London, England, U.K.
THE STORY: King Henry VIII's palace is said to be haunted by one of his executed wives, whose screams have reportedly been heard echoing throughout one of the galleries. Numerous visitors have fainted in one particular spot within the palace, and security cameras once recorded the fire doors bursting open and a mysterious unidentified figure closing them. Ooh, creepy!

GHOST HORSES

WHAT: Hotel Castello della Castelluccia
WHERE: Rome, Italy
THE STORY: Built between the 10th and 13th centuries by an Italian noble family, this hotel rests on the site of an ancient Roman villa. Three ghosts are thought to haunt the hotel, including the Roman emperor Nero, who restlessly wanders the gardens seeking somewhere to sleep. Guests have also reported hearing the hooves of ghostly horses who supposedly circle the castle at night.

SPOOKY SIGNALS

WHAT: St. Augustine Lighthouse and Museum
WHERE: St. Augustine, Florida, U.S.A.
THE STORY: When a cart carrying people and supplies tumbled into the ocean near this lighthouse, some victims disappeared forever—unless you believe the spooky tales. There have been reports of mysterious giggling in the lighthouse, ghostly faces peering out of windows, and a strange man in a blue lighthouse keeper's uniform.

WiLd Vacati⚛ns

Tree House Hotel!

SLEEP HERE!

HAINAN, CHINA

WHAT YOU'LL DO Sleep in tree houses overlooking the South China Sea; walk from tree to tree on a suspension bridge; admire some of the island's 600 butterfly species.

ACT LIKE A LOCAL Pick your snack. Hainan's tamarind trees produce tasty sweet-and-sour fruit to peel and eat.

SAY HELLO (in Mandarin)
ni hao (nee haow)

The Chinese invented toilet paper in the 1300s—but back then it was only for emperors.

Table tennis is one of China's most popular sports. Some players start training for the Olympics at 10 years old.